D1321409

World's
Air Fleets

Second (revised) edition, 1969

DAVID W. WRAGG

LONDON
IAN ALLAN

Second edition, 1969

S.B.N. 7110 0085 9

© IAN ALLAN LTD 1969

Published by Ian Allan Ltd, Shepperton, Surrey, and printed in the United
Kingdom by The Press at Coombelands Ltd, Addlestone, Surrey

FOREWORD

In preparing the second edition of *World's Air Fleets*, I have added a number of airlines excluded from the first edition which are now rather more frequent visitors to British airports, as well as up-dating airline histories, route network details, and fleet lists to reflect the changes which have taken place in the air transport industry over the past eighteen months or so. Again my grateful thanks must go to the airline officials who so kindly provided the information relating to their airlines, including all the photographs used in this book, and I must this time also thank those people who let me have their comments on the first edition.

February, 1969   DAVID W. WRAGG

Throughout this book, **F** following **Livery**
stands for **Fuselage**, and **T** for **Tail/tailplane**

Contents

ARIANA
Afghanistan

Ariana Afghan Airlines Co Ltd

During the early 1950s, the largest Indian charter airline, Indamer, operated special pilgrim charters from Kabul to Jeddah, and as a result of this experience decided to approach the Government of Afghanistan in 1955 with a proposal to establish an Afghan airline. Ariana was, as a result, formed that same year with Indamer holding a 49% interest, for which it had had to supply capital and equipment, and the Government of Afghanistan holding the remainder. Operations started in 1956 with DC-3s on internal routes within Afghanistan, but later that same year services to India and the Persian Gulf area followed.

In 1957, Ariana received part of aid provided by the United States for Afghanistan, and later that year, Indamer's interest was bought out by Pan American World Airways, Douglas DC-4s being introduced, helped by Pan American finance, and the DC-3s being refurbished. Services to Europe, by an extension of the Beirut service to Frankfurt, were started in 1959 with a Douglas DC-6B, but cut back to Beirut in 1961. Ariana's share of a US loan in 1963 provided a DC-6A and a Convair 340. Frankfurt and London were added to Ariana's route network in 1967. At the present time a fleet of two Douglas DC-6s, two DC-3s and a Convair 340 is operated.

International services from Kabul to:
Amritsa, Beirut, Damascus, Delhi, Frankfurt, Karachi, Lahore, London
Domestic services from Kabul to:
Herat, Jalabad, Kandabar, Kundiz, Mazar-i-Sharif
Fleet
YA-AAB	Douglas DC-3 Dakota	
YA-AAD	,,	,,
YA-DAN	Douglas DC-6B	
YA-DAO	,, DC-6A	
YA-EAP	Convair 340	

AEROLINEAS ARGENTINAS
Argentina

Aerolineas Argentinas, Empresa del Estado

Aerolineas Argentinas was formed in 1949 on the nationalization of all Argentine airlines, with the exception of LADE (operated by the Air Force). The backbone of the new airline was Aeroposta Argentina, a company that had started operations with Latécoère 25's in 1927 as a subsidiary of a French company, Cie. Générale Aéropostale, and that had expanded its original route between Buenos Aires and Asuncion (Paraguay) to a network of domestic and short international routes to neighbouring capitals. The Argentine Government had acquired 20% interest in Aeroposta in 1946.

Two other airlines involved in nationalization were ALFA (Aviacion del Litoral Fleuva Argentina), operating Short 'Sandringham' flying-boats on services along the Parana River, and ZONDA (Zonas Oeste y Norte de Aerolineas Argentinas) which had started operations in 1947 with DC-3's. This company had taken over the cabotage operations of Pan American-Grace Airways (Panagra). The Government had already acquired a 20% interest in each of these two companies prior to state ownership.

A fourth airline, FAMA (Flota Aero Mercante Argentina) was founded in 1946 with a one-third state holding to operate purely international services.

The merging of the four operators to form Aerolineas Argentinas gave the new airline a very mixed fleet, including Douglas DC-3's, DC-4's, and DC-6's, Convair 240's, Vickers 'Vikings', Avro 'Yorks', 'Lancastrians' and an 'Anson', and three ex-Aeroposta Junkers Ju52/3M tri-motors, all of which led to many difficulties during the early years. Then in 1959 Argentina became the fourth nation in the world, and Aerolineas Argentinas the first South American airline, to operate jet airliners, accomplished by the delivery of the first of six 'Comet' 4's. Short-range jet aircraft followed in 1962 with three Sud Aviation 'Caravelle' 6R's, before which nine (later increased to twelve) Hawker Siddeley 748 turbo-prop airliners were introduced. Boeing 707-387B jet airliners were taken into stock in 1966, and with the exception of six DC-4's, the present fleet is all jet or turbo-prop.

Antártida Argentina is one of four Boeing 707-387B's operated by Aerolineas Argentinas

Aerolineas Argentinas operates a comprehensive network of domestic services and international services are operated to other South American countries and to the United States and Europe. A notable feature of the airline's operations is the Buenos Aires–Madrid non-stop service introduced in August, 1967, which at 6,275 miles, is the longest non-stop scheduled flight in the world. Since 1955 privately-owned airlines have been permitted in Argentina and all of Aerolineas Argentinas' domestic routes, and those international services to neighbouring capitals, have competition from these operators. The airline's maintenance base also undertakes maintenance of some USAF transport aircraft.

Member of the International Air Transport Association

International services from Buenos Aires to:
Asuncion*, Bogotá, Dakar, Frankfurt, Lima, London, Madrid, Mexico City, Miami, Montevideo, New York, Paris, Port of Spain, Recife*, Rio de Janeiro*, Rome, Santiago de Chile*, São Paulo

* services via other points in Argentina.

Domestic route points

Bahia Blanca, Catamarca, Colonia Sarmiento, Comodoro Rivadavia, Condordia, Cordoba, Corrientes, Curuzú Cuatiá, Esquel, Formosa, Iguazú, Jujuy, La Rioja, Mar del Plata, Mendoza, Mercedes, Monte Caseros, Neuquen, Orán, Pasadas, Puerto de los Libres, Puerto Deseado, Rio Cuarto, Rio Galleagos, Rio Grande, Rosario, Salta, San Carlos de Bariloche, San Juan, San Julian, San Luis, San Rafael, Santiago del Estero, Santa Cruz, Santa Fé, Santa Rosa, Trelew, Tucumán, Ushuaia, Viedma, Villa Dolores

Livery F: white, blue, grey
T: blue and white

Fleet

Boeing 707-387B (*387C)

LV-ISA	*Antártida Argentina*	LV-ISD	*Proñon*
LV-ISB	*Almilan*	LV-*	
LV-ISC	*Betelgeuse*	LV-*	

Hawker Siddeley (de Havilland) Comet 4 (*4C)

LV-AHN	*Les Tres Marias*	LV-AHU	*Centaurus*
LV-AHS	*Alborada*	LV-AIB*	*Presidente Kennedy*

Sud Aviation S.E.210 Caravelle 6R

LV-HGX	*Aldebarón*	LV-III	*Antares*
LV-HGZ	*Rigel*		

Hawker Siddeley HS 748 Series 1

LV-HGW	*Ciudad de Bahia Blanca*	LV-HHG	*Ciudad de La Rioja*
LV-HHB	*Ciudad de Corrientes*	LV-HHH	*Ciudad de Meuquén*
LV-HHC	*Ciudad de Concordia*	LV-HHI	*Ciudad de Rio Gallegos*
LV-HHD	*Ciudad de Salta*	LV-IDV	*Ciudad de Montevideo*
LV-HHE	*Ciudad de Resistencia*	LV-IEE	*Ciudad de Santa Fé*
LV-HHF	*Ciudad de San Juan*	LV-IEV	*Ciudad de Gauleguaychú*

QANTAS
Qantas Airways Ltd

Australia

Although the history of Qantas Airways itself goes back to 1934, the airline's origins date back still further to 1920 and the formation of the Queensland and Northern Territory Aerial Service (QANTAS), although during the few months preceding the company's incorporation it was known first as "The Western Queensland Auto Aerial Service", and then as the "Australian Transcontinental Aerial Services Co.".

Initially the QANTAS fleet consisted of an Avro 504K and a BE2E with which the airline operated pleasure flights and special charters throughout Queensland while the directors pressed the Australian Government to grant a subsidy for scheduled services. After much pressure the necessary support was received, although the airline still had to tender for the right to operate the services, and operations began between Charleville and Cloncurry on 2nd November, 1922.

During the early years the airline had to struggle with severe equipment difficulties due to both delays in the delivery of new aeroplanes and to the necessity of cancelling orders for 'planes which failed to meet the severe operating conditions of the Queensland summer. It was only the expertise and determination of the new airline's engineering staff that kept the ageing fleet airborne, and services operating.

The airline survived, however, and, with the arrival of DH50's, which were a great improvement over the previous equipment, and for which the company held a manufacturer's licence, QANTAS prospered. Other activities started by the airline in the early days included two flying schools in 1926 and the establishment of a Flying Doctor Service in 1928 with a DH50 converted to a flying ambulance; although a Queensland doctor had used the company's aircraft for his visits to patients before this date.

In 1934 the airline was renamed "Qantas Empire Airways Ltd" and the following year QANTAS aircraft, four-engined DH86's, took over the Darwin–Singapore section of the Imperial Airways route to London, and which that airline had operated for QANTAS since the previous year. Several new types of aircraft were introduced by QANTAS during the 1934 to 1939 period, including the Short Empire 'C' Class flying boats which came in 1938. They were used later to form the nucleus of a Royal Australian Air Force flying boat squadron. Also during 1938, QANTAS moved its headquarters from Brisbane to Sydney, and from there operated the Brisbane–Singapore section of the route to London, the Australian airline's portion of this route later being extended to Karachi.

In association with the newly created British Overseas Airways Corporation, QANTAS operated a non-stop Perth–Colombo service, after the fall of Singapore during the Second World War. Other services operated during the war years were evacuation flights from New Guinea, and some essential Australian domestic air routes.

After the war, QANTAS embarked on a programme of expansion in order to establish a world-wide route network. Aircraft used during this period included ex-war 'Liberators', 'Catalina' flying boats, and new Douglas DC-4 'Skymasters', Short 'Sandringham' flying boats, the last of this type of aircraft to be operated by the airline. Lockheed 'Super Constellations' were introduced to the fleet in 1954, and four years later, one of them inaugurated the airline's round-the-world service.

In 1959, QANTAS became the first non-American airline to introduce Boeing 707 jet airliners, and the jet fleet has since grown by the addition of Boeing 707-338C's which have replaced the Boeing 707-138B's, a version unique to QANTAS. The airline's first, and only, turbo-prop equipment, Lockheed 'Electras', were also introduced in 1959. For the future, QANTAS has reserved delivery positions for four British-French jointly produced BAC/Sud Concordes and six of the American Boeing 2707 supersonic transports (SSTs); four Boeing 747's are also on order with another two on option.

The ownership of the airline passed to the Australian Government in 1947, and this position has remained unchanged since that date. QANTAS holds 32% of the shares in Malaysia-Singapore Airways (formerly Malaysian Airways), and 25% of the shares in Fiji Airways. The airline's name was changed to "Qantas Airways Ltd" late in 1967.

Member of the International Air Transport Association

QANTAS includes Boeing 707-338Cs (convertible passenger/cargo) aircraft in its jet fleet; here is VH-EBN in the new livery adopted in 1968

Services' route points:
Acapulco, Amsterdam, Athens, Auckland, Bahrain, Bangkok, Bermuda, Brisbane, Cairo, Calcutta, Christchurch, Colombo, Darwin, Djakarta, Fiji, Frankfurt, Hong Kong, Honolulu, Istanbul, Johannesburg, Karachi, Kuala Lumpur, London, Manila, Mauritius, Melbourne, Mexico City, Nassau, New Delhi, New York, Norfolk Island, Noumea, Perth, Port Moresby, Rome, San Francisco, Singapore, Sydney, Tahiti, Tehran, Tokyo, Vancouver, Vienna, Wellington

Livery F: white, red, grey   **T:** red

Fleet

Douglas DC-4 Skymaster
VH-EDA	*Pacific Trader*	VH-EDB	*Norfolk Trader*

Lockheed Electra L188C
VH-ECD	*Pacific Enterprise*

Boeing 707-338C
VH-EAA	*City of Toowoomba*	VH-EBO	*City of Townsville*
VH-EAB	*City of Canberra*	VH-EBP	*City of Alice Springs*
VH-EAC	*City of Sydney*	VH-EBQ	*City of Ballarat*
VH-EAD	*City of Melbourne*	VH-EBR	*City of Wollongong*
VH-EAE	*City of Brisbane*	VH-EBS	*Kalgoorlie*
VH-EAF	*City of Adelaide*	VH-EBT	*City of Bendigo*
VH-EAG	*City of Hobart*	VH-EBU	*City of Broken Hill*
VH-EAH	*City of Perth*	VH-EBV	*City of Tamworth*
VH-EAI	*City of Darwin*	VH-EBW	*City of Armidale*
VH-EAJ	*City of Geelong*	VH-EBX	*Port Moresby*
VH-EBN	*City of Parramatta*		

AUSTRIAN AIRLINES

Austria

Österreichische Luftverkehrs AG

Austrian Airlines was formed in 1957 after Austria had been without a national airline for almost twenty years since Ölag Österreichische Luftverkehrs AG, an airline formed in 1923, operating from Vienna to many Central European destinations, ceased operations on the German occupation of Austria in 1938.

The new airline's first international service was between Vienna and London with a Vickers 'Viscount' aircraft, and the present all-turbine fleet includes 'Viscounts' 'Caravelles' and Hawker Siddeley 748's operating on a network of domestic and international services, the latter extending throughout Europe and to the Middle East, with Boeing 707-operated trans-Atlantic services scheduled for 1969. The airline is owned in equal one-third shares by the Austrian Federal Government, the provincial governments, and private interests.

Member of the International Air Transport Association

One of three Austrian Airlines' Vickers Viscounts, OE-LAK, at Innsbruck

International Services from Vienna to:

Abadan, Amsterdam, Athens, Belgrade, Beirut, Brussels, Bucharest, Budapest, Cairo, Copenhagen, Damascus, Frankfurt, Geneva, Istanbul, Leipzig, London, Milan, Moscow, Munich, Paris, Prague, Rome, Salonica, Sofia, Stockholm, Tel Aviv, Warsaw, Zürich

from Innsbruck to:
Düsseldorf, Zürich, London

from Salzburg to:
Amsterdam, Frankfurt, London

from Graz to:
Frankfurt

from Linz to:
Frankfurt

12

Domestic services
Innsbruck–Salzburg–Vienna
from Vienna:
Graz, Linz, Klagenfurt
from Graz:
Linz

Livery F: white, red and grey **T:** red and white

Fleet
Vickers Viscount 837
OE-LAH *Franz Schubert*   OE-LAL *Wolfgang A. Mozart*
OE-LAK *Johann Strauss*

Sud Aviation S.E.210 Caravelle 6R
OE-LCA *Wien*   OE-LCO *Karnten*
OE-LCE *Tyrol*   OE-LCU *Steiemark*
OE-LCI *Salzburg*

Hawker Siddeley 748 (Belvedere)
OE-LHS *Franz Lehar*   OE-LHT *Anton Brückner*

SABENA   Belgium
Société Anonyme Belge d'Exploitation de la Navigation Aérienne

SABENA was founded in May 1923 as the successor to SNETA (Société Nationále pour l'Étude de Transports Aériens) an airline formed in 1919 to operate services to London, Paris and Amsterdam with ex-World War I aircraft.

SABENA began operations immediately with a newspaper service from Brussels to Lympne via Ostend, and in 1924 a service to Basle via Strasbourg was introduced with a three-engined Handley Page W.8. The following year an aircraft of this type flew to the Belgian Congo, the 75-hour journey being spread over 51 days, but it was not until 1935 that a regular Brussels–Leopoldville service was inaugurated with a Fokker F-VII which took five and a half days. This time was reduced to three days in 1936 with a Savoia-Marchetti S-73, and in 1938 was reduced further to 24 hours with a Savoia-Marchetti S-83; this aircraft was the fastest in commercial service at that time.

In the meantime SABENA had developed an extensive European network which included all the major cities as far north as Stockholm, and as far south as Vienna, which was reached in 1938. In 1939 SABENA took delivery of the Douglas DC-3. During the next few years, with World War II and Belgium occupied, the airline placed its fleet at the disposal of the Allied Powers.

Commercial services were restarted in 1946 with a fleet of Douglas DC-3's and DC-4's, the latter aircraft being used on international services to Africa and the United States. In 1947 SABENA became the first European airline to operate Douglas DC-6's, and another European "first" for SABENA occurred in 1949 when helicopter services were introduced. The airline became the first in the world to operate international helicopter services in 1953, and these services operated for thirteen years until 1966 (when the international services were abandoned). Helicopters first used were Sikorsky S-55's, followed by Sikorsky S-58's.

In 1956 the airline introduced Convair 440 'Metropolitans' on its European network, and in 1957 Douglas DC-7C's were put on the intercontinental services, these were the last piston-engined aircraft to be purchased by the airline. SABENA's first jet equipment, Boeing 707's were introduced in 1960, followed in 1961 by 'Caravelles' for the European routes. These two types together with Boeing 727's, Douglas DC-6's, DC-7C's and DC-3's form the present fleet, which will be supplemented in the 1970's by two BAC/Sud 'Concorde' SST.

SABENA is owned 65% by the Belgian Government, 25% by the Republic of Congo, and 10% by private shareholders. The airline developed an extensive network in the Belgian Congo over the years, and in 1961 helped to form Air Congo by providing technical assistance.

Member of the International Air Transport Association

International services from Brussels to:
Abidjan, Alicante, Amsterdam, Athens, Barcelona, Beirut, Bombay, Bucharest, Budapest, Bujumbura, Cairo, Casablanca, Cologne, Copenhagen, Dar-es-Salaam, Düsseldorf, Entebbe, Frankfurt, Guatemala, Geneva, Hamburg, Istanbul, Jeddah, Johannesburg, Kano, Kigali, Kinshasa, Lagos, Las Palmas, Lisbon, London, Lubumbashi, Luxembourg, Madrid, Malaga, Manchester, Mexico City, Milan, Montreal, Moscow, Munich, Nairobi, New York, Palma, Paris, Prague, Rome, Salonica, Stockholm, Stuttgart, Tangier, Tehran, Tel-Aviv, Tenerife, Tunis, Warsaw, Vienna, Zürich

Livery F: white, blue, grey **T:** blue

Fleet

Douglas DC-3 Dakota

OO-AUV	OO-AWK	OO-AWN	OO-CBU	OO-CBW
OO-AUX	OO-AWM	OO-AWZ		

Douglas DC-6B

OO-CTK	OO-CTN	OO-SDQ

Douglas DC-7C

OO-SFB	OO-SFC

Boeing 707-329

OO-SJA	OO-SJD	OO-SJE	OO-SJF	OO-SJG
OO-SJC				

Boeing 707-329C

OO-SJH	OO-SJJ	OO-SJZ

Sud Aviation S.E. 210 Caravelle 6R

OO-SRA	OO-SRC	OO-SRE	OO-SRG	OO-SRI
OO-SRB	OO-SRD	OO-SRF	OO-SRH	OO-SRK

Boeing 727-29

OO-STA	OO-STB	OO-STE

Boeing 727-29C

OO-STC	OO-STD	OO-

VARIG Brazil
SA. Empresa de Vicão Aerea Rio Grandense

VARIG started operations in 1927 with technical assistance from the German Condor Syndicate (a company formed by Lufthansa to operate the South American section of that airline's trans-South Atlantic air/sea service) whose Brazilian routes VARIG was to operate, initially with a Dornier 'Wal' flying-boat.

Although VARIG expanded, it remained a domestic operator confined mainly to South Brazil until 1951 when it acquired Aero Geral, another domestic operator with routes to Natal. International operations started in 1953 when a service to the United States was introduced, but expansion on international routes did not really gain impetus until 1961 when VARIG took over the REAL consortium, which included Aerovias Brasilia, Nacionale and Aeronorte. This virtually doubled the domestic network and quadrupled the international network. In 1965 VARIG began operations to Europe when it obtained the route network of Panair do Brasil which had been in financial difficulties finally culminating in bankruptcy when the Brazilian Government cancelled the airline's traffic rights and offered them to VARIG.

The present VARIG international network covers the Americas, Europe, Africa, and the Middle East, and the fleet includes an ex-Panair do Brasil leased Douglas DC-8, Boeing 707's, Convair 990A's, Lockheed 'Electras', Convair 240's Douglas DC-3's and Hawker Siddeley HS748's, introduced in spring 1968. The Lockheed 'Super Constellation' and Curtiss C-46 fleets are in the process of being sold. VARIG is an entirely private enterprise concern, owned 85% by employees and 15% by management.

Member of the International Air Transport Association

International services from Rio de Janeiro to:
Asuncion(S), Beirut, Bogota, Buenos Aires(S), Caracas(B), Frankfurt, Lima(S), Lisbon, London, Los Angeles, Madrid(R), Mexico City, Miami(B), Monrovia, Montevideo(S), New York, Panama, Paris, Rome(R), Santiago(S), Zürich(R)
B—via Belem   R—via Recife   S—via São Paulo
There are also connections from Rio de Janeiro to São Paulo from all flights
São Paulo–Curitiba–Iguassu Falls–Asuncion

Major domestic route points:
Belem, Brasilia, Natal, Recife, Rio de Janeiro, São Paulo

Livery F: white, blue, grey   **T:** white

Fleet

Douglas DC-3 (*Cargo)

PP-AKA	PP-VAW*	PP-VBH	PP-VBR	PP-YPI
PP-ANN	PP-VAX	PP-VBK	PP-VBT	PP-YPT
PP-ANU	PP-VAZ	PP-VBL	PP-VBW	PP-YPU
PP-ANV	PP-VBB	PP-VBN	PP-VCO	PP-YPY
PP-AVT	PP-VBF*	PP-VBO	PP-VCH	PP-YQQ
PP-AXL	PP-VBQ	PP-VBP	PP-VDM	

Convair 240

PP-VCN	PP-VCR	PP-VCW	PP-VCY	PP-VDG
PP-VCO	PP-VCU	PP-VCX	PP-VCZ	PP-VDH
PP-VCP				

Hawker Siddeley HS 748 Series II

PP-VDN	PP-VDQ	PP-VDS	PP-VDU	PP-VDW
PP-VDO	PP-VDR	PP-VDT	PP-VDV	PP-VDX
PP-VDP				

Douglas DC-8 Series 30 (leased)
PP-PDS   *Manuel de Barba Gato*

Boeing 707-441
PP-VJA   PP-VJJ

Boeing 707-341C
PP-VJS   PP-VJT   PP-VJX

Convair 990A Coronado
PP-VJF   PP-VJG

Lockheed L-188 Electra
PP-VJL   PP-VJN   PP-VJP   PP-VJV   PP-VJW
PP-VJM   PP-VJO   PP-VJU

TABSO
Bulgarian Civil Air Transport

Bulgaria

TABSO was formed in 1949 to take over the services of BVS which had been founded by the Bulgarian Government after the end of World War II and had started domestic operations in 1948. Initially the new airline was owned equally by Russia and Bulgaria, but in 1954 Bulgaria assumed full control, and the emphasis moved from domestic to international operations. The airline introduced services to Warsaw, Copenhagen, Frankfurt, Paris, Athens, Moscow and Beirut operating a mixed Li-2 (Russian-built DC-3's) and Ilyushin Il-14 fleet.

The route network was further expanded in 1962 with the introduction of the turbo-prop Ilyushin Il-18. These aircraft inaugurated a service to Tunisia and Algeria in 1963, and they also operate charter services from the rest of Europe to the Black Sea resorts. Three Tu-134's and six An-24's are also operated.

International services from Sofia to:

Algiers, Athens, Belgrade, Berlin (East), Bucharest, Budapest, Copenhagen, Damascus, Frankfurt, Istanbul, Kiev, London, Moscow, Paris, Prague, Tunis, Vienna, Warsaw

Domestic services from Sofia to:

Bourgos, Garna, Khaskovo, Ploudiv, Rose, Stara Zagora, Varna

Fleet

Ilyushin Il-14
LZ-ILA	LZ-ILC	LZ-ILE	LZ-ILF	LZ-ILG
LZ-ILB	LZ-ILD			

Antonov An-24
LZ-ANA	LZ-ANC	LZ-ANE	LZ-ANF	LZ-ANG
LZ-ANB				

Ilyushin Il-18
LZ-BED	LZ-BEL	LZ-BEO	LZ-BER	LZ-BET
LZ-BEG	LZ-BEM	LZ-BEP	LZ-BES	LZ-BEV
LZ-BEK	LZ-BEN			

Tupolev Tu-134
LZ-TUA	LZ-TUB	LZ-TUC

AIR CANADA

Canada

Air Canada was formed in 1937 as Trans-Canada Air Lines as a result of the Trans-Canada Air Lines Act which had been passed by the Canadian Parliament that year. The new airline was, and still is, owned 100% by Canadian National Railways, a Crown Corporation, after the failure of a plan for a mixed enterprise concern with Canadian Pacific Railways as the other shareholder.

The new airline purchased the Canadian Airways Company and with its fleet of two Lockheed 10a Electra and a single-engined Stearman bi-plane commenced operating a Vancouver–Seattle service. The following year saw the introduction of services from Winnipeg to Vancouver, Montreal and Toronto, and to Edmonton and Lethbridge. By the end of the year the fleet had grown to five Lockheed 10A's and nine of the larger Lockheed 14H's. In 1940 passenger services eastwards reached the Maritime Provinces providing Canada's first trans-continental air service.

During the first part of World War II TCA concentrated on expanding its network of domestic services. However, in 1943 the airline gained its first invaluable experience of trans-Atlantic operation when it commenced flying the Canadian Government Trans-Atlantic Air Service with Avro Lancastrians between Montreal and Prestwick. This service was intended to carry important passengers and Forces' mail to Europe.

The year the war ended, Trans-Canada Air Lines received a fleet of 30 Douglas DC-3's, and new routes followed, principally to the United States. Two years later the airline introduced the Canadair North Star (a Canadair—manufactured DC-4 with Rolls-Royce Merlin engines) and started to operate the trans-Atlantic routes in its own right. This expansion continued throughout the 1950's with new services to Europe, including, in 1957, a non-stop Toronto–London Super Constellation service. The Lockheed Super Constellations were introduced in 1954, and in 1955 TCA became the first North American operator of the Vickers Viscount turbo-prop airliner.

The airline's first jet equipment entered service in 1960, these were Douglas DC-8 Series 40's, and the following year TCA introduced the turbo-prop Vickers Vanguard to its routes. The present title was adopted in 1964 to reflect the fact that the airline was no longer merely a trans-continental operator. The first batch of Douglas DC-9's was also ordered in 1964 to begin Viscount replacement, and the present fleet consists of these aircraft with DC-8's, 'Vanguards' and 'Viscounts'. For the future Air Canada has reserved delivery positions for four BAC/Sud Concorde and six Boeing 2707 SST's, and ordered three Boeing 747 'Jumbo' jets and ten Lockheed L-1011 airbuses.

Member of the International Air Transport Association

CF-TLC, a Douglas DC-9 jet in service on Air Canada's North American routes

Route points—international and domestic

Antigua, Barbados, Bermuda, Boston, Calgary, Chicago, Cleveland, Copenhagen, Earlton, Edmonton, Fort William, Frankfurt, Fredericton, Freeport, Gander, Goose Bay, Halifax, Kingston (Jamaica), Lethbridge, London, London (Ontario), Miami, Moncton, Montego Bay, Montreal, Moscow, Nassau, New York, North Bay, Ottawa, Paris, Port Arthur, Prestwick, Quebec City, Regina, Rouyn-Noranda, Saguenay, Saint John, St. John's, Saskatoon, Sault Ste. Marie, Seattle, Sept-Iles, Shannon, Stephenville, Sudbury, Sydney, Tampa, Timmins, Toronto-Hamilton, Trinidad, Trois-Rivières, Val d'Or, Vancouver, Victoria, Vienna, Windsor (Ontario), Winnipeg, Yarmouth (Nova Scotia), Zürich

Livery F: white, red, grey, with black **T:** red

CF-TJM, a DC-8-54F used on the trans-Atlantic services

Fleet

Vickers Viscount 700

CF-TGI	CF-TGZ	CF-THI	CF-THQ	CF-THZ
CF-TGK	CF-THB	CF-THJ	CF-THR	CF-TIA
CF-TGS	CF-THC	CF-THK	CF-THS	CF-TIB
CF-TGT	CF-THD	CF-THL	CF-THU	CF-TIC
CF-TGU	CF-THE	CF-THM	CF-THV	CF-TID
CF-TGV	CF-THF	CF-THN	CF-THW	CF-TIE
CF-TGW	CF-THG	CF-THO	CF-THX	CF-TIF
CF-TGX	CF-THH	CF-THP	CF-THY	CF-TIG

Vickers Vanguard 952

CF-TKA	CF-TKF	CF-TKK	CF-TKP	CF-TKT
CF-TKB	CF-TKG	CF-TKL	CF-TKQ	CF-TKU
CF-TKC	CF-TKH	CF-TKM	CF-TKR	CF-TKV
CF-TKD	CF-TKI	CF-TKN	CF-TKS	CF-TKW
CF-TKE	CF-TKJ	CF-TKO		

Douglas DC-8 Series 41

CF-TJA	CF-TJC	CF-TJE	CF-TJH	CF-TJJ
CF-TJB	CF-TJD	CF-TJF	CF-TJI	CF-TJK

Douglas DC-8–53

CF-TIH	CF-TII	CF-TIJ

Douglas DC-8–54F Jet Trader

CF-TJL	CF-TJO	CF-TJQ	CF-TJR	CF-TJS
CF-TJM	CF-TJP			

Douglas DC-8 Series 61
CF-TJT   CF-TJV   CF-TJW   CF-TJX   CF-TJY
CF-TJU

Douglas DC-9–14
CF-TLB   CF-TLD   CF-TLE   CF-TLF   CF-TLG
CF-TLC

Douglas DC-9–32
Initial order for delivery by May, 1969, but those marked * are optional for
delivery by May, 1970

CF-TLH	CF-TLP	CF-TLX	CF-TMF	CF-TMN
CF-TLI	CF-TLQ	CF-TLY	CF-TMG	CF-TMO
CF-TLJ	CF-TLR	CF-TLZ	CF-TMH	CF-TMP
CF-TLK	CF-TLS	CF-TMA	CF-TMI	CF-TMQ*
CF-TLL	CF-TLT	CF-TMB	CF-TMJ	CF-TMR*
CF-TLM	CF-TLU	CF-TMC	CF-TMK	CF-TMS*
CF-TLN	CF-TLV	CF-TMD	CF-TML	CF-TMT*
CF-TLO	CF-TLW	CF-TME	CF-TMM	CF-TMU*

CP AIR   Canada
Canadian Pacific Airlines Ltd

Canadian Pacific Airlines is the air transport operating subsidiary of a $2,000-million group, originally formed to build and operate a trans-continental railway system, but now also including amongst its activities shipping, hotel, road transport, oil, gas and timber production, mining and property development.

A plan had been mooted by the Canadian Government during the 1930's for a joint state and private enterprise airline with Canadian Pacific as the private enterprise partner, but this came to nothing, and it was not until 1942 that Canadian Pacific Airlines was formed on the amalgamation of ten small independent, mainly bush, airlines; the largest of which was Canadian Airways of Winnipeg in which the Canadian Pacific Railway had held the controlling interest since 1930. The other airlines were Ginger Coote Airways of Vancouver, Yukon Southern Air Transport of Vancouver and Edmonton, Wings of Winnipeg, Prairie Airways of Moose Jaw, Mackenzie Air Services of Edmonton, Arrow Airways of Manitoba, Starratt Airways of Hudson, Quebec Airways, and Montreal and Dominion Skyways. The CPR had obtained a permit to operate aircraft commercially as far back as 1919. The decision to purchase the large number of smaller airlines had been taken in 1939, when many of them were in difficulty because of inadequate financing and inefficient aircraft ill-suited to their operations. The CPR had also assisted with the formation of the North Atlantic Ferry Service for delivery of bombers to the Royal Air Force in 1940, and during World War II, CPA operated six flying schools, and later, during the Korean War, some 700 military contract flights between Vancouver and Tokyo were operated.

Canadian Pacific's initial air transport effort was naturally aimed at continuing the bush service of its predecessors, but in 1949, the first two of its trans-Pacific services, to Sydney and Hong Kong, were started. In exchange for its Ontario and Quebec services, CPA obtained Air Canada's Mexico City route in

1955 (later extended to Buenos Aires), and the same year, the airline pioneered the polar route from Vancouver to Amsterdam. The last of CPA's bush operations was dropped in 1959, when the airline received authority to operate its first transcontinental service, using Bristol Britannias. More recently, the Canadian Government has allowed CPA's transcontinental operations to expand so that, by 1970, the airline will be able to provide 25% of the total capacity on these services. Currently, the airline's fleet name is being changed to CP Air as part of a marketing plan for the whole range of Canadian Pacific activities. A new livery was adopted during the winter of 1968-69.

At the present time, Canadian Pacific operates a fleet of Douglas DC-3's, DC-6 Cloudmasters, DC-8's and Boeing 737's on an extensive route pattern of domestic and international services.

Member of the International Air Transport Association

Domestic services

Vancouver–Calgary/Edmonton–Winnipeg–Toronto–Montreal
Vancouver–Penticton/Vernon–Castlegar–Nelson–Kimberley–Calgary
Vancouver–Prince George/Edmonton–Grande Prairie–Fort St John–Fort Nelson–Watson Lake–Whitehorse–Mayo–Dawson City
Vancouver–Prince Rupert–Whitehorse
Vancouver–Kamloops–Williams Lake–Quesnel–Prince George–Fort St John–Grande Prairie–Edmonton
Vancouver–Prince George
Vancouver–Sandspit–Prince Rupert–Terrace–Prince George–Smithers/Whitehorse

International services

Vancouver–San Francisco
Vancouver–Calgary–Mexico City–Lima–Santiago/Buenos Aires
Montreal–Toronto–Winnipeg–Vancouver–Tokyo–Hong Kong
Vancouver–Honolulu–Nandi–Auckland–Sydney
Vancouver–Calgary–Edmonton–Winnipeg–Windsor–Toronto–Montreal–Amsterdam–Santa Maria–Lisbon–Madrid–Rome–Amsterdam
Vancouver–Amsterdam

Livery F: white, red, unpainted **T:** red, white

Fleet

Douglas DC-3 Dakota
CF-CPX   CF-CRX   CF-CRZ

Douglas DC-6B Cloudmaster (a=DC-6A, c=cargo, *=leased)
CF-CUS*   CF-CZS c   CF-CZT   CF-CZU   CF-CZZ a
CF-CZQ c

Douglas DC-8 Series 43
CF-CPF   Empress of Rome   CF-CPI   Empress of Amsterdam
CF-CPG   Empress of Buenos Aires CF-CPJ   Empress of Mexico City
CF-CPH   Empress of Tokyo

Douglas DC-8–63 (* series 53, † 55F)
CF-CPO   CF-CPQ   CF-CPM*   Empress of Lisbon
CF-CPP   CF-CPS   CF-CPT†

Boeing 737
CF-CPB   CF-CPD   CF-CPU   CF-CPV   CF-
CF-CPC   CF-CPE

PACIFIC WESTERN
Pacific Western Airlines Ltd

Pacific Western, Canada's third largest airline, dates from 1945 when it was founded as British Columbia Airways. Operations started the following year, and the present title was adopted in 1953. In 1955, PWA purchased Queen Charlotte Airlines and Associated Airways, while in 1966 the airline sold its third-level services to Northward Aviation, an Edmonton-based company.

Currently, Pacific Western operates a network of scheduled regional services throughout Alberta, British Columbia, the Northwest Territories and Saskatchewan, from its base at Vancouver. North Atlantic inclusive tour and ad hoc passenger and freight charters are also operated. The fleet includes Boeing, Lockheed, Convair, Douglas, Grumman and de Havilland Canada types, with two Boeing 737's on order.

Fleet

CF-	Douglas DC-3 Dakota	CF-	de Havilland Canada Beaver
CF-PWB	,, DC-4	CF-	,, ,,
CF-PWJ	,, ,,	CF-	Grumman Goose
CF-PWA	,, DC-6B	CF-	,, ,,
CF-PWF	,, ,,	CF-	,, ,,
CF-NAI	,, DC-7C	CF-	Convair 640
CF-PWM	,, ,,	CF-	,, ,,
CF-PWO	Lockheed L-382B Hercules	CF-	,, ,,
CF-PWV	Boeing 707-138B	CF-	,, ,,
CF-	de Havilland Canada Otter		

WARDAIR
Wardair Canada Ltd

Wardair Canada Ltd was formed in 1952 as Wardair by Maxwell Ward, the current president and owner of 88% of the airline's capital, and commenced operations the following year replacing the bush charter services inaugurated in 1946 by a de Havilland Canada Fox Moth of the Polaris Charter Company. Wardair's first aircraft was a de Havilland Canada Otter, and the original task of serving survey groups, oil and mining companies, has now expanded to the level that two Bristol 170 Freighters, two de Havilland Canada Otters, two Twin Otters, a Beaver and a Piper Apache are required for this part of the airline's operations. However, an increasingly important part of Wardair Canada's workload is the intercontinental charter operations first started in 1962, a year after the present title was adopted, when the airline moved its main base from Yellowknife to Edmonton. Currently, the Boeing 727 and the Boeing 707 are both required for this work.

Livery F: white, red and blue, unpainted
      T: white, red

Fleet

CF-FAN	Boeing 707-311C
CF-FUN	Boeing 727-11
CF-TFX	Bristol 170 Freighter
CF-WAC	" "
CF-	de Havilland Canada Otter
CF-	" "
CF-	" Twin Otter
CF-	" "
CF-	" Beaver
CF-	Piper Apache

The Canadian independent, Wardair, operates this Boeing 707-311C, CF-FAN, on charter flights to Europe

AIR CEYLON Ceylon

Air Ceylon was formed in 1947 after the Ministry of Communications and Works had purchased three Douglas DC-3 Dakotas for this purpose. Initially, operations were within Ceylon and to India, but services to London and Sydney were introduced in 1949 after entering into an operating agreement with Australian National Airways, and two Douglas DC-4 Skymasters were purchased for these services.

In 1951, Air Ceylon became a corporation with the Ceylon Government holding 51%, and Australian National Airways 49%, of the capital. ANA's

22

interest was purchased in 1955 by KLM Royal Dutch Airlines, and from 1956, a service to Amsterdam was operated. This agreement terminated in 1961, when international services other than those to India were terminated until British Overseas Airways Corporation started a London–Colombo service in association with Air Ceylon in 1962, using one of BOAC's de Havilland Comet 4's; and this arrangement still exists, although a BAC VC10 is now used.

Since 1961, Air Ceylon has been owned entirely by the Ceylon Government. Current equipment includes a Nord 262 and Douglas DC-3 Dakotas, for domestic routes; a Hawker Siddeley HS 748 turbo-prop airliner for Indian services, and a Hawker Siddeley Trident 1E for services to Bangkok and Beirut; this airline may also have a Trident 2 joining it in the near future.

Member of the International Air Transport Association

International services from Colombo to:
Bahrain, Bangkok, Beirut, Bombay, Cairo, Kuala Lumpur, Kuwait, London, Madras, Rome, Singapore, Tehran

Domestic services from Colombo to:
Batticaloa, Gal Oya, Jaffna, Tiruchirapalli, Trincomalee

Livery F: white, red, yellow, grey
　　　　T: red, yellow

Fleet

4R-ACG	Douglas DC-3 Dakota
4R-ACI	,,　　　　　　,,
4R-	Hawker Siddeley Trident 1E
4R-ACJ	,,　　　　HS 748 Series 2
4R-ACL	Nord 262

A BOAC BAC VC10 is also used

4R-ACJ, Air Ceylon's Hawker Siddeley HS 748 Srs 2 is seen here at Colombo

LAN-CHILE
Línea Aérea Nacional de Chile

Chile

The story of LAN-Chile goes back to 1929 when the Government of Chile formed an airline, Linea Aeropostal Santiago-Arica under Air Force management and having an initial fleet of eight de Havilland 'Gipsy Moths'. The airline assumed its present name in 1932 when it became civilian-controlled. An assorted fleet including Ford Tri-Motors, Curtiss 'Condors', and Potez 56's, had been acquired during the airline's three-year existence, and with them LAN-Chile expanded its domestic routes.

The first international service, to Buenos Aires, was inaugurated in 1946 using newly acquired Douglas DC-3's. Development was still confined to domestic services using both the DC-3's and Martin 202's, and it was not until 1955 that the airline received its first four-engined equipment—Douglas DC-6B's. These aircraft opened routes to Lima and Guayaquil, and, in 1958, to Panama. LAN's first jet aircraft, 'Caravelles', arrived in 1962.

In 1964, after a change of Government, the airline was extensively re-organized and an attempt was made to reduce the subsidy which the airline received from the Government. By the end of 1966 the subsidy was vastly reduced and the airline embarked on a programme of modernization, with an order for eight DC-3 replacement Hawker Siddeley 748 turbo-prop airliners as a first step. The current fleet consists of 748's, DC-3's, DC-6's and 'Caravelles'. The airline is to expand shortly on to inter-continental services for which a Boeing 707 has been purchased from Lufthansa. Initially the airline will operate via Easter Island to Australia, but services to Europe are expected to follow.

Member of the International Air Transport Association

International services from Santiago de Chile to:
Buenos Aires, La Paz, Lima, Mendoza, Miami, Montevideo, Panama

Domestic services are operated from Santiago to some thirty points within Chile

Fleet
Douglas DC-3

CC-	CC-	CC-	CC-	CC-
CC-	CC-	CC-	CC-	CC-
CC-				

Douglas DC-6B

CC-	CC-	CC-	CC-	CC	
CC-	CC-	CC-	CC-	CC-	*

*Douglas DC-6A

Cessna 310
CC-

Sud Aviation S.E. 210 Caravelle 6R

CC-CCO	CC-CCQ	CC-CCP

Hawker Siddeley 748 Mk. 2

CC-CEC	CC-CEE	CC-CEG	CC-CEI	CC-CEJ
CC-CED	CC-CEF	CC-CEH		

Boeing 707-330B
CC-

AVIANCA
Aerovias Nacionales de Colombia SA

As SCADTA, the second airline in the world, and the first in the Americas to start operations, Avianca's history goes back to 1919 when a Junkers seaplane owned by the airline inaugurated a service between Barranquilla and Giradot. Because of the natural difficulties in surface travel in Colombia, the new airline's traffic potential enabled it to expand rapidly.

During its history Avianca has made many "firsts"; one of the airline's aircraft, a Fokker, won a prize offered by a newspaper for the first aircraft to land at Colombia's capital, Bogota, which is almost 9,000 feet up in the Andes. This was followed in 1925 by the first air service between North and South America when an Avianca flying boat flew from Barranquilla to Florida. Avianca also became the first South American airline to operate into Miami (1947) and New York (1948). In 1960 the airline introduced the first non-stop jet service between Miami and Bogota, followed, four years later, by the first non-stop jet service between New York and Bogota. Before this, the airline had introduced the first through jet services from New York to Bogota, Quito and Lima in 1961.

Today Avianca, which is a non-subsidized privately owned company in which Pan American World Airways has a 38% interest, operates a fleet of Boeing 720's and 727's, Douglas DC-4's and DC-3's, and Lockheed 'Super Constellations' on a network which includes North and South America, the Caribbean and Europe, as well as almost 40 towns within Colombia. In addition Avianca has three wholly-owned subsidiaries, Helicol, which operates general helicopter charters, Aerotaxi, which operates air-taxi services with Beechcraft, Cessna, and DHC 'Beaver' aircraft, and SAM which operates domestic scheduled services and international charters with DC-4 and C-46 aircraft.

Avianca of Colombia operates Boeing 720's on flights to the United States and Europe

During 1967 Avianca commenced services to Santiago de Chile, and may soon begin services to London. For its domestic routes, Avianca has a batch of Hawker Siddeley HS748 turbo-prop airliners on order to replace its DC-3 fleet.

Member of the International Air Transport Association

International services from Bogota to:

Buenos Aires, Caracas, Frankfurt, La Paz, Lima, Madrid, Mexico City, Miami, New York, Panama, Paris, Quito, San Juan, Santiago

Domestic (major route points only):

Arauca, Armenia, Barranca, Barranquilla, Bogota, Bucaramanga, Buenaventura, Cali, Cartagena, Cucuta, Ipiales, Leticia, Manizales, Medellin, Mitu, Monteria Neiva, Pasto, Pereira, Popaya, Puerto Leguizama, Puerto Carreno, San Andres' Santa Marta, Sogamosa, Tumaco, Turbo, Uriba, Villavicencio

Livery F: white, blue, red, grey   **T:** white, blue

Fleet

Lockheed L-1049G Super Constellation
HK-175	HK-176	HK-184

Douglas DC-3 Hiper conversion (* Freighter, c Convertible)
HK-101	HK-121	HK-140	HK-159	HK-1204*
HK-102	HK-122	HK-149	HK-329*	HK-1340
HK-107	HK-124c	HK-154	HK-508*	HK-1341
HK-111				

Douglas DC-4 (*C-54 Freighter)
HK-112	HK-171	HK-180	HK-728	HK-1027
HK-115	HK-172	HK-186	HK-729	HK-1028
HK-136	HK-173	HK-654*	HK-731	HK-1309*
HK-170				

Boeing 707-320B
HK-1402

Boeing 720B
KH-724	HK-725	KH-726

Boeing 727-59
HK-727	HK-1337	HK-1400	HK-1401

Fleet   Aerotaxi

de Havilland Canada Beaver
HK-182	HK-196	HK-951	HK-1014	HK-1070
HK-187	HK-211	HK-1004	HK-1018	HK-1135
HK-188	HK-248	HK-1012	HK-1044	HK-1259
HK-189	HK-249	HK-1013		

Beechcraft Queen Air
HK-1093	HK-1094	HK-1095	HK-1370

Fleet SAM

Douglas DC-4
HK-526	HK-529	HK-558	HK-767	HK-1065
HK-528				

Fleet   Helicol
Bell 47-D1

HK-199	HK-785	HK-973	HK-978	HK-981
HK-212	HK-904	HK-976	HK-979	HK-982
HK-783				

Bell 47-G

HK-198	HK-974

Bell 47-G3B

HK-784	HK-977	HK-1075	HK-1076

Bell 47-G4

HK-197	HK-782	HK-1301

Bell 47-G4A

HK-1298	HK-1349

Bell 47-J2A

HK-633	HK-657

Bell 204-B

HK-668	HK-1073	HK-1359	HK-1372	HK-1373
HK-1072	HK-1297			

Hiller 12-C
HK-887
Hiller 12-E4
HK-781

CYPRUS AIRWAYS
Cyprus Airways Ltd

Cyprus

Cyprus Airways was formed in 1947 to be owned by the Cyprus Government (40%) British European Airways (40%), and private interests (20%). At first the airline operated services to Athens and the Middle East with aircraft leased from BEA, but in 1948 it acquired three DC-3's of its own. Additional DC-3's were acquired in 1950 when Rome and several points in Arabia were added to the route network. By this time the airline was owned by the Cyprus Government (31)%, BEA (23%), BOAC (23%), and private interests (23%) as a result of an increase in the Company's capital.

The airline encountered serious setbacks in 1955 and 1956 when, on account of terrorist action and a drop in traffic, heavy losses were incurred. As a result, the airline abandoned its Arabian services and shelved plans to replace its DC-3's with its own 'Viscounts', and turned to the present system under which 'Viscounts' leased from BEA operate the services. The company is now owned by the Cyprus Government (53.2%), BEA (22.7%) and private interests (24.1%).

Member of the International Air Transport Association

International services only from Nicosia to:
Ankara, Athens, Beirut, Cairo, Istanbul, Jerusalem, London, Rhodes, Rome, Tel-Aviv

Livery F: blue
T: white

Fleet
2 Vickers Viscount 800's leased from BEA

CSA
Československé Aerolinie

Czechoslovakia

The history of CSA dates back to 1923 and the formation of a State air transport group, bearing the title Czechoslovak State Airlines, which used military aircraft—Brandenburg A-14's—military personnel, equipment and airfields. A trial flight was operated between Prague and Bratislava, scheduled services on this route following in 1924. The same year, the first Czech built and designed aircraft, the Aero 10, entered service between Prague and Košicé. The Aero aircraft factory also operated a route between Prague and Mariánské Lázně from 1925 to 1927 when the State airline took over the service.

During the next few years the airline developed rapidly and civil airports opened at Brno, Mariánské Lázně and Bratislava helping to eliminate the dependence on military aerodromes, and a succession of aircraft brought improvements in comfort, reliability and speed. Amongst the aircraft operated during this period were the de Havilland 50, the Farman 'Goliath', which was eventually manufactured under licence in Czechoslovakia, and the Czech designed and built Aero 23's and 38's. The State airline had tended to concentrate on domestic routes, and the development of international routes up to 1930 was left mainly to CLS (Československá Letecká Společnost), formed in 1927 and which had inaugurated its first routes to Rotterdam, Vienna and Berlin in 1928, followed in 1930 by Munich, Zürich and Basle. In 1930 CSA started its first international route to Zagreb, and in 1933 the airline joined the International Air Transport Association.

CSA became the first airline to offer a scheduled air link from West Europe to Russia in 1936 using Airspeed 'Envoys'. This aircraft became known as the "Russian Express" and the service took ten hours as against forty-five for a fast train. Also in 1936 CLS acquired Douglas DC-2's, in which it first used stewardesses, and followed these with DC-3's. Both airlines had quite extensive networks by 1938 when operations had to cease because of the German occupation.

The present Československé Aerolinie was formed in 1945 after the cessation of hostilities with a fleet of three salvaged ex-German Junkers Ju 52/3m's and a few lighter aircraft. Ex-military C-47 'Dakotas' were soon purchased and modified for the airline and operations began on a domestic route linking Prague with Brno and Bratislava in 1946. By the end of the year many of the pre-war European destinations were being served once more. Nationalization of the airline occurred in 1948.

The next type of aircraft to be operated by the airline was the Russian Ilyushin Il-12's and these were followed by Il-14's. In 1957 Tupolev Tu-104 jet airliners were introduced, and these are prominent in the present fleet with Il-18 turbo-prop airliners, twelve Tupolev Tu-134's and a number of Ilyushin Il-62's. Other activities of CSA include air-taxi services with Aero 45 and L200 'Morava' aircraft, and agricultural crop spraying with Czech built L-60's and Russian helicopters.

Member of the International Air Transport Association

International services from Prague to:
Alexandria, Amsterdam, Athens, Baghdad, Bamako, Beirut, Belgrade, Berlin (East), Bombay, Brussels, Budapest, Cairo, Chicago, Conakry, Copenhagen, Damascus, Djakarta, Geneva, Helsinki, London, Moscow, Milan, New York, Paris, Phom-Penh, Rabat (Morocco), Rangoon, Rome, Sofia, Stockholm, Vienna, Warsaw

Domestic services from Prague to:
Bratislava, Brno, Gottwaldov, Karlovy Vary, Košiće, Ostrava, Pieštany, Prešov, Prerov, Sliac

Livery F: white, red, grey   **T:** white

Fleet
Tupolev Tu-104A

OK-LDA	*Praha*	OK-NDD	*Pizen*
OK-LDC	*Brno*	OK-NDF	*Ceske Bodejovice*
OK-MDE	*Ostrava*		

Tupolev Tu-124

OK-TEA	*Melnik*	OK-TEB	*Centrotex*	OK-UEC *Mlada Boleslav*

Ilyushin Il-14

OK-LCA	OK-MCG	OK-MCL	OK-MCR	OK-MCW
OK-LCB	OK-MCH	OK-MCM	OK-MCS	OK-MCX
OK-LCC	OK-MCI	OK-MCN	OK-MCT	OK-MCY
OK-LCD	OK-MCJ	OK-MCO	OK-MCU	OK-MCZ
OK-LCE	OK-MCK	OK-MCP	OK-MCV	OK-OCA
OK-LCF				

Ilyushin Il-18

OK-NAA *Pieštany*	OK-OAC *Sliae*	OK-PAG	*Vysoke Trady*
OK-NAB *Košiče*	OK-PAE *Karlovy Vary*	OK-PAH	*Marianske Lazne*

Bristol Britannia 318 (on lease)
OK-MBB
Tupolev Tu-134

OK-	OK-	OK-	OK-	OK-
OK-	OK-	OK-	OK-	OK-
OK-	OK-			

Ilyushin IL-62

STERLING   Denmark
Sterling Airways A/S

Sterling Airways was formed in May 1962, as part of the travel agency, Tjaereborg Rejser A/S, which is the only shareholder in the airline, to operate inclusive tour charters from Scandinavia. Initially, a fleet of ex-Swissair Douglas DC-6 Cloudmasters was used, and today this fleet has grown to 8 DC-6's, 5 Sud Aviation Super Caravelles (with three on order for 1969 delivery, and another three for 1970 delivery), and one Fokker F-27 Friendship. Inclusive tour and worldwide ad hoc charters are still the airline's workload.

Sterling has its own engineering facilities at its base at Copenhagen Airport, and also owns several subsidiaries in Sweden, Norway and Luxembourg, although these are non-operating.

Livery F: white, red, unpainted
      T: white, red

Fleet
Douglas DC-6B Cloudmaster

OY-BAS	OY-BAU	OY-EAN	OY-EAR	OY-STP
OY-BAT	OY-BAV	OY-EAO		

The Danish charter operator, Sterling Airways, operates five Super Caravelles, one of which is in flight here

Sud Aviation S.E. 210 Super Caravelle
OY-STA   OY-STB   OY-STC   OY-STD   OY-STE
Fokker F-27 Friendship 500
OY-STO

EAST AFRICAN AIRWAYS   East Africa
East African Airways Corporation

East African Airways was formed in 1946, with British Overseas Airways Corporation's assistance and financial support, by the Governments of Kenya, Uganda, Tanganyika and Zanzibar. Initially operations were confined to East African routes on which the airline used a fleet of six leased de Havilland 'Dragon Rapide' biplanes. The corporation expanded rapidly however, and soon the 'Rapides' were replaced by 'Doves', in turn replaced by Lockheed 'Lodestars', which preceded DC-3's. Additional DC-3's were purchased in 1952.

In 1957, EAAC started international operations with Canadair DC-4M 'Argonauts' on services to London, Pakistan, India, Aden and Salisbury. The airline's first jet equipment, a de Havilland 'Comet' 4, was delivered in 1960, and in the autumn of that year the airline had two 'Comet' 4's operating on its international routes, including those to Europe. Prior to this a Bristol 'Britannia' was operated on these services. The current fleet for the international routes consists of four Super VC10's. Delivery of these "second generation" jet air-liners started in 1966, so that the 'Comet' fleet is relegated to purely African services, with a mixed Fokker F-27 'Friendship', de Havilland Canada Twin Otter and 'Dakota' fleet operating domestic routes within East Africa.

East African Airways Corporation is owned by the three East African Governments, Kenya, Uganda, and Tanzania, but the main shareholder is BOAC-Associated Companies with a 53% interest. Seychelles-Kilimanjaro Air Transport, an airline formed in 1960 that owns one DH 'Rapide', is a wholly owned subsidiary of East African Airways. The Comets may be replaced by BAC One-Eleven's in the near future, and more VC10's may be ordered.

Member of the International Air Transport Association

International services from Entebbe and Nairobi, with connections from Dar-es-Salaam to:
Addis Ababa, Aden, Benghazi, Blantyre, Bombay, Bujumbura, Cairo, Frankfurt, Karachi, London, Lusaka, Paris, Rome

East African regional and domestic route points:
Arua, Arusha, Dar-es-Salaam, Dodoma, Eldoret, Entebbe, Gulu, Iringa, Jinja, Kampala, Kasese, Kilwa, Kisumu, Kitale, Lindi, Lushoto, Mafia, Malindi, Mbeya, Mombasa, Moshi, Mtwara, Musoma, Mwanza, Nachingwea, Nairobi, Njombe, Pemba, Sao Hill, Songea, Soroti, Tabora, Tanga, Torora, Zanzibar

Livery F: white, green, yellow, red, black, grey   **T:** white

Fleet: 5H-Tanzania; 5X-Uganda; 5Y-Kenya
Vickers Super VC10
5H-MMT	5X-UVA	5X-UXJ	5Y-ADA

Hawker Siddeley (de Havilland) Comet 4
5Y-AAA	5X-AAO	5H-AAF

Fokker F-27 Friendship
5H-AAI	5X-AAP	5Y-AAB	5Y-AAC

de Havilland Canada Twin Otter (DHC-6)
5H-MNK	5H-MNR

Douglas DC-3 Dakota
5Y-AAE	5X-AAQ	5H-AAJ	5H-AAK	5H-AAL
5Y-AAF				

5X-UVA is one of two Uganda-registered members of East African Airways' Super VC10 fleet

FINNAIR
Finnair O/Y

Finland

Finnair was founded in 1923 by Bruno Lucander with one Junkers F-13 seaplane. Scheduled services started in 1924 when Tallin and Stockholm were served from Helsinki during the summer months, and during the winter temporary services were operated in Finland. The Helsinki–Tallin service was extended to Berlin for the summer of 1925, and the airline's performance during the exceptionally severe winter that followed when the boat services between Helsinki and Tallin were cancelled, and those between Helsinki and Stockholm severely delayed, convinced the Finnish Parliament of the value of air transport. As a result Finnair received a loan from the Government for the purchase of a Junkers G-24, together with subsidies for the Stockholm route, and for air mail services.

By 1928 the fleet consisted of five Junkers aircraft, four F-13's and a G-24, and that year a new service, the Scandinavian Air Express, was inaugurated linking Tallin and Helsinki to London and Paris via Stockholm, Malmö, Copenhagen and Amsterdam; the service took 24 hours. During the next few years several new routes were added to the airline's network, and Finnair also played a part in the development of night air mail services, helped in 1931 by the purchase of a three-engined Ju 52/3m which was able to establish its position using signals

Passengers board a Finnair Super Caravelle at Helsinki; a similar aircraft, OH-LSD is in the background

from a radio station. The opening of airports at Turku and Helsinki in 1935 and 1936 respectively enabled Finnair to convert to a landplane fleet. Before the outbreak of the Second World War, a domestic route network was built up using two DH 'Dragon Rapides'.

During the war years Finnair services had to be cut drastically, both because of wartime shortages and for political reasons. With the exception of the Stockholm service, flying was confined to the domestic routes. During 1944 and 1945, the airline had to suspend operations for six months and international services were not resumed until 1947 when flights were operated to Stockholm, although expansion occurred on the domestic services during the period 1945 to 1947 using Douglas DC-3's. The expansion of both domestic and international services continued throughout the 1950's. In the main, DC-3's were used on the domestic routes and Convair 440 'Metropolitans' on the international routes. In 1956 Finnair became the first Western European airline to receive permission to operate a service to Moscow.

Finnair entered the 1960's with the introduction of its first jets, Sud Aviation 'Caravelles', and today this type is used on all the airline's main routes. In 1966 Finnair ordered two Douglas DC-8 Super 62CF aircraft, with an option for a third, for expansion on to the North Atlantic route in May 1969.

The present Finnair fleet includes 'Caravelles', 'Metropolitans', and DC-3's. The airline is owned 73% by the State and 27% by private investors.

In 1962 Finnair purchased Veljekset Karhumäki O/Y, an aircraft repair firm, and through this obtained a 28.9% interest in Kar-Air O/Y, an airline that operated domestic routes and charter flights, and with which Finnair entered into an operating agreement in 1964. Kar-Air has authority to operate charters to the USA and Canada.

Member of the International Air Transport Association

International services from Helsinki to:
Amsterdam, Barcelona, Copenhagen, Frankfurt, Hamburg, Leningrad, London, Luxembourg, Malaga, Moscow, Oslo, Paris, Stockholm
Helsinki–Turku–Mariehamn–Stockholm
Vaasa–Umeå Vaasa–Sandsvall/Härnösand

Domestic route points:
Helsinki, Ivalo, Joensuu, Jyväskylä, Kajaani, Kemi, Kokkola Pietarsaari, Kuopio, Lappeenranta, Mariehamn, Oulu, Pori, Rovaniemi, Tampere, Turku, Vaasa

Livery F: white, blue, grey
 T: blue, white

Fleet
Douglas DC-3 Dakota

OH-LCD *Lokki*	OH-LCH
OH-LCE *Haanka*	OH-LCK
OH-LCG	

Sud Aviation S.E. 210 Caravelle

OH-LEA *Sinilintu*	OH-LEC *Sininuoli*
OH-LEB *Sinisiipi*	OH-LED *Sinipiika*

Convair 340/440

OH-LRA	OH-LRB	OH-LRC

Convair 440 (*owned by Kar-Air)

OH-LRD	OH-LRF	OH-LRG	OH-VKM*	OH-VKN
OH-LRE				

Douglas DC-8–62F
OH-   OH-

Sud Aviation S.E. 210 Caravelle 10B3

OH-LSA	Helsinki	OH-LSE	Lahti
OH-LSB	Tampere	OH-LSF	Pori
OH-LSC	Turku	OH-LSG	Jyväskylä
OH-LSD	Oulu	OH-LSH	Kuopio

KAR-AIR O/Y   Finland
Kar-Air O/Y (Karhumaki Airways)

As Karhumaki Airways, the operating company of the Karhumaki Group, which had been formed in the 1920's by three brothers who were interested in aircraft manufacture and operation, Kar-Air came into existence in 1950.

Initially, the airline operated six-seat de Havilland 'Dragon Rapides' on a service between Helsinki and Joensuu, and in 1951, two 12-seat Lockheed 'Lodestars' were purchased and the route extended to Sundsvall in Sweden via way of Jyväskylä and Vaasa. Later the Vaasa–Sundsvall section of route had to be dropped, although a new section between Tampere and Stockholm was added, and Douglas DC-3 Dakotas added to the fleet, providing much needed extra capacity.

The airline's present title was introduced in 1957, the same year as a Convair 440 Metropolitan was added to the fleet, soon followed by a second, and in 1961 and 1964, Douglas DC-6B 'Cloudmasters' were introduced to assist the expansion of Kar-Air into the air charter business. Finnair acquired a 28.9 per cent interest in Kar-Air in 1963, and operating agreements are in force between the two airlines, Kar-Air mainly devoting itself to charter activities with only two scheduled routes, and Finnair, as the Finnish flag carrier, scheduled services. Kar-Air flies charters as far afield as the United States, and uses a fleet of Douglas DC-6B's and DC-3's, one Convair 440, and one of the Lockheed 'Lodestars' (on survey work).

The Finnish charter operator, KAR-AIR, operates this Metropolitan, OH-VKM

Service
Helsinki–Tampere   Lappeenranta–Joensuu

Livery F: white, red, unpainted   **T:** white, red

Fleet
Douglas DC-3 Dakota
OH-VKA   OH-VKB   OH-VKC   OH-VKD

Douglas DC-6B Cloudmaster
OH-KDA*   OH-KDB   OH-KDC
* swing tail

Convair 440 Metropolitan
OH-VKM

Lockheed Lodestar
OH-VKU

AIR FRANCE   France
Compagnie Nationale Air France

The history of Air France goes back to 1933 when the airline was formed on the merger of five airlines, Farman Airlines, Cie. Internationale de Navigation Aérienne (CIDNA), Air Union, Air Orient and Aéropostale. Initially the French Government held a 25% interest in the new airline.

Farman Airlines dated from 1919 when this airline operated the first Paris–London passenger service, later followed by a Paris–Brussels service. On both of these routes the airline used a Farman 'Goliath' 13-seat aircraft, converted from a bomber. The airline was operating to most important European centres by 1930.

Air Union concentrated on services to the Mediterranean area of France, while Air Orient, as the name implies, operated to the Far East. Air Orient's first service was operated in 1931 from Marseilles to Saigon via Damascus. The journey took ten days, and the airline used a Loire-Olivier 242 on the Mediterranean section of the route, and a Bréguet 280 for the remainder.

Aéropostale was already owned by the French Government which had re-started the airline after its bankruptcy in order to maintain the mail services operated by the company. The history of Aéropostale dated from the early 1920's, and the airline had also played a part in the foundation of an ancestor airline in Aerolineas Argentinas.

Air France expanded rapidly after its formation, and by 1939 it had a fleet of some 90 aircraft, 15 of which were seaplanes. During the early years of the war the airline was devoted to the war effort, its activities including operating the Paris–London service on an hourly frequency during 1939. In 1942, however, the airline was reassembled in North Africa where it operated a network of services based on Algiers, Damascus and Dakar. At the end of the war the airline was nationalized, although provision was later made for 30% of the share capital to be held by private individuals and organizations.

Normal activities were resumed in 1946 when the airline restarted services to the French Colonies and inaugurated trans-Atlantic services. During the early 1950's the airline expanded its fleet at that time included Douglas DC-3's and DC-4's, 'Super Constellations', and, from the mid-1950's to the early 1960's, Vickers 'Viscounts'.

The present Air France network includes domestic, European and intercontinental services to all continents. Now operating a fleet which includes

35

Boeing 707's, 727's, Sud Aviation 'Caravelles', 'Super Constellations', Bréguet 763's, Douglas DC-4's and DC-3's, for use on the night mail service it operates for the French Post Office; which service is now receiving Fokker F-27's as replacements for the older aircraft. For the more distant future, Air France has ordered four Boeing 747 'Jumbo' jets and has options on eight BAC-Sud 'Concorde' and six Boeing 2707 SST's.

Air France is owned 70% by the State and 30% by private individuals and organizations at present. The airline has an interest in numerous associated companies. These include Air Inter, the French domestic airline, (25%), Air Vietnam (25%), Royal Air Cambodge (40%), Tunis Air (49%), Air Algerie (28%), Air Madagascar (30%), Royal Air Maroc (21%), and Middle East Airlines-Airliban (30%). A charter subsidiary, Société Aérienne Français d'Affrètement, was formed in July, 1966. The airline also has an interest in Air Afrique.

An in-flight shot of Air France's Boeing 707-328B, F-BHSV *Château de Vincennes*

Member of the International Air Transport Association

International services from Paris to:
Abadan, Acapulco, Accra, Aden, Alghero, Amman, Amsterdam, Ankara, Antigua, Athens, Auckland, Baghdad, Bahrain, Bangkok, Barcelona, Barbados, Basle, Beirut, Benghazi, Bergen, Berlin (West), Bermuda, Biarritz, Bilbao, Bogota, Bombay, Bordeaux, Boston, Bremen, Brisbane, Brussels, Cairo, Calcutta, Calgary, Caracas, Catania, Chicago, Cleveland, Cologne/Bonn, Colombo, Copenhagen, Corfu, Dakar, Dar-es-Salaam, Darwin, Delhi, Detroit, Dhahran, Djakarta, Doha, Dubai, Dublin, Dubrovnik, Düsseldorf, Edmonton, Entebbe,

Faroe, Fiji, Frankfurt, Freeport, Gander, Geneva, Georgetown, Gibraltar, Glasgow, Göteburg, Halifax (Nova Scotia), Hamburg, Hanover, Helsinki, Hong Kong, Honolulu, Istanbul, Jerusalem, Johannesburg, Kano, Karachi, Khartoum, Kingston (Jamaica), Kuala Lumpur, Kuwait, Lagos, Las Palmas, Leningrad, Lima, Lisbon, London, Los Angeles, Luanda, Lusaka, Madras, Madrid, Manchester, Manila, Mauritius, Mexico City, Miami, Milan, Montego Bay, Montreal, Moscow, Nairobi, Naples, Nassau, Ndola, New York, Nicosia, Oporto, Oslo, Palermo, Palma, Papeete, Perth (Western Australia), Prague, Rangoon, Reykjavik, Rome, Rotterdam, Salisbury (Southern Rhodesia), San Francisco, Sassari, Shannon, Singapore, Stavanger, Stockholm, Stuttgart, Sydney, Tangier, Tehran, Tel Aviv, Tripoli, Turin, Valencia, Vancouver, Venice, Vienna, Warsaw, Winnipeg, Zürich

Livery F: white, blue, grey **T:** white, blue

Fleet

Bréguet 763 Universel

F-BASN	F-BASQ	F-BASU	F-BASV	F-BASX
F-BASO				

Douglas DC-4

F-BBDA	F-BBDI	F-BBDP	F-BELJ	F-BILL
F-BBDD	F-BBDK	F-BBDQ	F-BHBX	

Currently the Douglas DC-3 Dakota fleet is being replaced by Fokker F-27 Friendship 500's

Lockheed L-1049G Super Constellation

F-BGNC	F-BGNI	F-BHBD	F-BHBI	F-BHMI
F-BGNG	F-BHBB			

Sud Aviation S.E. 210 Caravelle 3

F-BHRA	Alsace	F-BJTA	Antilles
F-BHRB	Lorraine	F-BJTE	Grenoble
F-BHRC	Anjou	F-BJTF	Orleannais
F-BHRD	Guyenne	F-BJTG	Roussillon
F-BHRE	Artois	F-BJTH	Franche-Comté
F-BHRF	Auvergne	F-BJTI	Navarre
F-BHRG	Berry	F-BJTJ	Bourdonnais
F-BHRH	Bourgogne	F-BJTL	Aunis et Saintonge
F-BHRI	Bretagne	F-BJTM	Maine
F-BHRK	Corse	F-BJTN	Comminges
F-BHRL	Dauphine	F-BJTO	Nivervnais
F-BHRM	Quercy	F-BJTP	Comtat Venaissin
F-BHRN	Gascogne	F-BJTQ	Champagne
F-BHRO	Ile-de-France	F-BJTR	Vercors
F-BHRP	Languedoc	F-BJTS	Principaute de Monaco
F-BHRQ	Limousin	F-BKGZ	Comte de Foix
F-BHRR	Lyonnais	F-BLKF	Angoumois
F-BHRS	Normandie	F-BNKA	(leased to Air Inter)
F-BHRT	Picardie	F-BNKB	(,, ,,)
F-BHRU	Poitou	F-BOHA	Comté de Nice
F-BHRV	Provence	F-BOHC	Pays Basque
F-BHRX	Savoie	F-	
F-BHRY	Touraine	F-	
F-BHRZ	Flandre		

Boeing 707-328

F-BHSB	Château de Chambard		F-BHSK	Château de Vizille
F-BHSC	Château de Fontainebleaux		F-BHSL	Château de Maintenon
F-BHSD	Château de Chenonceaux		F-BHSN	Château de Valençay
F-BHSE	Château de Rambouillet		F-BHSO	Château d'Anet
F-BHSF	Château de Blois		F-BHSP	Château de Villandry
F-BHSG	Château de Pau		F-BHSQ	Château de Compiègne
F-BHSH	Château d'Amboise		F-BHSR	Château de Cheverny
F-BHSI	Château de Josselin		F-BHSS	Château d'Uzes
F-BHSJ	Château de Chaumont		F-BHSU	Château de Versailles

Boeing 707-328B

F-BHSV	Château de Vincennes		F-BLCD	Chateau de Dampierre
F-BHSX	Château de Graignan		F-BLCE	Château d'Ussé
F-BHSY	Château de Luneville		F-BLCF*	Pelican II
F-BHSZ	Château de Kerjean		F-BLCG*	Château de Lude
F-BLCA	Château de Sully		F-BLCH*	Château de Hautefort
F-BLCB	Château de Chantilly		F-BLCI*	Château de Verteuil
F-BLCC*	Pelican I			

  *Boeing 707-328C (Cargo)

Boeing 727-228

F-BOJA	F-BOJC	F-BOJE	F-BOJG	F-BOJI
F-BOJB	F-BOJD	F-BOJF	F-BOJH	F-BOJJ

AIR INTER France
Lignes Aériennes Intérieures

Air Inter was formed in 1954 as a French domestic airline by Air France, SNCF (the French Railways) and the Compagnie de Transports Aériens, with banks, regional groups, and some private companies also providing some capital. Services were started in 1958 with chartered aircraft, but suspended after a few months, and it was not until June, 1960, that another attempt, this time successful, was made. The first route in 1960 was Paris–Toulouse, followed before the end of the year by Paris–Pau and Lille–Lyon–Nice, with services to Dinard, Quimper, La Baule, Tarbes, and Biarritz following shortly afterwards. These services were co-ordinated as far as possible with existing Air France and SNCF routes.

Major progress was made in 1962 with the decision to acquire five Vickers Viscount 708 turbo-prop airliners, introduced that same year, and with the establishment of a maintenance base at Orly Airport, outside Paris. Two more Viscounts followed in 1963, the same year as TAI, one of the owners, became a part of Union des Transports Aériennes, the major French private enterprise airline, and UTA naturally took over TAI's shares in Air Inter. 1964, saw the acquisition of further Viscounts, and also four of the small 26-seat Nord 262 turbo-prop airliner.

At present Air France and SNCF each have a 25% interest in Air Inter, with UTA having 15% and the rest being divided amongst French banks, local organizations, often Chambers of Commerce, and various private interests. The fleet includes 14 Viscounts, 10 Caravelles, 6 Fokker Friendships, with four on order, and four Nord 262s. A network of seasonal and all year services is operated, along with some charter flights.

F-BNKB is one of a number of Caravelle IIIs operated by the French domestic airline, Air Inter

Services from Paris to
  Ajaccio, Basle*, Bastia, Biarritz, Bordeaux, Brest, Clermont-Ferrand, Deauville, Dinard, Grenoble*, La Baule, Lille, Lorient, Lourdes, Lyon, Marseille, Metz, Montpellier, Nantes, Nice, Nîmes, Pau, Perpignan, Rennes, St Brieux, Strasbourg, Toulon, Toulouse, Vichy
      from Lyon to:
  Basle*, Clermont-Ferrand, Lille, Lorient, Nantes, Nîmes, Strasbourg
  Biarritz–Lourdes–Nice   Bordeaux–Toulouse–Marseille   St Brieux–Rennes
*__International__ service

Livery F: white, red, blue, unpainted
        T: white, red, blue

Fleet
Vickers Viscount 708 (*series 724)

F-BGNO	F-BGNR	F-BLHI	F-BMCH*	F-BOEB
F-BGNP	F-BGNT	F-BMCF*	F-BNAX*	F-BOEC
F-BGNQ	F-BGNU	F-BMCG*	F-BOEA	

Sud Aviation S.E. 210 Caravelle III (*leased from Air France)

F-BNKA*	F-BNKC	F-BNKE	F-BNKG	F-BNKI
F-BNKB*	F-BNKD	F-BNKF	F-BNKH	F-BNKJ

Fokker F-27–500 Friendship

F-	F-	F-	F-	F-
F-	F-	F-	F-	F-

Nord 262

F-BLHS	F-BLHT	F-BLHU	F-BLHV

CIE AIR TRANSPORT France

Formed in 1948, Cie. Air Transport was a partner of British United Air Ferries on cross-Channel services using Bristol 170's from 1961 till recently. Air ferry services are also operated on the Mediterranean using 'Carvairs'. French national railways (SNCF) are the majority shareholder with the remainder being held by French shipping and road haulage interests.

Services from Nîmes to:
  Ajaccio, Bastia, Corsica, Palma
      from Nice to:
  Corsica, Palma
Livery F: white, blue, grey   **T:** white, blue
Fleet
Aviation Traders Carvair ATL.98
F-BMHV   F-BOSU
Bristol 170 Mk. 32 Superfreighter

| F-BKBG | *Quatorze Juillet* | F-BLHH | *Dix-huit Juin* |
| F-BKBI | *Onze Novembre* | F-BPIN | |

ALL-AIR Germany (Federal)
Allegemeine Lufttransport GmbH

All-Air was formed on 1st September, 1966, by the Stinnes Industrial Group to operate worldwide passenger and freight charters from the airline's base at Frankfurt. Currently a fleet of three Douglas DC-4 Skymasters is employed on this work.

Two of ALL-Air's Douglas DC-4 Skymasters; D-ADAC is nearer the camera

Livery F: white, red, unpainted
     T: red, white
Fleet
Douglas DC-4 Skymaster
D-ADAB   D-ADAC   D-ADAD

BAVARIA FLUG
Bavaria Fluggesellschaft

Germany (Federal)

Originally formed in 1957 as an air taxi operator, Bavaria Fluggesellschaft has developed into an inclusive tour charter operator, first with Handley Page Heralds delivered in 1964 and more recently with BAC One-Eleven jets, initially with a leased Philippine Airlines' aircraft in 1967, then with its own aircraft in 1968. The workload of Bavaria Flug includes inclusive tour and ad hoc charters, with some airline contract flying for Deutsche Lufthansa. The air taxi business still exists, but only one Piper Apache is required for this activity.

Fleet

BAC One-Eleven 414
D-ANBI	D-ANDY

Handley Page Herald 200
D-BEBE	D-BIBI	D-BOBO

Piper PA-23 Apache 160
D-GISA

CONDOR
Condor Flugdienst GmbH

Germany (Federal)

The merging of Condor Luftreederei and Deutsche Flugdienst, a Lufthansa subsidiary, led to the formation of Condor Flugdienst, a wholly-owned Lufthansa subsidiary, in 1961; an airline with no connection with the pre-war Condor Syndicate which pioneered air services to, and within, South America.

The older of the two predecessor airlines was Deutsche Flugdienst, founded in 1955 and acquired by Deutsche Lufthansa in 1959, while Condor Luftreederei dated from 1957 when it was formed at Hamburg with two Convair 440 Metropolitans.

In 1964, Condor introduced scheduled services linking Düsseldorf with Bremen, Munster and Hanover, but these were abandoned in 1966 leaving the airline to concentrate on its chartered services, mainly inclusive tours work. At the present time, the airline operates a fleet of Boeing 707's, 727's, Fokker F-27 Friendships and Vickers Viscounts from its base at Frankfurt. Three Boeing 737's are on order.

Fleet

Boeing 707-330B
D-ABOV

Boeing 727-30 (* QC)
D-ABIK	D-ABIM	D-ABIP	D-ABIQ*	D-ABIR

Vickers Viscount 814
D-ANIP	D-ANOL	D-ANUN	D-ANUR

Fokker F-27 Friendship 400
D-BARI	D-BARO

LUFTHANSA
Germany (Federal)
Deutsche Lufthansa AG–German Airlines

The present airline started operations in 1955, but the history of Lufthansa dates back to the formation of a pre-war airline of the same name in 1926. This airline was formed by a merger of Deutsche Aero-Lloyd, shares of which were held by the Deutsche Bank and the Hamburg-Amerika Line and North German Lloyd shipping companies, with Junkers Luftverkehr, an operating subsidiary of the aircraft manufacturer. These airlines in turn had been formed from the rationalization of the operations of several smaller companies which were engaged in unprofitable competition, and the eventual merger between Aero-Lloyd and Junkers was the result of a similar situation which arose as the airlines expanded and their services overlapped.

The new airline's capital was held by regional airlines (27.5%), the German Government (26%), the provincial governments (19%) and various private interests (25%). The fleet of about 120 aircraft included some 80 single-engined types, while the route structure consisted of an extensive domestic network and international services as far as London and Stockholm.

Immediately the airline set about expanding its network, across the Atlantic and to the Far East, mainly for the carriage of mail. But in so doing, the airline did not neglect other advances, and while an associate, the Condor Syndicate, was paving the way for South American services with Dornier 'Wal' flying boats.

Lufthansa was the first operator of the Boeing 737; here is the first of the airline's aircraft, D-ABEA, while under construction

Lufthansa was busy in Germany attempting to improve its scheduled services by establishing beacons on its routes for night flying (Junkers had already operated some night flights prior to 1923) and building a chain of 73 radio stations along its routes as additional navigational aids.

Lufthansa did not confine itself to crossing the North Atlantic; at the same time as a sea/air service for mail was being operated over the North Atlantic (by the catapaulting of a small seaplane, carrying the mail, from a ship approaching either the American or European coasts), a sea/air service was being operated over the South Atlantic by which the mail went by air to Las Palmas. Here it was transferred to a steamer and taken to the first port of call across the Atlantic, and there transferred to a Dornier 'Wal' flying boat of the Condor Syndicate. The Dornier X twelve-engined flying boat made a flight to South America in 1932, and occasionally Zeppelins were used instead of the steamer.

In 1934 on the South Atlantic route and 1936 on the North Atlantic, flying boats were used for the actual crossing. A fleet of three ships converted to floating bases were used. The aircraft landed in the sea near one of these ships, was taken aboard for refuelling and servicing, and was then launched again by catapault. Still the North Atlantic crossing had to be made by the southern route via the Azores and Bahamas rather than by a more direct route because of the shorter trans-ocean section on the southern route. Aircraft used on the South Atlantic service included the Dornier 'Wal', and a larger version of the aircraft, the "10 ton Wal", while later on the diesel engined Dornier Do 18 and the Blohm and Voss Ha-139 four-engined flying boats were used on both

Lufthansa includes Boeing 707-430's in its jet fleet for inter-continental services.
Shown here is D-ABOF

routes. The overland sections of the routes in Europe were often flown by the tri-motored Junkers Ju52/3m; Lufthansa operated a total of 79 of this type.

By the outbreak of war when all routes, except those to neutral countries, were abandoned, the Lufthansa network reached to Santiago de Chile in the West and to Bangkok in the East. All services were suspended in 1945 and Eurasia, an associate in which Lufthansa held a one-third interest, and the Chinese Transport Ministry the remainder, became China Air Transport, the Nationalist Chinese Airline. Lufthansa finally began to be liquidated in 1951.

In 1952 the Federal Government, with the approval of the Allied Powers, agreed to the establishment of a company to prepare for a German airline, Luftag. In 1954 the airline re-adopted its present title, and in 1955 operations started with eight 'Super Constellations', four Convair 340's and three DC-3's. Captains were provided for the 'Super Constellations' by Trans World Airlines and Eastern Airlines, and for the other aircraft by BEA, in order to assist the new airline which, of course, had no crews with experience of modern aircraft. Services to most of the more important European centres were started in 1955, and a service to New York was also begun that year. By 1958 the South American route reached Santiago again, and in 1964 a polar route to Tokyo was introduced; now the airline serves all six continents.

Vickers' 'Viscount' turbo-prop airliners were introduced in 1958, and Boeing 707 jet airliners were introduced in 1960. Lufthansa has standardized on Boeing jet aircraft and the present fleet includes 707's and 727's, and the airline was the first to use the Boeing 737. An option is held on three Boeing 2707's and three BAC/Sud 'Concorde' SST's.

Member of the International Air Transport Association

International services from Frankfurt to:
Amsterdam, Anchorage (H), Athens (M), Baghdad (M), Barcelona, Bangkok, Beirut (M), Boston, Brussels, Buenos Aires, Cairo (M), Calcutta, Chicago, Copenhagen (DH), Dakar, Dar-es-Salaam (M), Delhi, Dharhan, Entebbe (M), Geneva, Guayaquil, Hong Kong, Istanbul (M), Johannesburg, Karachi, Khartoum (M) Kingston (Jamaica), Kuwait, Las Palmas, Lima, Lisbon, London*, Madrid, Mexico City, Milan (HSMD), Montevideo, Montreal, New York (HSMC), Nairobi, Nice, Palma (D), Paris (HSMCD), Philadelphia, Prague, Rio de Janeiro, Rome (HMD), San Francisco, Santa Cruz, Santiago de Chile, São Paulo, Stockholm (D), Sydney, Tokyo (H), Tripoli, Tunis, Vienna (M), Zürich (HCD)
C—also from Cologne D—also from Düsseldorf H—also from Hamburg M—also from Munich S—also from Stuttgart * from Hamburg, Stuttgart, Munich, Cologne, Dusseldorf and Bremen
Dusseldorf-Rotterdam
There are connections to many international services from Berlin (West), Bremen, Cologne, Düsseldorf, Hamburg, Hanover, Munich, Stuttgart

Lufthansa is not allowed to operate into Berlin

Domestic services from Frankfurt to:
Bremen, Cologne, Düsseldorf, Hamburg, Hanover, Munich, Nuremberg, Stuttgart
from Bremen to:
Düsseldorf, Hamburg, Munich, Nuremberg, Stuttgart
from Düsseldorf to:
Hamburg, Hanover, Munich, Nuremberg, Stuttgart
from Hamburg to:
Cologne, Hanover, Munich, Nuremberg, Stuttgart

Domestic services from Hanover to:
  Munich, Nuremberg, Stuttgart
                    from Munich to:
  Cologne, Nuremberg, Stuttgart
                    from Stuttgart to:
  Cologne, Nuremberg

Livery F: white, blue, grey
         T: white, yellow and blue   (emblem: flying crane)

Fleet

Boeing 707-430

D-ABOB	Hamburg	D-ABOF	München
D-ABOC	Berlin	D-ABOG	Bonn
D-ABOD	Frankfurt		

Boeing 707-330B

D-ABOT	Düsseldorf	D-ABUG	Essen
D-ABOV		D-ABUH	Dortmund
D-ABOX	Köln	D-ABUK	Bochum
D-ABUB	Stuttgart	D-ABUL	Duisburg
D-ABUD	Nürnberg	D-ABUM	Bremen
D-ABUF	Hannover		

Boeing 707-330C

D-ABUA	Europa	D-
D-ABUE	Amerika	D-
D-ABUI	Asia	

Boeing 727-30 ('Europa Jet')

D-ABIB	Augsburg	D-ABIL	Lübeck
D-ABIC	Saarbrücken	D-ABIN	Münster
D-ABID	Braunschweig	D-ABIS	Freiburg
D-ABIF	Mannheim	D-ABIT	Heidelberg
D-ABIG	Kiel	D-ABIV	Kassel
D-ABIH	Wiesbaden		

Boeing 727-30QC ('Europa Jet')

D-ABBI	Mainz	D-ABIU	Ulm
D-ABIA	Pforzheim	D-ABIW	Bielefeld
D-ABIG	Oberhausen	D-ABIX	Würzburg
D-ABII	Wuppertal	D-ABIY	Aachen
D-ABIJ	Krefeld	D-ABIZ	Gelsenkirchen
D-ABIO	Hagen		

Boeing 737-130 ('City Jet')

D-ABEA	D-ABEG	D-ABEL	D-ABEP	D-ABET
D-ABEB	D-ABEH	D-ABEM	D-ABEQ	D-ABEU
D-ABEC	D-ABEI	D-ABEN	D-ABER	D-ABEV
D-ABED	D-ABEK	D-ABEO	D-ABES	D-ABEW
D-ABEF				

Vickers Viscount 814

D-ANAB	D-ANAD	D-ANAM	D-ANEF	D-ANIZ
D-ANAC	D-ANAF			

Boeing 747-30 (early 1970 delivery)

D-ABYA	D-ABYB	D-ABYC

LTU
Lufttransport-Unternehmen GmbH & Co KG

Germany (Federal)

It was as Lufttransport Union that LTU was formed in 1955 to operate inclusive tour and freight charters. The present title was adopted in 1958. Apart from tne charter work for which the airline was founded, since 1960 LTU has undertaken third-level scheduled service operations on behalf of Deutsche Lufthansa, the Federal German flag carrier, although there is no financial connection between the two airlines. The current fleet includes Sud Aviation Caravelle jets, Fokker Friendship and Nord 262 turbo-prop airliners, and a Cessna 310, while the latest addition is a Fokker Fellowship.

D-ABAP, one of Lufttransport-Unternehmen's Caravelle IIIs in flight

Domestic services from Düsseldorf to:
Bremen, Hanover, Saarbrucken

Livery F: white, red, unpainted
T: white

Fleet
Sud Aviation Caravelle III
D-ABAF	D-ABAM	D-ABAP

Fokker F-27 Friendship
D-BAKA	D-BAKI	D-BAKU

Fokker F-28 Fellowship
D-	D-	(option)

Nord 262
D-CADY

Cessna 310
D-

SÜDFLUG INTERNATIONAL   Germany (Federal)
Südflug International GmbH

Südflug is a wholly-owned subsidiary of the German national airline, Deutsche Lufthansa, and specializes in cargo and passenger charters, for which CAB authority for trans-Atlantic charters is held. Currently a fleet of six Douglas DC-7C/Fs, a Douglas DC-8 (delivered in autumn 1968) and two DC-9's is operated. The airline was originally formed in 1952 with the company president, Captain R. A. Bückle, holding 50% of the capital, the remainder being divided between the Touropa and Scharnow travel agencies.

Fleet
Douglas DC-7C
| D-ABAC | D-ABAK | D-ABAN | D-ABAR | D-ABAS |
| D-ABAD | | | | |

Douglas DC-8
D-ADIM
Douglas DC-9-32
| D-ACEB | D-ACEC |

TRANSPORTFLUG   Germany (Federal)
Transportflug GmbH

Transportflug currently operates three Douglas C-54 on freight charter work, for which activity the company was formed in 1965.

Fleet
Douglas C-54
| D-ABAG | D-ACAB | D-ADAR |

GHANA AIRWAYS   Ghana
Ghana Airways Corporation

Ghana Airways was formed in July 1958, to take over the Ghana services of the West African Airways Corporation shortly after the Gold Coast achieved its independence (and simultaneously changed its name to Ghana). The airline was formed as a limited liability company with the British Overseas Airways Corporation holding a 40% interest and the Ghanaian Government holding the remainder—and being responsible for any losses incurred by Ghana Airways.

The predecessor of Ghana Airways, West African Airways Corporation, was formed in 1946 by the four colonies which comprised British West Africa: Nigeria, the Gold Coast, Sierra Leone and Gambia. Scheduled services were started in 1947 and by 1948 the airline was operating domestic routes within the Gold Coast and Nigeria as well as an inter-capital service between Lagos and Accra, and a service to Freetown, Bathurst and Dakar. In 1950 the airline introduced Bristol 'Wayfarers' on a trans-Africa route, which was withdrawn some three years later as unsuccessful, and on the Dakar route. All other routes were operated by de Havilland 'Doves'. In 1952, six Handley Page 'Marathons' were introduced, but withdrawn the following year as unsatisfactory.

In 1956, Douglas DC-3's and de Havilland 'Herons' replaced the 'Wayfarers' and 'Doves'. Almost immediately after formation, Ghana Airways entered into an agreement with BOAC to operate a pool service to London using aircraft leased from BOAC. Initially a Boeing 'Stratocruiser' in Ghana Airways colours was used, but this was replaced a few months later by a Bristol 'Britannia' 102 turbo-prop airliner which operated the service twice weekly, once via Madrid and once via Tripoli and Rome. From then until October 1960, the West African Airways Corporation operated the Ghana Airways' domestic and regional services under contract.

In 1961 the Government of Ghana assumed full control of the airline which then became the Ghana Airways Corporation. Two years later, in 1963, the corporation received the first of eight Ilyushin Il-18 turbo-prop, and an Il-14 piston, airliners. The airline then embarked on a very ambitious, but commercially uneconomic expansion that included a service to Moscow and a trans-Africa service, with plans to operate to North and South America, the Far East, and Australia. The Russian aircraft were unsuccessful in commercial service owing to their exceptionally short engine life and maintenance problems. In 1966, after a change in Government, these aircraft were returned to the Soviet Union. The Moscow and trans-Africa services were suspended at the same time.

The airline currently operates a fleet of one VC10, Viscounts and DC-3's on services within Ghana and Africa, and to Europe. In an attempt to keep the corporation on a sound commercial footing, one of two VC10's was leased to Middle East Airlines but was destroyed by military action in 1968 at Beirut airport.

Member of the International Air Transport Association

9G-ABO, a Rolls-Royce-engined Vickers VC10 of Ghana Airways standing on the apron at Accra airport, is the only one now in the fleet

International services from Accra to:
  Abidjan, Bathurst, Beirut, Cairo, Dakar, Freetown, Lagos, London, Monrovia, Rome, Zürich

Domestic services
  Accra–Kumasi–Tamale   Takoradi–Kumasi

Livery F: white, blue, grey
      T: white with red and green

Fleet

9G-AAC	Douglas DC-3C Dakota		9G-AAW	Vickers Viscount 838	
9G-AAD	,,	,,	9G-AAU	,,	,,
9G-AAE	,,	,,	9G-ABO	,, VC-10	,,
9G-AAF	,,	,,			

OLYMPIC
Olympic Airways SA

Greece

Olympic Airways became operational in 1957 as successor to TAE National Greek Airlines which had been formed in 1951 by the merger of Hellos—serving several European and Middle Eastern destinations, TAE—concentrating mainly on domestic routes, and Aero Metaforai Ellados. All these airlines had been formed shortly after the end of World War II. TAE National Greek Airlines experienced financial difficulties in 1955 and was acquired by the Government.

The new airline, Olympic Airways, was, and still is, owned by the millionaire Greek shipowner, Aristotle Onassis. With his backing the new airline began to expand rapidly, Douglas DC-6B's and de Havilland 'Comet' 4B's being ordered to supplement the initial fleet of a Fairchild 'Argus', a Douglas DC-4 and fourteen Douglas DC-3's all of which were taken over from TAE National Greek Airlines when Onassis accepted the Greek Government's offer to form the new airline. The 'Comets' were introduced in 1960, and set a record of three hours 13 minutes for the London–Athens service. New routes were then added and the airline expanded throughout Europe, the Middle East and the Mediterranean, as well as building up an extensive domestic network.

The present fleet includes 'Comets', Boeing 707's with which a service to New York was started in June 1966, Douglas DC-3's, DC-4's and DC-6B's. A Sud-Aviation Super Frelon helicopter is used on a summer service between Athens and certain Greek Islands.

Member of the International Air Transport Association

SX-DAL *Queen Olga*, one of the fleet of Hawker Siddeley (de Havilland) Comet 4B's operated by Olympic Airways, at Athens

International services from Athens to:
Amsterdam, Beirut, Cairo, Frankfurt, Istanbul, London, New York, Nicosia, Paris, Rome, Tel-Aviv

Domestic services from Athens to:
Agrinion, Alexandroupolis, Chania, Chios*, Corfu, Herakleon, Ioannina, Kalamataa, Kavala, Kos, Kozani, Larissa, Lefkas, Lemnos, Mykonos*, Mytilini Preveza, Rhodos, Salonica, Samos, Skiatnos*, Thira*, Volos
*summer helicopter services

Livery F: white, blue, grey   **T:** blue
Fleet
Boeing 707-320C

SX-DBA	*City of Athens*	SX-DBC	*City of Knossos*
SX-DBB	*City of Corinth*	SX-DBD	

Hawker Siddeley (de Havilland) Comet 4B

SX-DAK	*Queen Frederica*	SX-DAO	*Princess Sophia*
SX-DAL	*Queen Olga*	G-ARJL	
SX-DAM	*Queen Sophia*		

Sud Aviation SA-321-F Super Frelon

MALÉV   Hungary
Magyar Légiközlekedési Vállalat

In March 1946 Malév was formed as the Hungarian-Soviet Airlines Company (Maszovlet), and operations were started later the same year. Initially the airline operated only domestic routes using Ilyushin Il-12 aircraft, but by 1950 international services had been inaugurated from Budapest to Prague, Bucharest, Belgrade and Warsaw. A service to Venice did not last very long.

In 1954 control of the airline passed entirely into Hungarian hands, and the present title was adopted. The airline continued to expand, services being introduced to Vienna and many other West European centres, including London in 1961. Malév's first intercontinental service, to Cairo, was started in 1963, fowolled by Damascus in 1965 and Beirut in 1966.

The present fleet consists of six Ilyushin Il-18's, seven Il-14's and five Tupolev Tu-134's, some Ilyushin Il-62's are on order.

A Malév Ilyushin Il-18 turbo-prop airliner taking off from Budapest's Ferihegy airport

International services from Budapest to:
Amsterdam, Athens, Beirut, Belgrade, Berlin, Brussels, Bucharest, Cairo, Copenhagen, Damascus, Dubrovnik, Frankfurt, Helsinki, Kiev, London, Milan, Moscow, Munich, Nicosia, Paris, Prague, Rome, Salzburg, Sofia, Stockholm, Tirana, Vienna, Warsaw, Zagreb, Zürich

Livery F: white, blue, grey
T: white

Fleet

Iyushin Il-14
| HA-MAA | HA-MAC | HA-MAE | HA-MAH | HA-MAI |
| HA-MAB | HA-MAD | HA-MAF | | |

Ilyushin Il-18
| HA-MOA | HA-MOE | HA-MOF | HA-MOG | HA-MOH |
| HA-MOC | | | | |

Tupolev Tu-134
| HA- | HA- | HA- | HA- | HA- |

ICELANDAIR
Flugfelag Islands HF

Iceland

Icelandair was formed in 1937 as Flugfelag Akureyrar HF, and operated a seaplane service from Reykjavik to Akureyri. The airline continued to operate on domestic routes intil 1945, when a 'Catalina' seaplane inaugurated the airline's first international service, to Glasgow. A second service, to Copenhagen, was started shortly afterwards.

Regular services were started from Reykjavik to Prestwick and Copenhagen in 1946 using converted 'Liberators' leased from Scottish Aviation, and two years later the airline obtained its own four-engined aircraft, Douglas DC-4 'Skymasters'. Other aircraft followed; in 1957 Icelandair purchased two Vickers 'Viscounts', and in 1961 and 1963, two Douglas DC-6B 'Cloudmasters' strengthened the total number of owned aircraft.

The present fleet includes Douglas DC-3's, a DC-4, and DC-6B's, Fokker F-27 'Friendships' and a Boeing 727. The international route network extends to Greenland—where Icelandair also operates charters during the summer, Great Britain and Scandinavia. The airline also operates to thirteen domestic points. The present title was adopted in 1950, the same year as the Icelandic Government obtained a 13.2% shareholding. The other important shareholder is the Icelandic Steamship Co., owning 39.6% of Icelandair's capital.

Member of the International Air Transport Association

International services from Reykjavik to:
Bergen, Copenhagen, Glasgow, Kulusuk, London, Narssarssuaq, Olso, Vagar

Major domestic service points:
Akureyri, Eglisstadir, Fagurhólsmyri, Hornafjördhur, Húsavik, Isafjördhur, Kópasker, Patreksfjördhur, Saudarkrókhur, Vestmannaeyjar, Pórshöfn

Livery F: white, blue and red, grey
     T: white

Fleet

Douglas DC-3 Dakota
TF-ISA *Glofaxi*   TF-ISB *Gunnfaxi*   TF-ISH *Gljafaxi*

Douglas DC-4
TF-FID *Straumfaxi*

Douglas DC-6B
TF-FIP *Solfaxi*   TF-ISC *Skyfaxi*

Fokker F-27 Friendship
TF-FIJ   *Blikfaxi*   FT-FIK *Snarfaxi*   TF-FIL

Boeing 727-08C
TF-FIE *Gullfaxi*

LOFTLEIDIR
Icelandic Airlines (Loftleidir HF)

Iceland

Loftleidir was formed on 10th March, 1944, with one Stinson seaplane which was used on routes within Iceland. During the first few years, aircraft operated by the company included a 'Catalina' and Douglas DC-3's, and in 1946 a Douglas DC-4 'Skymaster' was added to the fleet. This aircraft inaugurated the airline's first international service, to Copenhagen in 1947, and the following year the airline received authority to operate to the United States.

The domestic operations were withdrawn in 1952, but also during that year the airline started its present service to the United States from Europe via Iceland. Since then these services, which are operated on a non-IATA low-fare basis, have provided the great bulk of the airline's work, and have been steadily increased over the years. In 1960 the airline introduced Douglas DC-6's, bought with a government guaranteed loan, and in 1964 the airline introduced the turbo-prop Canadair CL-44 (Rolls-Royce 'Tyne'-engined developments of the Bristol 'Britannia'). The current fleet consists of these two aircraft types, the CL-44's having been converted to CL-44J standard.

Services, international only, from Reykjavik to:
    Copenhagen, Glasgow, Helsinki, London, Luxembourg, New York, Oslo, Stavanger, Stockholm

Livery F: white, blue, grey
     T: white, with blue and red

Fleet

Canadair CL-44J (known as Rolls-Royce 400)
TF-LLF *Leifur Eiriksson*   TF-LLH *Gudridur Thorbjarnardottir*
TF-LLG *Vilhjalmur Stefansson*   TF-LLI *Bjarni Herjolfsson*

Douglas DC-6B
TF-ISC
TF-LLA *Thorvalda Erickson*   TF-LLC *Thorfinnur Karlsefni*
TF-LLB *Snorri Sturluson*   TF-LLJ *Eirikur Raudi*
                                    TF-LLE *Snorri Thorfinnsson*

AIR-INDIA India

Air-India's history extends back to 1932 and the formation of Tata Airlines by Air-India's present chairman, J. R. D. Tata, to operate airmail services. During the first few years, mail provided almost all the payload needed for the company's aircraft and it was not until 1938 that passenger loads justified the use of de Havilland 'Rapides'.

The intervention of war ended all airmail flying in India for its duration and all air transport services were operated for the Government and armed forces. However, from the experience of operating larger and more modern aircraft during the war, Tata Airlines was able to expand rapidly afterwards, becoming a public company and changing its name to Air-India Ltd. in 1946. The airline also received assistance from Trans World Airlines in the training of cabin crew for the fleet of C-47's and C-54's, in return acting as general agents for the American company.

Two months after India's independence, the airline changed its name to Air-India International Ltd. and the Government took a 49% shareholding with an option on another 2%. Later that year the airline inaugurated its first international service between Bombay and London. The number of flights on this route was soon increased and it was followed in 1950 by another international service between Bombay and Nairobi. In 1953 all Indian airlines were nationalized and the aircraft and services of Air-India and six other purely domestic airlines were merged into two corporations, Indian National Airlines Corporation for domestic routes, and Air-India International Corporation for international routes. Rapid expansion of international routes followed and in 1954 Lockheed 'Super Constellations' were introduced into the fleet.

The airline's name was changed again in 1962 to Air-India, the present title.

Today over twenty years after Constellation *Malabar Princess* inaugurated a Bombay–London service, Air-India operates a small, but modern, fleet of Boeing 707's on an intercontinental network. The airline's maintenance base at Bombay was the first Boeing 707 maintenance facility in the Near/Middle East—Asia to receive an American Federal Aviation Agency Approved Repair Station Certificate. For the future the airline has secured delivery positions for two BAC/Sud 'Concordes' and three Boeing 2707 SST's.

Member of the International Air Transport Association

One of Air-India's fleet of Boeing 707-337B's in flight

Services from Bombay and Delhi to: (some connections to Calcutta and Madras): Aden, Bahrain, Bangkok, Beirut, Brussels, Cairo, Djakarta, Dubai, Frankfurt, Geneva, Hong Kong, Kuala Lumpur, Kuwait, London, Mauritius, Moscow, Nairobi, Nandi, New York, Paris, Perth (Western Australia), Prague, Rome, Singapore, Sydney, Tehran, Tokyo, Zürich

Livery: F white, red, grey
      T: red

Fleet

Boeing 707-437
VT-DJI *Nandi Devi*	VT-DNY *Dhaulagiri*
VT-DJJ *Gauri Shankar*	VT-DNZ *Nangaparbat*
VT-DJK *Everest*	

Boeing 707-337B (* 337C)
VT-DPM *Makala*	VT-LSI *Lhotse*
VT-DVA *Annapoora*	VT-DVB*

IRANAIR
Iran National Airlines Corporation

Iran

The predecessor of Iranair, Iranian Airways, was formed in 1944 as a private company with Trans World Airlines holding 10% of the share capital. Charter services were introduced in 1945, and scheduled services followed in 1946, including the first international services to Baghdad, Cairo and Beirut. The following year, Paris, Athens and Rome were added to the international network. In 1949, Iranair acquired Eagle Airlines, a small company formed the year before, that operated one de Havilland 'Dove'.

During the 1950's the airline operated Douglas DC-3's and DC-4's, with some Convair 240's, and in 1959, the first turbine aircraft, Vickers 'Viscount' 700's, were introduced. In 1961, at Government behest, the airline merged with the near-bankrupt Persian Air Services, an airline dating from 1954, and which had received assistance from both SABENA and KLM Royal Dutch Airlines. After this merger Iranian Airways was extensively re-organized in 1962, becoming a wholly state-owned corporation. As part of the re-organization, the airline signed a three year technical assistance agreement with Pan American in 1964.

Currently Iranair operates a fleet of Boeing 727's, Vickers 'Viscounts', Douglas DC-6's, and DC-3's on both regional, domestic, and international routes to India, Pakistan and Europe. The Boeing 727's inaugurated the London service in 1966.

Member of the International Air Transport Association

International services from Tehran to:
Baghdad, Bombay, Dhahrain, Doha, Dubai, Kabul, Karachi, London

Domestic services from Tehran to:
Abadan, Bandar-Abbas, Bushira, Gachsaran, Harradan, Isfahan, Kerman, Kermashah, Khark, Lengeh, Meshed, Shiraz, Tabriz, Zahedan

Fleet
Douglas DC-3 Dakota

EP-ACU	EP-ADG	EP-ADL	EP-AGH

Douglas DC-6 (* 6A; † 6B)

EP-AES	EP-AEU†	EP-AEW	EP-AEX	EP-AEY
EP-AET	EP-AEV*			

Vickers Viscount 700

EP-AHC	EP-

Boeing 727-86

EP-IRA	EP-IRB	EP-IRC	EP-IRD

IRAQI AIRWAYS   Iraq

Iraqi Airways was formed by the Government of Iraq in 1945 as a branch of the State Railways. Operations started the following year when a service was inaugurated between Baghdad and Basra by de Havilland 'Rapide' biplanes. By the end of 1946, services had been introduced from Baghdad to Beirut, Damascus, Lydda and Cairo with Douglas DC-3's. From then until 1960 the airline received assistance from the British Overseas Airways Corporation.

The airline expanded steadily, in 1947, Tehran and Kuwait were added to the route network. The following year saw services to Bahrain, Cyprus, and Athens being introduced. In 1957, when the airline received its first four-engined aeroplanes, the turbo-prop Vickers 'Viscount' 700, the fleet consisted of DH 'Doves' and Vickers 'Vikings' which had replaced the 'Rapides' and DC-3's. New services were introduced with the 'Viscount', including a service to London via Istanbul and Vienna in 1956.

Currently Iraqi Airways operates Vickers 'Viscounts' and Hawker Siddeley 'Trident' 1E's, which were first introduced in 1965. The airline's services extend to Europe, to India and Pakistan, as well as throughout the Middle East.

Member of the International Air Transport Association

International services from Baghdad to:
Amman, Bahrain, Beirut, Cairo, Damascus, Delhi, Frankfurt, Geneva, Istanbul, Karachi, Kuwait, London, Prague, Tehran, Vienna

Domestic services from Baghdad to:
Basrah, Kirkuk, Mosul

Livery F: white, green, grey
T: green and white

Fleet

YI-ACK	Vickers Viscount 735
YI-ACL	,, ,,
YI-ACM	,, ,,
YI-ACU	,, ,,
YI-AEA	Hawker Siddeley Trident 1E
YI-AEB	,, ,,
YI-AEC	,, ,,

AER LINGUS-IRISH INTERNATIONAL   Ireland
Aer Lingus–Irish International Airlines

Aer Lingus-Irish International Airlines is really two airlines; Aer Lingus formed in 1936 which operates services within Europe and the British Isles, and Aerlinte Eireann, formed in 1947 to provide a trans-Atlantic service, although operations did not start until 1958.

Aer Lingus's original base was at Baldonnel, now Casement Airport, and it was from there in May 1936, that the airline introduced its first service, Dublin–Bristol, with its only aircraft, a five-seat de Havilland DH84 'Dragon Rapide'. The new airline had a staff of twelve and the entire stock of spare parts could just fill a biscuit tin—a far cry from the present staff of more than 5,000 and the large spares holding which modern airliners require.

Before the end of 1936 the airline's Bristol service had been extended to London and a new service to Liverpool was inaugurated. Expansion continued until, the outbreak of war in Europe in 1939 when, although Eire was neutral, operation had to be confined to a Dublin–Liverpool service with Manchester as an alternative terminus when weather conditions prevented use of Liverpool. The expansion of Aer Lingus continued after the war until today it operates a wide network of services from three airports in Eire and from Belfast to North America.

St. Mel is one of four BAC One-Eleven airliners operated by Aer Lingus

Aerlinte Eireann's first routes linked Dublin and Shannon with New York and Boston by Lockheed 'Super Constellation'. The airline has since expanded and modernized, all trans-Atlantic services being operated by Boeing jets. Its most recent service is from Belfast to New York.

The present combined fleet of twenty-six aircraft carry between them just under 1¼ million passengers a year. The fleet includes the Boeing 707's and 720's of Aerlinte Eireann, and the 'Viscounts' and BAC 'One-Elevens' of Aer Lingus. Aer Lingus has eight Boeing 737 aircraft in course of delivery.

Member of the International Air Transport Association

Services—Aer Lingus from Dublin to:
Amsterdam, Barcelona, Belfast, Birmingham, Blackpool, Boston, Bristol, Brussels, Cardiff, Chicago, Copenhagen, Cork, Düsseldorf, Edinburgh, Frankfurt, Glasgow, Isle of Man, Jersey, Leeds, Bradford, Liverpool, London, Lourdes, Malaga,

Manchester, Montreal, Munich (via Brussels), New York (via Belfast), Paris, Rennes, Rome, Shannon, Zürich

from Cork to:
Barcelona, Birmingham, Bristol, Cardiff, Dublin, Jersey, London, Lourdes Manchester, Paris

from Shannon to:
Boston, Chicago, Dublin, London, Manchester, Montreal, New York, Paris
There are also numerous international connections via Dublin

Livery F: white, green, grey **T:** white

Combined Fleet
names are given here in English only

EI-AJI	St Gall	Vickers Viscount 808
EI-AJJ	St Columban	,, ,,
EI-AJK	St Kilian	,, ,,
EI-AKL	St Colmcille	,, ,,
EI-AKO	St Colman	,, ,,
EI-ALA	St Patrick	Boeing 720-048
EI-ALC	St Brendan	,, ,,
EI-ALG	St Kieran	Vickers Viscount 808
EI-AMA	St Conleth	,, ,,
EI-AMW	St Laurence O'Toole	Boeing 707-348C
EI-ANE	St Mel	BAC One-Eleven
EI-ANF	St Malachy	,, ,,
EI-ANG	St Declan	,, ,,
EI-ANH	St Ronan	,, ,,
EI-ANO	St Brigid	Boeing 707-348C
EI-ANV	St Enda	,, ,,
EI-AOE	St Dymphna	Vickers Viscount 803
EI-AOG	St Finian	,, ,,
EI-AOH	St Fiacre	,, ,,
EI-AOI	St Fergal	,, ,,
EI-AOJ	St Flannen	,, ,,
EI-AOM	St Felim	,, ,,
EI-APD	St Finbar	,, ,,
EI-APG	St Senan	Boeing 707-348C
EI-ASA		Boeing 737-248
EI-ASB		,, ,,

St. Laurence O'Toole is an Aer Lingus Irish International Airlines Boeing 707-348C for use on the North Atlantic routes

EL AL
Israel
El Al Israel Airlines Ltd

The national airline of Israel, El Al (Hebrew for "To the Skies" or "Onward and Upward") was formed on 15th November, 1948, and operations began in July 1949, when Douglas DC-4 'Skymasters' flew on services to Rome and Paris. The airline's route network developed during the following year with the addition of Athens, Vienna, Zürich, London, Nairobi, Johannesburg and New York; services across the Atlantic were begun with Lockheed 'Constellations'. Other routes followed; El Al was soon operating to every major city in Western Europe.

In 1957 El Al introduced turbo-prop airliners—four Bristol 'Britannia' 300's—on the North Atlantic services via London. The 'Britannia' set a record for the New York–London service, and placed the relatively small airline amongst the best in the international class. El Al maintained this position when, in January 1961, it introduced its first pure jet airliners, Boeing 707-420's. Later that year the Boeings began the first non-stop service between New York and Tel Aviv.

Since 1961, El Al has purchased additional Boeing jets, 720's in 1962 and 707-320's in 1964, and these aircraft with the original 707-420's form the present fleet. El Al is owned by the Government of Israel (50% plus), the Government-owned ZIM Shipping Company, and the Histadrut Federation of Labour. A purely international airline, El Al has a 50% interest in Arkia, the Israeli domestic airline formed in 1950, whose fleet is four Handley Page 'Herald' 200's and two Douglas DC-3's. El Al has secured options on two Boeing 2707 SST's.

An unusual feature of El Al is that it operates only six days a week, as no El Al aircraft arrive or depart at Lod, the Airport for Tel Aviv, on the Sabbath. Member of the International Air Transport Association

El Al's fleet of Boeing 707's includes several of the Rolls-Royce Conway powered 707-458 version, like 4X-ATA, here

Services, international only from Tel Aviv to:
Amsterdam, Athens, Brussels, Copenhagen, Frankfurt, Istanbul, Johannesburg, London, Munich, Nairobi, New York, Nicosia, Paris, Rome, Tehran, Vienna
Livery F: white, blue, grey   **T:** blue

Fleet				
4X-ABA	Boeing 720-058B		4X-ATB	Boeing 707-458
4X-ABB	,,	,,	4X-ATC	,, 707-358B
4X-ATA	,,	707-458	4X-ATR	,, ,,
			4X-ATS	,, ,,

ALITALIA
Alitalia Linee Aeree Italiane

Italy

Alitalia was formed in 1946 as one of two airlines backed by the Italian Government through the Institute for Industrial Reconstruction (Istituto Ricostruzione Industriale), the other airline being Linee Aeree Italiane (LAI) which was formed with a technical and financial agreement with Trans World Airlines. Alitalia was also formed with a similar agreement with a foreign airline, British European Airways. Under the agreement, BEA held a 30% interest in Alitalia and was able to appoint five representatives to its board.

The two airlines developed separately, and during their expansion absorbed all other Italian air carriers. In 1957 the two airlines merged at IRI's behest, partly to eliminate some overlapping of the two route networks which had developed, although in general the two airlines were complementary to each other. LAI operated domestically, within Europe, to Egypt, and to North America, while Alitalia also operated domestically and within Europe, but to the Middle East, Africa, and South America too. In 1958, a year after the merger, (in which period Alitalia had devoted much time and effort to rationalization) the fleet of the combined airline consisted of six Douglas DC-7C's, operating mainly across the North Atlantic, eight Douglas DC-6B's, three DC-6's and twelve DC-3's, six Vickers 'Viscounts' and six Convair 440 'Metropolitans'. Two years later, in 1960, Alitalia took delivery of its first jets, both the long-range Douglas DC-8, and the shorter-range Sud Aviation 'Caravelle'.

The present Alitalia fleet of DC-8's, 'Caravelles', and 'Viscounts' covers domestic and European services, and intercontinental services to North and South America, Africa, Asia, and Australia. Presently in delivery are 28 Douglas DC-9's; for the more distant future, Alitalia has an option on six Boeing 2707 SST's.

Alitalia is now owned by the Istituto Ricostruzione Industriale, having a 96.2% shareholding, and FIAT. Alitalia has a 90% interest in Aero Trasporti Italiani, the Italian domestic operator formed in 1964 to take over the routes of

I-DIWA is a Rolls-Royce Conway-engined Series 40 DC-8

another Alitalia subsidiary Societè Aérea Mediterranea, in which Alitalia has a 95% shareholding. The airline also owns 62.6% of the capital of Elivie, the Italian helicopter operator, and holds a 50% interest in Somali Airlines.

In March 1967, Alitalia was awarded a contract to provide technical and management assistance to Zambia Airways on its withdrawal from Central African Airways.

Member of the International Air Transport Association

International services from Rome to:

Accra, Addis Ababa, Abidjan, Aden, Algiers, Amman, Amsterdam (M), Asmara, Athens, Bangkok, Barcelona (M), Beirut, Benghazi, Bombay, Boston (M), Brussels (M), Buenos Aires, Cairo, Calcutta, Caracas (M), Chicago (M), Copenhagen (M), Dakar (M), Damascus, Dar-es-Salaam, Delhi, Dhahran, Düsseldorf, Entebbe, Frankfurt, Geneva (M), Hamburg, Hong Kong, Istanbul, Johannesburg, Kampala, Karachi, Khartoum, Kinshasa, Lagos, Leopoldville, Lima (M), Lisbon (M), London (MG), Lusaka, Madrid (M), Malta (C), Mogadishu, Montevideo, Montreal (M), Moscow, Munich (M), Nairobi, New York (M), Nice, Paris, Prague (M), Rio de Janeiro, Salisbury (Southern Rhodesia), Santiago de Chile, São Paulo, Singapore, Stockholm, Stuttgart (M), Sydney, Tehran, Tel-Aviv, Tirana, Tokyo, Tripoli, Tunis (P), Vienna (M), Zürich (M)

C–via Catania   G–via Genoa   M–via Milan   P–via Palermo

Domestic route points

Alghero, Bari, Brindisi, Cagliari, Calabria, Catania, Comiso, Genoa, Milan, Naples, Palermo, Pantelleria, Pisa, Reggiodi, Rome, Taranto, Trieste, Turin, Venice, Verona

Livery F: white, dark and light blue, grey   **T:** green, white, red

Fleet

Vickers Viscount 785

I-LARK	I-LIFT	I-LIRC	I-LIRP	I-LITS
I-LIFE	I-LILI	I-LIRG	I-LIRS	I-LIZO
I-LIFS	I-LINS	I-LIRM	I-LIRT	I-LOTT

Douglas DC-8 Series 40

I-DIWA	Amerigo Vespucci	I-DIWO	Marco Polo
I-DIWB	Antonio Pigafetta	I-DIWP	Alvise ca da Mosto
I-DIWE	Cristoforo Colombo	I-DIWR	Nicoloso da Recco
I-DIWG	Luca Tarigo	I-DIWU	Giovanni Caboto
I-DIWI	Giovanni da Verazzano	I-DIWS	Leone Pancaldo
I-DIWL	Nicolo Zeno	I-DIWT	Emanuele Pessagno
I-DIWM	Ugolino Vivaldi		

Sud Aviation S.E. 210 Caravelle 6N

I-DABA	Regolo	I-DABW	Betelgeuse
I-DABE	Rigel	I-DABZ	Spica
I-DABF	Mizar	I-DAXA	Altair
I-DABG	Arturo	I-DAXE	Aldebaran
I-DABI	Sirio	I-DAXI	Antares
I-DABL	Fomalhaut	I-DAXO	Deneb
I-DABR	Bellatrix	I-DAXT	Polluce
I-DABS	Dubhe	I-DAXU	Canopo
I-DABT	Denebola	I-DABM	Procione
I-DABU	Vega	I-DABP	Castore
I-DABV	Acrux		

Douglas DC-9–32 (* Freighter)

I-DIBC	Lampedusa	I-DIKL	Panarea
I-DIBD	Montecristo	I-DIKM	Tavolara
I-DIBJ	Capraia	I-DIKN	Nisida
I-DIBN	Palmaria	I-DIKO	Pantelleria
I-DIBQ	Pianosa	I-DIKP	Marettino
I-DIKA	Capri	I-DIKR	Torcello
I-DIKB	Caprera	I-DIKS	Filicudi
I-DIKC	Ponza	I-DIKT	Usticia
I-DIKD	Giglio	I-DIKU	Ischia
I-DIKE	Elba	I-DIKV	Vulcano
I-DIKF*	Atlante	I-DIKW	Giannutri
I-DIKG*	Anteo	I-DIKZ	Linosa
I-DIKI	Murano	I-DIKY	Alicudi
I-DIKJ	Lipari		

SAM
Società Aerea Mediterranea SpA

Italy

Società Aerea Mediterranea bears the same name as an Italian airline ancestor of Alitalia that was formed in 1928 to operate a service between Brindisi and Valona. Alitalia holds 95 per cent of the capital of the present SAM, and there the connection with Alitalia's ancestor ends as the existing airline was not formed until 1960, when Alitalia provided 70 per cent of the capital of the then new air charter carrier.

Initially SAM operated three Douglas DC-6Bs, but ex-Alitalia Douglas DC-3s found their way into the fleet for the period prior to 1964 when SAM operated several ex-Alitalia domestic services, which disappeared with the DC-3s on the formation of Aero Trasporti Italiani by Alitalia as a domestic service operator. Today, SAM concentrates on inclusive tour and ad hoc charter services, with two scheduled freight services operated for Alitalia, and operates a fleet of seven Douglas DC-6B's. The airline has two Sud Caravelle jet airliners on order.

International services:
  Rome–Milan–Frankfurt; Rome–Tripoli

Livery F: silver, light blue, red, white
  T: white, red, green

Fleet
Douglas DC-6B

I-DIMA	I-DIMD	I-DIMI	I-DIMP	I-DIMU
I-DIMB	I-DIME			

JAL
Japan Air Lines Co Ltd

Japan Air Lines was formed in 1951 when permission was given by the Supreme Commander, Allied Powers, for the operation of domestic routes by a Japanese airline on the condition that the aircraft and crews would be supplied by a non-Japanese operator. Five companies bid for the right to start services and Japan Air Lines was nominated to operate services on condition that it formed a union with its four competitors in order to strengthen the new airline.

The predecessor of Japan Air Lines was Dai-Nippon Airways, an operator formed by the amalgamation of the Japan Air Transport Company and several other operators in 1938, and which operated throughout World War II until 1945 when it was disbanded.

Initially JAL services were operated by Martin 202's of Northwest Orient Air Lines, but in 1952 Japan Air Lines was allowed to operate its own aircraft using Japanese crews. Two Douglas DC-4's were placed into service, and two de Havilland 'Comet' 2's were ordered, but never delivered. The same year JAL received permission to operate international services, a start being made with a Tokyo–San Francisco route. Government capital for the airline's expansion was made available by the acquisition of a 50 per cent interest in the company, and this has since been increased to 58 per cent.

In 1956 JAL ordered long-range aircraft in the form of Douglas DC-7C's and DC-8 Series 30's. In 1959, after consolidating its Pacific and Asian services, JAL started a Tokyo–Paris polar service using Air France Boeing 707's pending delivery, the following year, of the airline's own jet aircraft. A second Tokyo–Europe route via Hong Kong was opened in 1962. Authority for flights across the Atlantic between New York and London was obtained in 1965 and JAL started a round-the-world service in March, 1967. A service to Mexico via Vancouver and San Francisco was introduced from Tokyo in time for the 1968 Olympic Games.

For the future, Japan Air Lines envisages the operation of services to Europe via Moscow in a couple of years, but more immediately, a service to Sydney is planned for October, 1969. The company has secured delivery positions for three BAC/Sud Concordes and five Boeing 2707 SSTs, with six Boeing 747 Jumbo jets on order.

JAL has a 7.6 per cent shareholding in All-Nippon Airways and plans to absorb Japan Domestic Airways, whose domestic trunk route JAL already operates, by 1971; a 7.6 per cent shareholding in JDA is presently held by JAL.

The airline also has a 56 per cent interest in Southwest Air Lines of Ryukyu Islands.

Member of the International Air Transport Association

A Boeing 727, similar to those used by Japan Air Lines on domestic routes

JA8021, a Convair 880 Coronado that operates the domestic and regional routes

International services from Tokyo to:
Amsterdam, Anchorage, Brussels, Bangkok, Cairo, Calcutta, Copenhagen, Delhi, Djakarta, Frankfurt, Geneva, Hamburg, Hong Kong, Honolulu, Karachi, London, Los Angeles, Manila, Mexico City, Moscow, New York, Paris, Rome, San Francisco, Seoul, Singapore, Sydney, Taipei, Tehran, Vancouver

Domestic services from Okinawa to :
Fukuoka, Osaka, Sapporo
Stops are made on some Asian services at Fukuoka, Okinawa, Osaka, and Nagoya

Livery F: white, red and blue, grey   **T:** white and blue

Fleet
Douglas DC-6B

JA 6201	*City of Tokyo*	JA 6207	*City of Fukuoka*
JA 6203	*City of Nara*	JA 6208	*City of Supporo*
JA 6206	*City of Nagoya*		

Douglas DC-8 Series 32 (* series 33)

JA 8001	*Fuji*	JA 8005*	*Miyajima*
JA 8002	*Nikko*	JA 8006*	*Kamakura*

Douglas DC-8 Series 53 (* series 55; † freight)

JA 8007	*Yoshino*	JA 8014*†	*Asama*
JA 8008	*Matsushima*	JA 8015*	*Seto*
JA 8009	*Shima*	JA 8016*	*Shikotsu*
JA 8010	*Kirishima*	JA 8017*	*Bandai*
JA 8011	*Towada*	JA 8018*†	*Ise*
JA 8012	*Akan*	JA 8019*	*Aso*
JA 8013	*Haruna*		

Douglas DC-8–62 (* series 61; † series 62F)

JA 8031	*Awaji*	JA 8036†	*Wakasa*
JA 8032	*Shiga*	JA 8037	*Yashima*
JA 8033	*Amakusa*	JA 8038*	*Iza*
JA 8034	*Daisen*	JA 8039*	*Tukuba*
JA 8035	*Taisetsu*	JA 8040	*Hida*

Convair 880M

JA 8021	*Sakura*	JA 8026	*Yanagi*
JA 8022	*Matsu*	JA 8027	*Sumire*
JA 8024	*Kiku*	JA 8028	*Kikyo*
JA 8025	*Ayame*		

Boeing 727-46 (*-89)

JA 8307	Tone	JA 8315*	Yoda
JA 8308	Kamo	JA 8318	Tama
JA 8309	Chikugo	JA 8319	Kitakami
JA 8310	Ishikari	JA 8320	Sagami
JA 8311	Kiso	JA 8325	Shinano
JA 8312	Tokachi	JA 8326	Kumano
JA 8314*	Tenryu		

JA8007, a DC-8 used on inter-continental services

ALIA
The Royal Jordanian Airlines

Jordan

Alia Royal Jordanian Airlines commenced operations from Amman to Jerusalem, Beirut, Cairo, Kuwait and Jeddah on 15th December, 1963, with a fleet of two Handley Page 'Heralds' and a Douglas DC-7. The new airline was formed by Royal Decree, replacing Air Jordan, and is named after King Hussein's daughter, Princess Alia (the name means "high flying"). Ownership is divided equally between private and state interests.

A second DC-7 was obtained in July, 1964, followed a year later by the first of two Sud Aviation 'Caravelle' 10R's with which a new service from Amman and Jerusalem to Rome was introduced in September, 1965. The second 'Caravelle' arrived in February, 1966, by which time the Handley Page 'Heralds' had been phased out.

Paris and London were added to Alia's network in June and August 1966, and the 'Caravelles' are used on this route. The fleet now includes three Caravelles

JY-ACT *Jerusalem*, one of Alia's three Caravelles here at Amman

and a Fokker Friendship. With the exception of major engine overhauls, all maintenance is dealt with at Alia's own base at Amman.

Member of the International Air Transport Association

International services from Amman and Jerusalem to:
   Beirut, Cairo, Jeddah, Kuwait, London, Paris, Rome

Fleet

JY-ACS	*Amman*	Sud Aviation S.E. 210 Caravelle 10R
JY-ACT	*Jerusalem*	,, ,,
JY-ACV		,, ,,
JY-ACU		Fokker F-27 Friendship 200

KUWAIT AIRWAYS   Kuwait
Kuwait Airways Corporation

It was as the Kuwait National Airways Company that Kuwait Airways commenced operations in 1954 with two DC-3 aircraft on routes to Iraq, Syria, the Lebanon, Jordan and Iran.   The airline was an immediate success and two 'Hermes' aircraft were introduced in 1955, followed in 1957 by DC-4's.   Also in 1957, the name of the company was changed to Kuwait Airways Company.

In 1958 BOAC became responsible for the technical management of the airline for a period of five years.   Shortly afterwards Vickers 'Viscounts' were introduced and India and Pakistan added to the route network.

During the period from its formation until 1962 the airline's capital had been divided equally between the Kuwait Government and private companies.   In that year, however, the remaining 50% passed to the state and the present title was adopted.   Also in 1962 the airline obtained its first jet equipment in the form of a leased 'Comet', and the following year one of these aircraft was purchased. There are now three of them plus two 'Tridents', three 707's and three DC-6B's in the fleet operating over a route network stretching from London to Bombay.

Member of the International Air Transport Association

Services from Kuwait to:
   Abadan, Amman, Baghdad, Bahrain, Beirut, Bombay, Cairo, Damascus, Doha, Dubai, Frankfurt, Geneva, Karachi, London, Paris, Sharjah, Tehran

Livery F: white, blue, grey   **T:** blue and white

Fleet

9K-ABA	Douglas DC-6B	
9K-ABB	,, ,,	
9K-ABC	,, ,,	
9K-ACA	Hawker Siddeley (de Havilland) Comet 4C	
9K-ACE	,,	,,
9K-ACF	,,	Trident IE
9K-ACH	,,	,,
9K-ACI	,,	Comet 4
9K-ACJ	Boeing 707-369C	
9K-ACK	,, ,,	
9K-ACL	,, ,,	

MEA/AIR LIBAN
Lebanon

Middle East Airlines Air Liban SAL

Middle East Airlines was formed in 1945 with a fleet of three de Havilland 'Rapide' biplanes. The new airline had established routes from Beirut to Baghdad, Aleppo, Cairo, Lydda, Haifa, Damascus and Amman by mid-1946 and the fleet had to be supplemented by two Douglas DC-3's. The Palestine crisis in 1948 forced the airline to terminate the Haifa and Lydda services, but the effect of this was countered by the introduction of services to Ankara and Istanbul. A third DC-3 was purchased in 1949 and the 'Rapides' sold.

Also during 1949 MEA began the first of its associations with large international carriers: Pan American World Airways acquired a 36% interest and in return provided three more DC-3's for the airline. This arrangement was terminated in 1955 to enable MEA to get the assistance required to introduce more modern aircraft. This assistance came from BOAC, which acquired a 48.5% shareholding and assisted with the purchase of three Vickers 'Viscounts', the establishment of a maintenance base at Beirut, and, in 1960, leased two 'Comet' 4's to the airline for charter work pending delivery of MEA's own 'Comet' 4C's. Scheduled services started with the 4C's in 1961. During the period of the agreement with BOAC, Middle East Airlines expanded into the air freight business, first with a Bristol 170 in 1956, and later with three Avro 'Yorks'. The agreement with BOAC ended in 1961, partly because MEA had to face competition from British European Airways.

MEA became independent of foreign airline investment from 1961 to 1963, indeed the tables were turned during this period by its holding a 30% interest in Jordan Airways. However, this agreement was terminated in 1963, the year in which Air France acquired a 30% interest in MEA when the latter was merged with Air Liban. Air France had a controlling interest in Air Liban, the Lebanese aviation concern.

Air Liban had operated DC-4 services in the Middle East and to West Africa, and after the merger, Air France and MEA co-operated on the development of services between France and the Lebanon. One effect of the Air France interest in MEA is the airline's fleet of 'Caravelles'.

For the future Middle East Airlines has taken two 1971 delivery positions for the BAC/Sud 'Concorde' supersonic transport. Three Douglas DC-8's were ordered, but the order was later cancelled because of conditions attached to its payment that included the 'forced' adoption of a 'buy American policy' and Boeing 707-320's are now on order. MEA entered into a pooling agreement with another Lebanese operator, Lebanese International Airlines, early in 1967 with a view to a possible merger in the near future, but this agreement terminated in March 1968 without a merger, and a new agreement had to be arranged in July 1968, for the gradual take-over of LIA's fleet and services.

MEA's fleet suffered badly in an Israeli attack at Beirut Airport on 28th December, 1968, when a Viscount, a 707, three Comets, two Caravelles and a leased VC10 were destroyed.

Member of the International Air Transport Association

Services from Beirut to:

Abidjan, Accra, Aden, Addis Ababa, Aleppo, Ankara, Athens, Baghdad, Bahrain, Benghazi, Bombay, Brussels, Cairo, Copenhagen, Damascus, Dharan, Doha,

OD-AEE, an MEA Caravelle at Beirut

Dubai, Frankfurt, Geneva, Istanbul, Jeddah, Jerusalem, Karachi, Khartoum, Kuwait, London, Lagos, Monrovia, Munich, Nicosia, Paris, Rome, Tehran, Vienna, Zürich

Livery F: white, red, grey   **T:** white with red and green

Fleet

OD-ACV	Vickers Viscount 700
OD-ADD	,, ,,
OD-ADT	Hawker Siddeley (de Havilland) Comet 4C
OD-AEO	Sud Aviation S.E. 210 Caravelle 6N
ET-AAH	Boeing 720B (leased)

TMA
Trans Mediterranean Airways SAL

Lebanon

Trans Mediterranean Airways was formed in 1953 as an air freight charter operator using a fleet of six Avro 'Yorks'. In 1959 another two 'Yorks' and two Douglas DC-4's were added to the fleet. Scheduled cargo operations started in 1960 and today the airline operates scheduled cargo services throughout the Middle East and to Europe, and *ad hoc* charters anywhere, with a fleet of Douglas DC-6's and DC-4's.

Member of the International Air Transport Association

Fleet

Douglas DC-4 Skymaster

OD-ADI	OD-AOK

Douglas DC-6

OD-AEG	OD-AER	OD-AET	OD-AEV	OD-AEU
OD-AEL	OD-AES			

KINGDOM OF LIBYA AIRLINES   Libya

Kingdom of Libya Airlines was formed in 1964 by Royal Decree and started operations almost a year later with a service to Tripoli. The airline took over the activities of NAA Libiavia and United Libyan Airlines.

At present Kingdom of Libya Airlines operates a network of domestic and international services with a fleet of 'Caravelles' and 'Friendships' (on lease from Aero Trasporti Italiani). Technical assistance is being given by Autair International Airlines, a British company.

Member of the International Air Transport Association

International services from Tripoli to:
Athens*, Beirut*, Cairo*, Geneva (B), London (B), Malta, Rome (B), Tunis
*via Benghazi   B–from Benghazi via Tripoli

Domestic services from Tripoli to:
Benghazi, Ghadames, Mersa Brega, Sebha
from Benghazi to:
Beida, Mersa Brega, Tobruk

Fleet

5A-DAA	Sud Aviation S.E. 210 Caravelle 6R
5A-DAB	,, ,,
5A-DAE	,, ,,
I-ATIM	Fokker F.27 Friendship (on lease)
PH-FSD	,, ,, ,,
5A-DAC	Lear Jet
5A-DAD	,,

LUXAIR   Luxembourg
Société Anonyme Luxembourgeoise de Navigation Aérienne

Luxair was formed in 1962, as the national airline of the Grand Duchy of Luxembourg, and the main shareholders, apart from the Luxembourg Government, are the steel industry and the banks. The airline is a successor to Luxembourg Airlines which received assistance from the British company, Scottish Aviation, between 1948 and 1951 and the American, Seaboard and Western Airlines (now Seaboard World Airlines) between 1952 and 1960.

The airline operates to several major European centres and, under an agreement with Trek Airways, a Luxembourg–Johannesburg service is operated with Trek 'Constellations' in Luxair colours. Luxair's own fleet includes three Fokker F-27 'Friendships' and a Vickers 'Viscount' 810.

Services from Luxembourg to:
Athens, Brussels, Frankfurt, London, Milan, Nice, Palma, Paris, Split, Vienna

Livery F: white, turquoise blue, grey   **T:** white

LX-LGA, one of Luxair's small fleet of F-27 Friendships

Fleet

LX-LGA	*Prince Henri*	Fokker F-27 Friendship
LX-LGB	*Prince Jean*	,, ,,
LX-LGC		Vickers Viscount 810
LX-LGD	*Prince Guillaume*	Fokker F-27 Friendship

THE MALTA AIRLINES Malta, GC

The Malta Airlines (Malta Airways Co. Ltd. and its associate, Air Malta Ltd.) was formed in 1946 with British Overseas Airways Corporation holding a 34% interest which passed to British European Airways in 1948. The airlines have no fleet of their own, BEA providing the aircraft for a jointly licensed Malta–Rome–London service, and Malta Airlines services to Tripoli and Catania. Plans have been prepared for BEA to sell its shareholding and for the Malta Airlines to buy its own jet airliners, probably Douglas DC-9's. The base is at the modernized Luqa Airport in the south of the island.
Member of the International Air Transport Association

Services from Malta to:
  Catania, London, Rome, Tripoli (Libya)
Fleet
  None; BEA aircraft are employed at present

AERONAVES DE MEXICO Mexico
Aeronaves de Mexico SA

Mexico's Government-owned airline, Aeronaves de Mexico, was formed in 1934 as a private enterprise with a small fleet of Beechcraft aeroplanes. On the 14th September of that year the airline was granted an 'experimental permit' by the Mexican Government to operate a scheduled service between Mexico City and Acapulco, now Mexico's bustling tourist resort but then only a small fishing village. The airline later received a permanent licence for this service.

In 1940 Pan American World Airways acquired a 40% interest in Aeronaves. The following year new services were inaugurated to Mazatlán and La Paz, but more notably, 1941 was the year in which the airline acquired Transportes Aéreas de Pacifico, the first of many small airlines to be acquired by Aeronaves during its development. Aeronaves de Mexico was further expanded in 1943 when Taxi Aéreo de Oaxaca was taken over, giving Aeronaves a route network to the north, west, and south of Mexico City. In 1944 when Líneas Aéreas Jesus Sarabia went out of business, the company acquired that airline's route rights.

Other acquisitions followed, including in 1952 Líneas Aéreas Mexicanas SA (LAMSA), a domestic operator of no small importance with a history dating from 1934, purchased when the American company, United Air Lines, decided to sell its interest. This gave Aeronaves services to several important centres in northern central Mexico. Aerovias Reforma was bought in 1954, and this acquisition gave Aeronaves several routes to Mexico's northern border. They were particularly valuable at a time when the airline had no international services of its own, due in part to the difficulties of obtaining international permits. One of the routes acquired from Aerovias Reforma, Mexico City–Tijuana (a Mexican border town 30 miles south of San Diego in California) became the airline's most important route at the time. Aeronaves introduced two Lockheed 'Constellations' leased from Pan American on it during the mid 1950's to cater for the rapidly increasing tourist traffic. The remainder of the fleet then consisted mainly of Douglas DC-3 and DC-4 aircraft.

In 1957 the Pan American shareholding was sold to Mexican interests. Later in 1957 the company received permission to operate its first international route from Mexico City to New York, and this marked the start of a change of emphasis from domestic to international services. This process had been helped the previous year when Aeronaves had, at government request, formed Aerolineas Mexicanas to operate some unprofitable routes in the national interest.

The airline's promising development was imperilled in 1959 by a strike by Mexican airline pilots. The economic effects of this strike were so disastrous that the Mexican Government had to take over Aeronaves to keep it operating. A government administrator was appointed with a brief to ensure that all the airline's expenses were covered without loss as soon as possible. As a result, the airline was completely re-organized, including fleet standardization on Douglas DC-6's and DC-3's with two Bristol 'Britannia' 302's. In addition a Douglas DC-8 was ordered for the New York service. Domestic fares were increased.

An Aeronaves de Mexico Douglas DC-8 as used by the airline on its long-haul routes

In 1960 Aeronaves had to acquire Aerolineas Mexicanas and Trans Mar de Cortes, both of which had gone bankrupt. Although with the acquisition of Aerolineas Mexicanas, Aeronaves was in effect repossessing many unprofitable routes, Trans Mar de Cortes operated into Los Angeles, a valuable addition to the Aeronaves network.

In 1961 Aerovias Guest was purchased by Aeronaves when Scandinavian Airlines System, which had been assisting Aerovias Guest, sold its interest to Aeronaves. This gave Aeronaves traffic rights to South America and a profitable Mexico City–Miami service.

The present Aeronaves de Mexico fleet consists of Douglas DC-8 and DC-9 jets, and DC-3's for the more lightly trafficked routes. For the more distant future, the airline has options on two Boeing 2707 SST's. The airline will commence operations to London in the very near future, although before then it is likely that the remainder of the Aerovias Guest routes on which Aeronaves suspended operations because of a shortage of suitable aircraft will be resumed.

Member of the International Air Transport Association

International services from Mexico City to:
Caracas, Detroit, Los Angeles*, Madrid, Miami, Montreal, New York, Panama, Phoenix, Rome, Toronto, Washington
*also from Acapulco and La Paz
also—Hermosillo–Tucson

Main domestic route points:
Acapulco, Chihuahua, Ciudad Juárez, Ciudad Obregón, Guadalajara, Hermosillo, La Paz, León, Mazatlán, Mexico City, Monterrey, Tijuana, Torréon

Livery F: white, orange, grey   **T:** white

Fleet
Douglas DC-3 Dakota

XA-	XA-	XA-	XA-	XA-
XA-	XA-	XA-	XA-	XA-
XA-	XA-			

Douglas DC-8 Series 51

XA-NUS	XA-PIK	XA-SIA	XA-SIB	XA-SID

Douglas DC-9 Series 10

XA-SOA	XA-SOD	XA-SOF	XA-	XA-
XA-SOC	XA-SOG	XA-SOY	XA-	

ROYAL AIR MAROC Morocco
Cie Nationale de Transport Aériens–Royal Air Maroc

Royal Air Maroc was formed in 1953 as Air Maroc on the merger of another company of the same name with Air Atlas. This fusion came about at the request of the Government of Morocco which had been attempting to merge the two airlines since 1951 in order to eliminate some duplication of services and ensure the future of a national airline. Up to that time, the two companies had been experiencing certain financial difficulties.

Air Atlas had been formed in 1946 under the sponsorship of the French Resident-General as a regional and domestic operator with some services to the South of France. Initially the airline operated a fleet of ten Junkers Ju52/3m's which were supplemented by 'Martinets' for short haul services and replaced in 1948 by Douglas DC-3's on the main routes to Marseilles and Bordeaux.

Air Maroc was formed in 1947 as a private company to undertake air charter work; these operations started the following year with Douglas DC-3's. Scheduled services were started in 1949, and by the time the merger with Air Atlas came, the airline was operating from Casablanca to several major European centres, including Paris and Geneva.

Upon merger, the Government of Morocco acquired a 34% interest, while Air France, a major shareholder in Air Atlas, held an equal shareholding. The airline acquired its present title in 1956 when it became the national airline of Morocco on the country's independence. Currently, Royal Air Maroc is owned 64% by the Moroccan State, 21% by Air France, 7.6% by Cie. Gale Transatlantique, 5% by Aviaco, and 2.4% by other private interests. The fleet includes four 'Caravelles' and a Douglas DC-3 operating from Casablanca (where the airline's predecessors also had their bases) to Europe and North Africa. Services were introduced to London early in 1967.

International services from Casablanca to:
Algiers, Bordeaux, Frankfurt, Geneva, Gibraltar, London, Lyon, Madrid, Malaga, Marseilles, Milan, Nice, Oran, Paris

Domestic services from Casablanca to:
Agadir, Fes, Marakech, Meknes, Mellila, Oujdei, Tangier, Tetuan

Fleet

CN-CCL	Douglas DC-3 Dakota	
CN-CCV	Sud Aviation S.E.210 Caravelle	
CN-CCX	,,	,,
CN-CCY	,,	,,
CN-CCZ	,,	,,

KLM
Koninklijke Luchtvaart Maatschappij NV
(KLM/Royal Dutch Airlines)

Netherlands

Formed in 1919 at The Hague, KLM inaugurated its first scheduled service between Amsterdam and London the following year using a single-engined two-passenger biplane. This route is the oldest scheduled air service in the world to be operated by the same company. The airline's first intercontinental air service started in 1929 between Amsterdam and Djakarta using a Fokker F-VIIB tri-engined monoplane. Since then the airline has grown until now its route network is the world's third largest. KLM was the first European airline to operate the Douglas DC-2 and DC-3 aircraft before World War II, and afterwards the airline introduced trans-Atlantic services using the Douglas DC-4 in a fleet of 18 DC-4s and 30 DC-3s.

50.5 per cent of KLM's share capital is held by the Dutch Government and the remainder is held by private interests. The airline owns several other commercial operators including KLM Aerocarto, specializing in air surveys; ALM Dutch Antillean Airlines, founded in 1964 to take over KLM's West Indian services; NLM Dutch Airlines, founded in 1966 to operate domestic services experimentally with Fokker F-27s leased from the Royal Netherlands Air Force, and KLM Nordzee Helikopters which will operate helicopter supply services to North Sea drilling rigs. KLM also has a 25 per cent interest in Martin's Air Charter, formed in 1958, operating inclusive tour and executive charter services.

KLM's present fleet includes Douglas DC-8 and DC-9 jets. These replaced the piston-engined Douglas DC-7Fs and turbo-charged Lockheed Electras in the winter of 1968-9. An option is held for three Boeing 2707s and three BAC/Sud Concordes. In 1968 KLM entered into an agreement with SAS and Swissair covering Boeing 747 maintenance, and with Swissair covering DC-9 maintenance.

Member of the International Air Transport Association

PH-DNB *City of Brussels*, one of KLM's fleet of Douglas DC-9-10's for short haul routes

Services from Amsterdam to:
Abadan, Abidjan, Accra, Amman, Anchorage, Ankara, Aruba, Athens, Baghdad, Bangkok, Barcelona, Basle, Beirut, Belgrade, Benghazi, Berlin, Birmingham, Bonn, Brazzaville, Bremen, Brussels, Bucharest, Budapest, Buenos Aires, Cairo, Calcutta, Caracas, Cologne, Conakry, Copenhagen, Curaçao, Delhi, Dhahran, Djakarta, Dublin, Düsseldorf, Frankfurt, Geneva, Glasgow, Guayaquil, Hamburg, Hanover, Houston, Istanbul, Johannesburg, Kano, Karachi, Kinshasa, Kristiansand, Kuala Lumpur, Kuwait, Lagos, Las Palmas, Lima, Linz, Lisbon, London*, Madrid, Malaga, Manchester, Manila, Mexico City, Milan, Monrovia, Montevideo, Montreal, Moscow, Munich, New York, Nice, Nuremburg, Oslo, Panama City, Palma de Majorca, Paramaribo, Paris, Port of Spain, Prague, Rio de Janeiro, Rome, Rotterdam, Santiago de Chile, Singapore, Sofia, Stavanger, Stockholm, Stuttgart, Sydney, Tehran, Tel-Aviv, Tokyo, Tripoli (Libya), Tunis, Vienna, Warsaw, Zagreb, Zürich
*direct service from Rotterdam also

Livery F: white, blue, grey   **T:** dark and light blue

Fleet
Douglas DC-8 Series 32
PH-DCA *Albert Plesman*
PH-DCB *Daniel Bernoulli*
PH-DCC *Sir Frank Whittle*

PH-DCE *Thomas Alva Edison*
PH-DCF *Anthony Fokker*
PH-DCG *Giuglielmo Marconi*

C*

Douglas DC-8 Series 53
PH-DCI *Sir Isaac Newton*
PH-DCK *Admiral Richard E. Byrd*
PH-DCM *Henry Dunant*
Douglas DC-8 Series 54-F
PH-DCS *Alfred Nobel*
PH-DCT *Pierre Baron de Coubertin*
Douglas DC-8–63
PH-DEA *Amerigo Vespucci*
PH-DEB *Christopher Columbus*
PH-DEC *Marco Polo*
PH-DED *Leifur Eriksson*
Douglas DC-9 Series 15
PH-DNA *Amsterdam*
PH-DNB *Brussels*
PH-DNC *Luxemburg*
Douglas DC-9–32 (*series 33)
PH-DNG *City of Rotterdam*
PH-DNH *City of Zürich*
PH-DNI *City of Istanbul*
PH-DNK *City of Copenhagen*
PH-DNL *City of London*
PH-DNM* *City of Madrid*
PH-DNN* *City of Vienna*

PH-DCN *Albert Schweitzer*
PH-DCO *Sir Alexander Fleming*
PH-DCV *Bali*

PH-DCU *Sir Winston Churchill*
PH-DCW *Gerard Mercator*

PH-DEE *Abel Tasman*
PH-DEF *Henry Hudson*
PH-DEG *Jan van Riebeeck*

PH-DND *Bonn*
PH-DNE *Rome*
PH-DNF *Paris*

PH-DNO* *City of Oslo*
PH-DNP* *City of Athens*
PH-DNR* *City of Stockholm*
PH-DNS *City of Arnhem*
PH-DNT *City of Lisbon*
PH-DNV *City of Warsaw*
PH-DNW *City of Moscow*

Alfred Nobel, a KLM Douglas DC-8-54F 'Jet Trader' in flight

MARTINAIR HOLLAND   Netherlands
Martin's Luchtvervoer Maatschappij NV

Martinair was formed in 1958 by Mr. J. Martin Schröder, one of the two current joint-presidents, as Martin's Air Charter (MAC). Prior to forming the airline, Martin Schröder had operated pleasure flights with Piper and Auster aircraft. Initially, MAC did not have any aircraft of its own, equipment being hired as required, and so it was not until 1961 that the first aircraft, an ex-BEA Douglas DC-3 Pionair, was acquired. A Douglas DC-4 and a de Havilland Dove soon followed. Apart from charter work, MAC also undertook a considerable volume of airline contract flying for KLM-Royal Dutch Airlines during the early 1960s.

In 1963, four Dutch shipping companies acquired interests in MAC, one of which also owned another airline, Fairways of Rotterdam, which was acquired by MAC, together with its two DC3s, in 1964. Also during 1964, KLM acquired a 25% interest in MAC, and two Douglas DC-7Cs and a Convair 340 were added to the fleet. Currently, Martinair operates a fleet of two Douglas DC-9's, one DC-8, three DC-7C's, one DC-6A and four DC-3's, and two Convair 640's (Rolls-Royce Dart turbo-prop conversions of the 340/440).

Fleet

Douglas DC-3 Dakota
| PH-MAB | PH-MAG | PH-SCC | PH-SSM |

Douglas DC-6A
PH-MAM

Douglas DC-7C
| PH-DSC | *Gele Zee* | | PH-DSO | *Bering Zee* |
| PH-DSL | *Oost Zee* | | | |

Douglas DC-8–32
PH-DCD *Nikolaus August Otto*

Convair 640
| PH-CGD | PH-MAL |

Douglas DC-9
| PH-MAN | PH-M |

TRANSAVIA
Transavia Holland NV

Netherlands

One of Europe's newest air charter operators, Transavia Holland was formed in 1966 as a subsidiary of Amsterdamse Crediet Maatschappij NV. The airline specializes in inclusive tour charters, although ad hoc charters are operated, and holds CAB authority to operate trans-Atlantic charters. A fleet of five Douglas DC-6s and one Boeing 707-320C is operated from Amsterdam's Schiphol Airport.

An underwing shot of one of Transavia Holland's Douglas DC-6s

Fleet
Douglas DC-6A
PH-TRA   PH-TRB

Douglas DC-6B
PH-TRC   PH-TRD   PH-TRE

Boeing 707-320C
PH-TRF (leased from Executive Jet Aviation)

NIGERIA AIRWAYS
WAAC Nigeria Ltd

Nigeria

The predecessor of Nigeria Airways, the West African Airways Corporation was formed in 1946 by the Governments of the British West African colonies, Nigeria, the Gold Coast, Sierra Leone and Gambia, to continue the operation of services inaugurated by the Royal Air Force during the Second World War. Scheduled services started the following September when the new airline took over the Lagos–Kano service of Nigeria Air Services and operated this route with extensions to Freetown, Bathurst and Dakar.

In 1950 the Colonial Office requested that the airline should operate a trans-Africa service to Khartoum, and for this and the Dakar service, the airline purchased several Bristol 'Wayfarers'; all other routes were operated by de Havilland 'Doves'. The trans-Africa route proved a failure and was abandoned in August, 1953. Also during 1953, the airline withdrew the six Handley Page 'Marathons', in service since only the previous year, as they proved unsuited to the airline's operations. In 1956 the 'Wayfarers' and 'Doves' were replaced by Douglas DC-3's and de Havilland 'Herons', and four years later, the airline's routes became all DC-3 operated.

Fokker F-27 'Friendships' were introduced in 1963, initially on the Dakar service, but now these aircraft also operate on domestic routes.

Since 1957, Nigeria Airways and BOAC have operated a "pool" service to London using BOAC aircraft. Initially this service was operated with Canadair 'Argonauts', followed by Boeing 'Stratocruisers', Bristol 'Britannias', de Havilland 'Comets'; today Vickers VC 10's are used. A similar service to New York is operated with Pan American World Airways using Douglas DC-8's.

The airline has held its present title since 1958 on dissolution of the West African Airways Corporation. Initially ownership of Nigerian Airways was with the Nigerian Government (51%), British Overseas Airways Corporation (32⅔%) and Elder Dempster Lines (16⅓%), but since 1st May, 1961, the Nigerian Government has had complete control of the airline.

Member of the International Air Transport Association

International services from Lagos to:
Abidjan, Accra, Bathurst, Dakar, Frankfurt, Freetown, Leopoldville, London, Monrovia, Rome

Domestic services from Lagos to:
Benin, Calabar, Douala, Enugu, Fort Lamy, Gossu, Jos, Ibada, Kaduna, Kano, Port Harcourt, Sokoto, Tilko, Yola

Shown on the ground is 5N-AAZ, a Fokker F-27 Friendship of Nigeria Airways

BRAATHENS SAFE   Norway
Braathens South American and Far East Airtransport A/S

Although Ludvig Braathen, the Norwegian shipowner, applied for licences to operate air services from Oslo to London and New York before World War II, permission being refused by the Norwegian authorities, it was not until 1946 that Braathens SAFE was formed, and a fleet of three Douglas DC-4 'Skymasters' delivered early in 1947 (a fourth DC-4 and a DC-3 were purchased later in 1947). The crews for the aircraft received their training in the United States, and KLM trained 40 mechanics for the airline's maintenance base.

Initially the airline flew charter services (including ship's crew charters) between Europe and the Middle East, but these charter flights were soon extended to the Far East. In 1949, Braathen received a five year authority to operate a scheduled service to Hong Kong using 'Skymasters'. These aircraft took four days for the journey, a considerable saving on the time taken by the flying boat, the only other Europe-Far East flight available at the time. The Far East route was extended on a regular, but non-scheduled basis, from Oslo via Reykjavik to Caracas in Venezuela. At the same time, "South American and Far East" was added to the company's title. During its period of operation, the Hong Kong–Caracas route (further extensions into South America were impossible for

77

political reasons) was claimed by Braathens to be the world's longest air route.

In 1952 the Norwegian Government warned Braathens that his airline would not have its authority for the Far East service renewed in 1954 because of Norway's commitment to SAS which forbade any competition with SAS on international routes by any Scandinavian airline. Braathens SAFE was allowed, however, to operate domestic services and these started in 1952 with de Havilland 'Herons', which were soon supplemented, and eventually replaced, by DC-3's.

In 1954 when the Far East service was terminated Braathens found that the air charter business could not justify the purchase of two Lockheed 'Super Constellations' which the airline had on order, so it was cancelled. As the four DC-4's had been sold already, an agreement was made with Loftleidir Icelandic Airlines under which Braathens leased one of that airline's aircraft.

Since 1954 Braathens SAFE has expanded the air charter side of its business, and apart from traditional charters to the East with ships' crews, many of which originate from Rotterdam, the airline also operates inclusive tour and educational charters (including a weekly service to England). The domestic services have also expanded, helped in 1958 by absorbing the services of VLS, which had suspended operations, and by the introduction of the Fokker F-27 Friendship in 1960. A further expansion of these services will take place in 1967 when the network is extended north from Trondheim to Bodø and Tromsø. This will be in competition with SAS and Braathens SAFE had to wait for a change in Government before authority could be received.

The present fleet includes six Fokker Friendships, used mainly on the domestic services with five Fokker F-28 Fellowship jet airliners on order which will replace five or six of the F-27s, and two Boeing 737's which will replace four or five of the DC-6's, both types being delivered during the first half of 1969. The airline's maintenance base at Sola, Stavanger, not only undertakes all maintenance on the company's fleet, but also maintains and overhauls the aircraft of several other airlines and the Norwegian Air Force.

Braathens South American and Far East Airtransport is owned by the Braathens shipping companies in which the Braathens family holds 82.5% of the share capital.

LN-SOU is one of the eight Fokker F-27 Friendships used by Braathens SAFE in Norway and probably due for early replacement

Services from Oslo to:
Ålesund, Kristiansand, Stavanger, Trondheim
Oslo–Kristiansand–Farsund–Stavanger Oslo–Røros–Trondheim   Stavanger–
Bergen–Ålesund–Trondheim
Trondheim–Bodø–Tromsø

Livery F: white, red, grey **T:** white

Fleet
Douglas DC-6B
LN-SUB	LN-SUH	LN-SUK	LN-SUM	LN-SUT
LN-SUD	LN-SUI			

Fokker F-27 Friendship
LN-SUA	LN-SUF	LN-SUG	LN-SUL	LN-SUW
LN-SUE				

Fokker F-28 Fellowship
LN-SUC	LN-SUN	LN-SUO	LN-SUX	LN-SUY

Boeing 737-205
LN-SUP	LN-SUS

PIA   Pakistan
Pakistan International Airlines Corporation

Pakistan International Airlines was formed in 1954 by the Pakistan Government, and commenced operations later that year on a non-stop inter-wing service between East and West Pakistan using three Lockheed 'Super Constellations'. The predecessor of PIA was Orient Airlines, a company that had started operations in northern India in 1946, and since Pakistan's independence had flown inter-wing, domestic, and international services with 'Dakota' and 'Convair' aircraft until 1954 when the airline became restricted to domestic routes. In 1955, the year in which PIA services reached London, Orient Airlines and Pakistan International Airlines finally merged.

PIA's first turbo-prop 'planes, Vickers 'Viscounts', were introduced in 1959, and were followed in 1960 by Fokker F-27 'Friendships'. The airline also started jet operations in 1960 with a Boeing 707 leased from Pan American World Airways, and with this aircraft PIA started a service to New York in 1961. Later the 707 was returned to Pan American on receipt of Pakistan International's own Boeings of the 720 type. The service to New York had to be suspended in 1963 due to a shortage of capacity on other routes, but PIA still managed to expand its route network, notably by routeing a service to Europe via Moscow, and by becoming the first non-Communist airline of any importance to operate regular services to Canton and Shanghai.

A notable feature of PIA's domestic routes in East Pakistan for some time was the helicopter services operated with Sikorsky S-61N's. These services had to be switched to fixed wing aircraft in 1966 after two accidents reduced the S-61N fleet from three to one, although by this time traffic had developed to a worthwhile level to favour the construction of runways for fixed wing aircraft.

The present fleet consists of Hawker Siddeley 'Trident' 1E's, Boeing 707's and 720's, Fokker 'Friendships', Lockheed 'Super Constellations' and Douglas DC-3's. The airline is owned 89.3% by the Pakistan Government, and 10.7% by private interests.

Member of the International Air Transport Association

AP-AUG, one of Pakistan International's fleet of Hawker Siddeley Trident IE tri-jets

International services from Karachi to:
 Baghdad, Bahrain, Bangkok (D), Beirut, Cairo, Canton (D), Dhahran, Doha, Dubai, Frankfurt, Geneva, Istanbul, Jeddah, Kuwait, London, Moscow, Nairobi, Paris, Rome, Shanghai (D), Tehran
 D—via Dacca

Domestic inter-wing services to:
 Karachi—Dacca

West Pakistan route points:
 Chitral, Gilgit, Gwadar, Hyderabad, Jiwani, Kabul, Karachi, Lahore, Lyallpur, Mohenjodaro, Multan, Nawabshah, Panjgur, Pasni, Peshawar, Quetta, Rawalpindi, Skardu, Sui, Sukkur

East Pakistan major route points:
 Chittagong, Comilla, Dacca, Ishurdi, Jessore, Khatmandu, Sylhet

Livery F: white, green, grey
 T: green

Fleet
Boeing 707-34C
AP-AUN   AP-AUO   AP-AUP

Boeing 720-040B
AP-AMG   AP-AMJ   AP-ATQ

Hawker Siddeley HS 121 Trident 1E (*in use by Pakistan Air Force)
AP-ATK   AP-ATL   AP-ATM   AP-AUG*

Fokker F-27 Friendship 200 (* Series 400)
AP-ALM   AP-ALO   AP-ALX   AP-ATT*   AP-AUR
AP-ALN   AP-ALW   AP-ATO   AP-ATU   AP-AUS

Lockheed L-1049C/H Super Constellation
AP-AFR   AP-AFS   AP-AJY   AP-AJZ

Douglas DC-3 Dakota
AP-AJH   AP-AJT   AP-ATJ

APSA
Aerolineas Peruanas SA

Peru

Aerolineas Peruanas was formed on 16th September, 1956, by a group of Peruvian industrialists and Air Force Officers, with support from Transportes Aéreos Nacionales (TAN) of Honduras, to operate international services from Peru after the bankruptcy of two other international airlines.

Initially the airline operated two Curtiss C-46's and a Douglas DC-6 leased from TAN on services to Miami and Buenos Aires. Other services followed, including Bogota in 1962, and today the airline operates to most important centres in Latin America and to the United States with two Convair 990A's, a DC-7B, a DC-6, and a C-46. 77% of the airline is owned by Peruvian interests and 23% by the Shelton Estate, which also controls TAN.

Although APSA does not operate into the United Kingdom at present, the airline is considering opening services to Europe, and London is likely to be one of the destinations served.

Member of the International Air Transport Association

International services only from Lima to:
Bogota, Buenos Aires, Caracas, Guayaquil, Los Angeles, Mexico City, Miami, Panama, Santiago, Tegucigalpa

Fleet

OB-R-765	Convair 990A Coronado	OB-	Douglas DC-6
OB-R-728	,, ,,	OB-	Curtiss C-46
OB-	Douglas DC-7B		

LOT POLISH AIRLINES
Polskie Linie Lotnicze

Poland

LOT Polish Airlines was formed on 1st January, 1929, by the Government of Poland to take over the two private enterprise airlines, AEROTARG, dating from 1921, and AER-LLOYD (1922) both of which operated domestic services. LOT continued the operation of these services, and, in 1930, introduced the first international services to Bucharest, Sofia, Salonica and Athens. This progress continued throughout the 1930's, until by 1939 the airline was operating to most central European capitals with a mixed Lockheed 'Electra' and Douglas DC-2 fleet that had replaced the Polish-designed PWS-24's of the mid-'thirties and the licence-built Fokker F-VII's of 1929.

During the Second World War occupation of Poland, airline operations were suspended. The airline was reformed on 6th March, 1945, with ten ex-Polish Air Force Li-2's, and operations commenced later that year. In common with most East European airlines at this time, LOT received Russian assistance.

Operating Li-2's, DC-3's and four-engined Languedoc aircraft, international services were resumed to Berlin (East) and Paris in 1946, and Budapest, Bucharest, Belgrade, and Copenhagen in 1947. In the years that followed, Brussels, Sofia, Moscow, Prague, Vienna, Athens, Zürich, Amsterdam and Rome were added

The Polish airline, LOT, operates Ilyushin Il-18 turbo-props, one of which, SP-LSF is shown here

to the international network, while the more modern Ilyushin IL-12's and Il-14's and Convair 240's were acquired.

The present LOT fleet consists of Ilyushin Il-18 and Antonov An-24 turbo-prop airliners, Ilyushin Il-14's and Tupolev Tu-134's.

Member of the International Air Transport Association

International services from Warsaw to:
Amsterdam, Athens, Beirut, Belgrade, Berlin (East), Budapest, Bucharest, Brussels, Cairo, Copenhagen, Frankfurt, Helsinki, London, Milan, Moscow, Paris, Prague, Rome, Sofia, Stockholm, Vienna, Zagreb, Zürich

Domestic services from Warsaw to:
Gdansk, Katowice, Koszalin, Rzeszów
from Gdansk to:
Cracow, Wroclaw

Fleet

Ilyushin Il-14
SP-LNA	SP-LNC	SP-LNE	SP-LNH	SP-LNK
SP-LNB	SP-LND	SP-LNG	SP-LNI	

Ilyushin Il-18
SP-LSA	SP-LSC	SP-LSE	SP-LSG	SP-SLI
SP-LSB	SP-LSD	SP-LSF	SP-LSH	

Antonov An-24
SP-LTA	SP-LTC	SP-LTE	SP-LTG	
SP-LTB	SP-LTD	SP-LTF	SP-LTH	SP-LTK

Lisunov Li-2
SP-	SP-	SP-	SP-	SP-

Tupolev Tu-134
SP-	SP-	SP -	SP-	SP-

TAP   Portugal
Transportes Aéreos Portugueses, SARL

Transportes Aéreos Portugueses was formed in 1944 by the Portuguese Department of Civil Aviation, although services did not start until two years later with Douglas DC-3 services to Madrid, and later the same year, Angola and Mozambique. The European network expanded during the next few years, reaching London in 1949, and in 1953 TAP acquired the status of a private company to give its management greater commercial freedom.

In the meantime DC-4's had been introduced. They were replaced on the African routes by Lockheed 'Super Constellations' in 1955, by which time the fleet had grown to six DC-3's, three DC-4's and three 'Super Constellations'. In 1959 a pool arrangement was agreed with British European Airways covering the London route on which both airlines utilized BEA's 'Viscounts'. The following year a similar arrangement was reached with Air France covering the Paris route and using 'Caravelles', while 'Comet' 4B's were introduced on the London service. In 1961 a pool arrangement was agreed with Panair do Brasil covering a route to Rio de Janeiro; keeping to the principle of the other agreements, the aircraft used were Panair's Douglas DC-7's.

TAP's first jets, Sud Aviation 'Caravelles', were taken into stock in 1962 and the airline began to operate on the London and Paris routes with its own aircraft once more, although the pool arrangements stayed in force. The long-range jet Boeing 707-382B's were introduced in late 1966, and medium range Boeing 727-82's were introduced early in 1968.

Member of the International Air Transport Association

International services from Lisbon to:
Beira, Bissau, Buenos Aires, Brussels, Frankfurt, Funchal, Geneva, Ilha do Sal, Johannesburg, Las Palmas, London*, Luanda, Lourenço Marques, Madrid, New York, Paris, Porto Santo, Recife, Rio de Janeiro, Santa Maria
*also Faro–London

Domestic services:
Lisbon–Faro   Lisbon–Oporto

Livery F: white, red, grey   **T:** white

CS-TCB, a Caravelle belonging to TAP at Lisbon

Fleet
Boeing 707-382B

CS-TBA	*Santa Cruz*		CS-TBC	*Luanda*
CS-TBB	*Santa Maria*		CS-TBD	*Luvrencico Marzia*

Boeing 727-82 (*82C)

CS-TBK	*Açores*		CS-TBN*	*Porto*
CS-TBL	*Madeira*		CS-TBO	*Costa do Sol*
CS-TBM	*Algarve*			

Sud Aviation S.E. 210 Caravelle 6R

CS-TCA	*Goa*		CS-TCC	*Diu*
CS-TCB	*Damao*			

TAROM
Transporturile Aeriene Romine

Romania

TAROM was formed in 1946 by the Governments of Romania and Russia, ownership being divided equally between the two countries, to operate domestic and regional services with a fleet of Li-2's. The predecessor of TAROM was LARES, formed in 1932 by the Romanian Government; operations were suspended on the outbreak of war.

By 1954, when ownership of TAROM passed entirely to the Romanian Government, international services had been introduced to Prague, Budapest, and Warsaw. International services were progressively expanded after 1954 with the introduction of Ilyushin Il-14's which replaced the Li-2's. In 1955, a service to Moscow was inaugurated, and in the years that followed Vienna, Zurich, Brussels, Copenhagen and Paris were added to the airline's network.

TAROM'S first turbine aircraft, Ilyushin Il-18 turbo-prop airliners, arrived in 1962 to replace the Il-14's on international services as well as introducing new services to Belgrade, Sofia, Athens, Frankfurt and Warsaw (they had been suspended for a few years) and supplementing Il-14's on domestic routes. In spring, 1968, the airline introduced its first jets, British-built BAC One-Elevens—Antonov An-24's complete the fleet.

International services from Bucharest to:
Athens, Belgrade, Brussels, Copenhagen, Frankfurt, London, Moscow, Paris, Prague, Sofia, Warsaw, Zürich

Domestic services from Bucharest to:
Arad, Bacău, Baia Mare, Caranșebes, Cluj, Constanța, Craiova, Deva, Iași, Oradea, Satu-Mare, Suceava, Târgu, Mureș, Timișoara, Tulcea

Fleet
Ilyushin Il-18

YR-IMA	YR-IME	YR-IMF	YR-IMH	YR-IMR

Antonov An-24

YR-AMX	YR-AMY	YR-AMZ

BAC One-Eleven 400

YR-BCA	YR-BCC	YR-BCD	YR-BCE	YR-BCF
YR-BCB				

SAUDI ARABIAN AIRLINES
Saudi Arabian Airlines Corporation

Saudi Arabia

Saudi Arabian Airlines Corporation was formed in 1945 as a government agency managed by Trans World Airlines, and commenced air charter operations the following year. The first scheduled services were inaugurated in 1947 when Cairo and Dhahra were served from Jeddah. At this time the Corporation had a fleet of five Douglas DC-3's, but by the end of the year this had doubled. In 1948 services were introduced to Damascus and Beirut. Throughout this period expansion also took place on the domestic services.

The fleet was supplemented in 1951 by the arrival of five Bristol 'Wayfarers' (all-passenger versions of the Bristol Freighter) and in 1952 the airline purchased several Douglas DC-4's, and since then has also added DC-6B's and Convair 340's to the fleet. The present fleet includes these aircraft plus Douglas DC-3's, and Boeing 720's introduced in 1962, with Douglas DC-9's and Boeing 707's delivered in 1967. Services to London were started in the spring of 1967. Trans World Airlines continues to provide commercial and financial assistance.

International and domestic route points:
Abadan, Aden, Amman, Anaiza, Baghdad, Bahrein, Basra, Beirut, Bisho, Buraida, Cairo, Damascus, Dhahra, Doha, El Russ, Giza, Gurayut, Hail, Hodeida, Jeddah, Khamis, Kharj, Khartoum, Kuwait, London, Maima, Mushait, Nejran, Port Sudan, Rudadh, Sakaka, Shagra, Tabuk, Taif, Taraif, Turubah, Wejh, Yenbo, Zilfe

Fleet
Douglas DC-3 Dakota (*cargo)

HZ-AAB*	HZ-AAE	HZ-AAK	HZ-AAM	HZ-AAR
HZ-AAC*	HZ-AAJ	HZ-AAL	HZ-AAP	HZ-AAX
HZ-AAD				

Douglas DC-6A

HZ-ADA	HZ-ADB	HZ-ADC (DC-6B)

Douglas DC-9-10

HZ-AEA	HZ-AEB	HZ-AEC

Convair 340

HZ-AAT	HZ-AAV	HZ-ABB	HZ-ABD	SA-R4
HZ-AAU	HZ-AAY	HZ-ABC		

Boeing 707-368C

HZ-ACC	HZ-ACD

Boeing 720-068B

HZ-ACA	HZ-ACB

SAS
Scandinavian Airlines System

Scandinavia

Although Scandinavian Airlines System only dates from 1946 the history of the airline goes back to 1918 and the formation of the Danish airline, DDL. This company can lay claim to being the world's oldest commercial airline by virtue of the fact that it is the only one still in existence to have signed the first International Air Transport Agreement at The Hague in 1919.

The other two parent companies of SAS, the Swedish ABA and the Norwegian DNL were formed in 1924 and 1927 respectively. During the years preceding World War II the three airlines, in competition, operated a wide assortment of aircraft, including Avro biplanes, Friedrichshafen flying boats, and Fokkers and Junkers with ski undercarriages as well as the more conventional wheels and floats.

Although all three airlines were capable of operating their own European networks it was soon apparent that their ultimate aim, trans-Atlantic services, could only be operated in unison. In 1938 the first steps were taken towards a merger which was to be delayed by the outbreak of war. The three governments, including the Norwegian Government in-exile, did not, however, allow their efforts to slacken and in 1944 SILA, a Swedish airline formed by ABA to operate trans-Atlantic services, obtained authority from the United States Government to operate such a service and ordered ten Douglas DC-4's. It was with converted Boeing B-17 bombers, however, that SILA and DDL operated the first post war trans-Atlantic commercial service in 1945.

The following year SAS was formed, with a two-sevenths shareholding each for DDL and DNL and three-sevenths for SILA-ABA, but only for inter-continental operations, and was known as OSAS, Overseas Scandinavian Airlines System. Merger of European routes occurred in 1948 with the resulting creation of European Scandinavian Airlines System (ESAS) and this combined with OSAS in 1951 to form SAS under an agreement which expires in 1975. Included in the agreement is a condition limiting each member nations' share to 50% private investment and 50% state investment.

The new airline's route network had already expanded rapidly, having reached South America in 1946, East Africa in 1947, Thailand in 1949, and Japan in 1951, In 1953 South Africa was reached, but it was in 1954 that the airline made history by inaugurating the first polar commercial air route, initially with Douglas DC-6's to the West Coast of the United States. This was followed in 1957 by a DC-7 polar route to the Far East which cut the journey time by half. In November 1967, SAS introduced a "Trans Asian Express" service from Copenhagen to Bangkok and Singapore via Tashkent (technical stop only); this direct route to the Far East cuts off 1,350 miles from the previous most direct route. In 1968 this service was extended to Djakarta.

It was also during 1957 that the airline became the first non-French airline to order the 'Caravelle' and this aircraft features prominently in today's fleet which also includes DC-8's, DC-9's and Convair 'Metropolitans'. This latter type of aircraft is also included in the fleet of Linjeflyg, the Swedish domestic subsidiary owned half by SAS and half by ABA (itself a SAS shareholder) and dating from 1957 when it was formed to operate newspaper services. Other operators associated with SAS are Greenlandair (25% SAS) and, in the Far East, Thai International (30%).

There is also a very close association with Swissair involving technical co-operation and standardization of aircraft types together with the pooling of certain services to all parts of the world. In 1968, this agreement was extended to include technical co-operation with KLM on the Douglas DC-9, and the Boeing 747 when it enters service in 1970.

SAS has two Boeing 747 'Jumbo' jets on order.

Member of the International Air Transport Association

SE-DAF *Sven Viking*, a Swedish-registered Caravelle of the tri-nation Scandinavian Airlines System

Services from Copenhagen to:

Abadan, Amsterdam, Anchorage, Athens, Bangkok, Barcelona, Beirut, Brussels, Buenos Aires, Cairo, Calcutta, Chicago, Damascus, Djakarta, Dublin, Düsseldorf, Entebbe, Frankfurt, Geneva, Glasgow, Hamburg, Helsinki, Johannesburg, Karachi, Khartoum, Lisbon, London, Los Angeles, Madrid, Malaga, Manchester, Manila, Milan, Monrovia, Montevideo, Montreal, Moscow, Nairobi, New York, Nice, Palma, Paris, Prague, Rio de Janeiro, Rome, Santiago, São Paulo, Seattle, Singapore, Stuttgart, Tehran, Tokyo, Turku-Åbo, Vienna, Zürich

Certain of the above services are routed via Bergen, Göteburg or Stavanger; all have connections from Oslo and Stockholm

African and Far East services in pool with Swissair

Scandinavian services from Copenhagen to:

Göteburg–Oslo, Aalborg–Kristiansand–Stavanger–Bergen, Stockholm, Malmö, Nörrköping, Helsingborg
from Oslo to Stockholm

Danish domestic services from Copenhagen to:

Aarhus, Aalborg, Haderslev, Herning, Odense, Rønne, Sønderborg, S. Strømfjord, Vejle

Norwegian domestic services from Oslo to:

Ålesund, Alta, Andenes, Bardufoss, Bergen, Bødo, Farsund, Kirkenes, Kristiansand, Lakselv, Røros, Skien, Stavanger, Tromsø, Trondheim

Swedish domestic services from Stockholm to:

Borlänge, Göteburg, Halmstad, Helsingborg, Jönköping, Kalmar, Karlstad, Kiruna, Kristianstad, Luleå, Malmö, Örnsköldsvik, Ötersund, Ronneby, Skellefteå, Sundsvall, Umeå, Visby
also Visby–Norrköping

Domestic destinations include those served by:
Linjeflyg (Sweden), Braathens SAFE and Fjellfly (Norway), and Falck's Flyvetjeneste and Cimberair (Denmark), but not by Greenlandair

Livery F: white, red, grey   **T:** white
Fleet
Convair 440 Metropolitan

LN-KLA	Atle Viking	OY-KPF	Ingemund Viking
LN-KLB	Ivar Viking	SE-BSO	Edmund Viking
LN-KLD	Ragnar Viking	SE-BSP	Rollo Viking
LN-KLE	Snorre Viking	SE-BSR	Bjarne Viking
LN-KLF	Birger Viking	SE-BSS	Holger Viking
LN-KLG	Sigurd Viking	SE-BST	Tor Viking
OY-KPA	Hans Viking	SE-BSU	Steiner Viking
OY-KPB	Egil Viking	SE-BSX	Sverker Viking
OY-KPD	Ravn Viking	SE-BSY	Assur Viking
OY-KPE	Sune Viking		

Douglas DC-8 Series 55

LN-MOH	Harald Viking	SE-DBD	Folke Viking
OY-KTC	Gorm Viking†		

†all freight

Douglas DC-8 Series 32

LN-MOA	Haakon Viking	SE-DBB	Ottar Viking
OY-KTA	Dan Viking	SE-DBC	Visbur Viking
OY-KTB	Bue Viking	LN-MOT	Olav Viking
SE-DBA	Rurik Viking		

Sud Aviation S.E.210 Caravelle III

LN-KLH	Finn Viking	OY-KRG	Alf Viking
LN-KLI	Einar Viking	SE-DAA	Eskil Viking
LN-KLN	Trygve Viking	SE-DAB	Ingemar Viking
LN-KLP	Trond Viking	SE-DAC	Arne Viking
LN-KLR	Hall Viking	SE-DAD*	Torolf Viking
OY-KRA	Vagn Viking	SE-DAE*	Alric Viking
OY-KRC*	Faste Viking	SE-DAF	Sven Viking
OY-KRD	Ulf Viking	SE-DAG	Dag Viking
OY-KRE*		SE-DAH	Torgny Viking
OY-KRF	Torkil Viking	SE-DAI	Alrik Viking

*leased to Thai International

Douglas DC-8–62 (*Series 62F; † Series 63)

LN-MOO	Sverre Viking	SE-DBE	Anund Viking
LN-MOU†	Leif Viking	SE-DBF	Ingvar Viking
OY-KTD	Knud Viking	SE-DBG	Jorund Viking
OY-KTE*	Skjold Viking	SE-DBH†	Ring Viking

Douglas DC-9–41 (*Series 32)

LN-RLK	Erlind Viking	OY-KGW*	Ossur Viking
LN-RLS*	Lodin Viking	SE-DBT	Agne Viking
LN-RTF	Gunnar Viking	SE-DBU	Hjalmar Viking
LN-RTG	Stein Viking	SE-DBW	Aldils Viking
OY-KGA	Heming Viking	SE-DBX	Arnljiot Viking
OY-KGB	Toste Viking	SE-DBY*	Yngve Viking
OY-KGC	Helge Viking	SE-DBZ*	Kettil Viking
OY-KGU*	Gaut Viking		

LN–Norway   OY–Denmark   SE–Sweden

SAA
South African Airways

South African Airways was formed in 1934 when the Railways Administration took over Union Airways, a privately financed company, unable to match the investment required for a rapidly expanding airline. Union Airways had started operations in 1929 carrying mail from Port Elizabeth to Cape Town, Johannesburg and Durban in five de Havilland 'Gipsy Moths'. This fleet was soon inadequate for the traffic available and the first of the Junkers aircraft which were to predominate in the pre-war SAA fleet were delivered. They were F-13's and a W-34. Another airline, South West African Airways, founded in 1932 and absorbed by South African Airways in 1935, also operated a Junkers F-13 and two A-50's.

The years between the formation of SAA and the outbreak of World War II saw the rapid expansion of the airline. Services were operated throughout South and South West Africa, and to Rhodesia, Tanganyika and Uganda, while the fleet expanded to include eleven Junkers Ju 52/3m's and eighteen Ju 86's. This fleet was increased by the addition of twenty-eight Lockheed 'Lodestars' which entered service service before the war.

Although some services were operated until 1940, eventually all civil aviation in South Africa ceased during the war and SAA's fleet and employees were taken over by the South African Air Force. Operations were restarted on a limited scale in 1944 with some 'Lodestars' released by the SAAF. They were soon supplemented by Douglas DC-3's and DC-4 'Skymasters' and Avro 'Yorks' with which SAA started intercontinental operations by introducing a service to London in 1945.

In 1950 Lockheed 'Constellations' were placed on the London service which they operated until replaced by Douglas DC-7B's in 1956, except for a short period in 1953 when de Havilland 'Comet' 1's were leased from BOAC, but with South African crews.

During 1956 South African Airways ordered its first, and only, turbo-prop aircraft, Vickers 'Viscounts'. The airline re-entered the jet age, permanently, in 1960 with the introduction of Boeing 707's.

Until 1963 SAA's services to Europe had been routed through central Africa, but in that year several states banned overflights by South African aircraft and the airline had to find an alternative route. This was done without the cancellation of any service, and the new coastal route, with some stops at Lisbon and Madrid, has proved popular with passengers.

ZS-DYN, a Boeing 727 of South African Airways shortly after take-off

The present fleet includes Boeing 707 jets on services to Europe and Australia, with Boeing 727's, Vickers Viscount turbo-props, and Douglas DC-3's and DC-4's on regional and domestic routes (from which the propeller aircraft will be retired early in 1969 in favour of Boeing 737 jets). The airline started weekly operations across the South Atlantic to Rio de Janeiro and New York on 28th February, 1969. Three Boeing 747 'Jumbo' jets are on order.

Member of the International Air Transport Association

A Boeing 707 is prepared for flight

International services from Johannesburg to:
Athens, Bulawayo, Cocos Islands, Frankfurt (W), Gaberones, Las Palmas(W) Lisbon, London (W), Laurenço Marques, Luanda(W), Madrid, Mauritius, Paris, Perth, Rome, Salisbury (D), Zürich
W–via Windhoek   D–via Durban

Domestic services from Johannesburg to:
Bloemfontein, Cape Town, Durban, East London, Kimberley, Port Elizabeth, Windhoek
from Cape town to:
Alexander Bay, Durban, East London, George, Grahamstown, Kimberley, Oudtshoorn, Plettenberg Bay, Port Elizabeth, Queenstown, Windhoek
from Port Elizabeth to:
Bloemfontein, Durban, George, Grahamstown, Kimberley, Oudtshoorn, Plettenberg Bay, Queenstown
from East London to:
Bloemfontein, Durban
from Kimberley to:
Bloemfontein, Keetmanshoop, Upington
from Durban to:
Bloemfontein

Livery F: white, blue, grey
          T: orange

Fleet
Douglas DC-3 Dakota
ZS-BXF   *Vasberade*   ZS-DJB   *Simonsberg*
ZS-BXG   *Piketberg*
ZS-BXI   *Elandskop*

Douglas DC-4
ZS-AUB *Auteniqua*

Vickers Viscount 813
ZS-CDT *Blesbok*
ZS-CDU *Bosbok*
ZS-CDV *Rooibok*
ZS-CDW *Waterbok*

ZS-CDX *Wildebees*
ZS-CDY *Gemsbok*
ZS-CDZ *Hartbees*

Boeing 707-344 (*344B)
ZS-CKC *Johannesburg*
ZS-CKD *Cape Town*
ZS-CKE *Durban*
One aircraft on order

ZS-DYL* *Bloemfontein*
ZS-EKV* *Windhoek*
ZS-EUX *Port Elizabeth*

Boeing 727-44
ZS-DYM *Tugela*
ZS-DYN *Limpopo*
ZS-DYO *Vaal*
ZS-DYP *Orange*
Two aircraft on order

ZS-DYR *Letaba*
ZS-EKW *Komati*
ZS-EKX

Boeing 737-244
ZS-SBL
ZS-SBM

ZS-SBN

TREK
Trek Airways (Pty) Ltd

South Africa

Trek Airways was formed in 1953 to operate low-fare services between South Africa and Europe at non-IATA rates. The airline is now South Africa's largest long-haul charter airline, and operates a Johannesburg–Luxembourg scheduled service once a week, which has been routed via Luanda and Cape Verde since the ban on overflying by South African aircraft imposed by several African states in 1963. Currently, three Starliners, two ex-World Airways and one ex-Air France, are employed by the airline, which is based at Johannesburg. Trek's aircraft are registered in Luxembourg, and various agreements are in existence with Luxair.

Service:
Johannesburg–Luxembourg

Fleet
Lockheed L-1649 Starliner
LX-LGX   LX-LGY   LZ-LGX

AIR SPAIN

Spain

Spain's newest air charter airline, Air Spain, received its first aircraft, a Bristol 'Britannia', in October, 1966. The airline operates inclusive tour and freight charters on a worldwide basis with a fleet of three 'Britannias', two of them formerly flying in British Eagle colours, and the other ex-El Al Israel Airlines.

The new Spanish charter operator, Air Spain, operates three Bristol Britannia 300's one of which, EC-BFK, is shown in this impression

Livery F: white, blue and yellow, grey   **T:** white

Fleet

EC-BFJ	*Atlantico*	Bristol Britannia 312		
EC-BFK		,,	,,	,,
EC-BFL	*Cantabrico*	,,	,,	313

AVIACO
Aviacion y Comercio SA

Spain

Aviaco was formed in 1948 by a group of Bilbao businessmen as an all-cargo charter operator using Bristol 170's. This business was not profitable and the airline started all-passenger operations in 1950 when it was awarded licences for domestic routes linking Bilbao, Madrid and Barcelona. An international route to Marseilles and services to the Canary and Balearic Islands followed.

At this time the airline operated the Bristol 170's, converted to 'Wayfarer' passenger standard, and ex-Air France Languedoc 161's which were purchased in 1952. Also during 1952 the airline extended its domestic routes with the introduction of a number of services based on Madrid. In 1960, Convair 440's and Douglas DC-3's replaced the Languedoc 161's and some de Havilland 'Herons' (purchased for some domestic routes), and 'Caravelles' and DC-6's were leased from SABENA. The airline began vehicle ferry services to Palma in 1964 with Aviation Traders 'Carvairs' (converted DC-4's).

At present Aviaco operates a number of domestic routes, services to the Canary Islands, the Balearic Islands and North Africa with a fleet of Convair 440's, DC-4's and 'Carvairs'. The airline also operates a Bilbao–London service jointly with BKS Air Transport. Aviaco is owned by Iberia (66.6%), Instituto Nacional de Industria, and private interests.

Aviaco's EC-ARQ, a Convair 440 Metropolitan

International services from Seville to:
Madrid–Casablanca
Lisbon, Tangier, Tetuan
Barcelona–Brussels, Palma–Brussels, Palma–Marseilles, Palma–Algiers, Alicante–Oran, Bilbao–London

Domestic services from Madrid to:
Alicante, Badajoz, Barcelona, Bilbao, Cordoba, Granada, San Sebastian, Seville, Vigo
also to Tenerife and Las Palmas   Malaga–Seville   Seville–Las Palmas

Fleet

Convair 440 Metropolitan

EC-APT	EC-APV	EC-AQK	EC-ARP	EC-ARQ
EC-APU				

Douglas DC-4

EC-ACD	EC-ACE	EC-ACF	EC-AEK	EC-APQ

ATL 98 Carvair

EC-AXI	EC-AZA

IBERIA
Linéas Aereas de España SA

Spain

The present Iberia was formed in 1938 to acquire LAPE, an entirely State owned airline that had run into difficulties. LAPE itself had been formed in 1931 to absorb a predecessor airline, CLASSA, in which the State had a majority shareholding. CLASSA was formed in 1929 by the amalgamation of the three pioneer Spanish airlines—CETA, Union Aerea Española and the original Iberia Air Transport, which was formed in 1927.

On its formation Iberia acquired a network of domestic routes, some whose operations had been suspended, and a service between Madrid and Paris. The airline had a fleet in which the Junkers Ju52/3m tri-motor predominated. The airline was awarded exclusive Spanish air traffic rights for twenty years by the Spanish Government, which acquired a 51% shareholding. During the second World War the airline ran into difficulties through the fuel shortage and this forced it to reduce services. As a result, the State acquired the remaining 49% of a by now increased share capital.

After the war, expansion of the airline's international routes started in earnest with Douglas DC-3's, starting a thrice weekly London service in 1946, and DC-4's with which the airline started its trans-Atlantic services. These aircraft were soon supplemented by Lockheed 'Super Constellations' for the Atlantic routes, and by Convair 440 'Metropolitans' for European services. The airline's first jets, Douglas DC-8's, entered service in 1961 over the Atlantic, followed in 1962 by 'Caravelles' for the European routes. Douglas DC-3 replacement Fokker Friendships were first introduced in late 1967, and the present fleet includes these aircraft with Douglas DC-8's and DC-9's, Convair Metropolitans and Sud Caravelles. The airline has three Boeing 747's on order, and options on three Boeing 2707 SST's.

Iberia has a 66.6% interest in Aviaco, another Spanish airline.

Member of the International Air Transport Association

EC-ARL, one of Iberia's fleet of Caravelles, in flight

International services from Madrid to:
Bogota, Brussels (L), Buenos Aires, Caracas (L), Casablanca, Copenhagen (L), Frankfurt (L), Havana, Lima, Lisbon, London (L), Mexico City, Milan, Montevideo, New York, Paris, Rio de Janeiro, Rome, San Juan de Puerto Rico (L), Santiago de Chile, Stockholm (L), Tangier, Zürich
L–either via, or from, Las Palmas
from Barcelona to:
Brussels, Copenhagen (P), Düsseldorf (P), Frankfurt, Geneva (P), London (P), Milan, Paris (P), Rome, Stockholm (P)
P–some flights from Palma via Barcelona

from Malaga to:
Brussels, Casablanca, Copenhagen, London, Stockholm, Tangier
from Seville to:
Casablanca, Tangier
from Tenerife to:
Casablanca

Domestic services from Madrid to:
Barcelona, Ibiza, Las Palmas, Malaga, Palma, Seville, Tenerife, Valencia
from Barcelona to:
Malaga, Palma, Seville, Valencia
from Malaga to:
Seville, Tenerife, Valencia
Las Palmas—Melilla

Services operated by Aviaco are excluded

Livery F: white, red, grey
T: white

Fleet

Convair 440 Metropolitan

EC-AMR	EC-AMU	EC-APZ	EC-ATC	EC-ATF
EC-AMS	EC-AMV	EC-ARS	EC-ATD	EC-ATG
EC-AMT	EC-APY	EC-ART	EC-ATE	EC-ATI

Douglas DC-8 Series 52

EC-ARA	Velázquez	EC-ATP	Sorolla
EC-ARB	El Greco	EC-AUM	Zurbarán
EC-ARC	Goya	EC-BAV	Julio Romero de Torres
EC-ASN	Murillo	EC-BMV	Pedro Barruguete

Sud Aviation S.E.210 Caravelle 6R

EC-ARI	Albéniz	EC-AVZ	Sarasate
EC-ARJ	Chapí	EC-AXU	Alfonso X El Sabio
EC-ARK	Granados	EC-AYD	Juan Criséstomo Arriaga
EC-ARL	Manuel de Falla	EC-AYD	Jose Mariá Usandizaga
EC-ATV	Maestro Victoria	EC-BBR	Padilla
EC-ATX	Turina	EC-BIA	Jeronimo Jiminez
EC-AVY	Amadeo Vives		

Sud Aviation S.E.210 Caravelle 10R

EC-BDC	Hiarión Eslave	EC-BID	Tomas Breton
EC-BDD	Jesús Guridi	EC-BIE	Padre Antonio Soler
EC-BIB	Teobaldo Power	EC-BIF	Francisco Torrega
EC-BIC	Emilio Arrieta		

Douglas DC-9-30

EC-BIG	Madrid	EC-BIO	Bilbao
EC-BIH	Barcelona	EC-BIP	Santiago de Campastela
EC-BII	Seville	EC-BIQ	Malaga
EC-BIJ	Santa Cruz de Tenerife	EC-BIR	Valencia
EC-BIK	Las Palmas	EC-BIS	Alicante
EC-BIL	Zaragoza	EC-BIT	San Sebastian
EC-BIM	Santander	EC-BIU	
EC-BIN	Palma de Mallorca		

Fokker F-27 Friendship 500

EC-BMS	Ebro	EC-BMX	Mino
EC-BMT	Tajo	EC-	
EC-BMV	Guadalquivir	EC-	
EC-BMW	Duero	EC-	

Douglas DC-8–63

EC-BMY	EC-BMZ

SPANTAX
Spantax SA

Spain

Spantax was formed in October 1959, to supply air transport to companies searching for oil in the Spanish Sahara. In 1962 the company obtained permission to operate inter-island charters in the Canary and Balearic Islands, as well as full traffic rights for international charter services.

Today Spantax operates inclusive tour charters from all parts of Europe to Iberia, North Africa, the Canary Islands and the Balearic Islands, and *ad hoc* charters to all parts of the world. The airline also operates regular services within Mauritania, and undertakes contract flying for several major scheduled service airlines.

The present fleet includes two Convair 990's, five Douglas DC-7's, two DC-6's, five DC-4's, nine Dakotas, two Fokker F-27 'Friendships' and a Beechcraft Model 18. Principal owners are Rudolfo Bay Wright, the chairman and managing director, and Miss Marta Estades, director and commercial manager.

EC-ATR, one of the five Douglas DC-7C's operated by the Spanish independent, Spantax, on long distance charter flights

Livery F: white, blue, grey
      T: white

Fleet

Douglas DC-3 Dakota

EC-AQB	EC-AQF	EC-ATT	EC-BED	EC-BEL
EC-AQE	EC-ASP	EC-AXS	EC-BEG	

Douglas DC-4 Skymaster

EC-ACD	EC-ACE	EC-ACF	EC-APQ	EC-AUY

Douglas DC-6 (*DC-6B)

EC-AZX	EC-BBK*

Convair Coronado 990A

EC-BJC	EC-BJD	EC-BNM

Douglas DC-7C

EC-ATQ	EC-ATR	EC-BBT	EC-BDL	EC-BDM

Beechcraft Model 18
EC-ASJ

Fokker F-27 Friendship

EC-BFU	EC-BNJ

TRANS EUROPA
Trans Europa Compania de Aviacion SA (TECA)

Spain

An airline of recent formation, TECA was founded in July 1965, by Eugenio Dieste, the president, and commenced operations in the following September. The main activity of the airline is inclusive tour charters for passengers into Spain from the rest of Europe, although cargo charters are also operated with the fleet of eight Douglas aircraft, equally divided between DC-4 and DC-7C.

Fleet

EC-BBH	Douglas DC-7C		EC-BDK	Douglas DC-4	
EC-BCH	,,	,,	EC-BEB	,,	,,
EC-BCI	,,	,,	EC-BER	,,	,,
EC-BCJ	,,	DC-4	EC-BJK	,,	DC-7C

SUDAN AIRWAYS

Sudan

Sudan Airways was formed in 1946 by the Sudanese Government and operations began the following year with assistance from Airwork, a British airline, using a fleet of three de Havilland 'Doves' on domestic services connecting several of the more important centres in the Sudan. This route network expanded until by 1959 Sudan Airways was operating to several points in the Middle East, Africa and Europe with a fleet of four 'Doves', seven Douglas DC-3 'Dakotas', and a Vickers 'Viscount' turbo-prop airliner.

The airline introduced three Fokker F-27 'Friendship' turbo-prop airliners in 1962, and the following year the first pure-jet, a de Havilland 'Comet' 4C, was introduced. The 'Comet' has enabled further expansion to take place, both by increasing frequencies and by the addition of further destinations to the route network, including Frankfurt, Addis Ababa and Nairobi.

Member of the International Air Transport Association

International services from Khartoum to:
Addis Ababa, Aden, Asmara, Athens, Beirut, Cairo, Entebbe, Fort Lamy, Frankfurt, Jeddah, London, Luxor, Nairobi, Rome

Domestic services from Khartoum to:
Asmara, Atbara, Dongola, El Fasher, El Obeid, Er Roseires, Juba, Kassala, Khashm El Girba, Kosti, Malakal, Merowe, Nyala, Port Sudan, Wad Medani, Wau

Livery F: white, green, grey with black   **T:** yellow

Fleet

ST-AAA	Fokker F-27 Friendship	ST-AAX	Hawker Siddeley (de Havilland)
ST-AAH	Douglas DC-3 Dakota		Comet 4C
ST-AAI	,, ,,	ST-AAY	Fokker F-27 Friendship
ST-AAK	,, ,,	ST-ADB	de Havilland Canada Twin Otter
ST-AAR	Fokker F-27 Friendship	ST-ADC	,, ,,
ST-AAS	,, ,,	ST-ADO	,, ,,
ST-AAW	Hawker Siddeley (de Havilland) Comet 4C		

FALCONAIR
Falconair Charter AB

Sweden

Falconair Charter was formed early in 1967 and commenced operations for that summer with three ex-Philippine Air Lines' Vickers Viscount 784D's operating on ad hoc and inclusive tour charter flights from Malmö. The airline is owned by Messrs. Stig and Lars Berglöf, Tommy Jexell, Kurt Klausson, Kjell-Åke Larsake, and Bo Irving.

Two ev-Eastern Airlines Lockheed Electras were introduced in January 1969, on lease from International Aerodyne.

Livery F: white, yellow, white   **T:** yellow (emblem: falcon's head)

Fleet
Vickers Viscount 784D
SE-CNK   SE-CNL   SE-CNM
Lockheed L-118 Electra
SE-FGA   SE-FGB

TSA
Transair Sweden AB (TSA)

Sweden

Transair Sweden (TSA) was formed in 1951, initially operating three Airspeed Consuls on newspaper flights from Stockholm to the south of Sweden. The first passenger charter flights started in 1953 with two Douglas DC-3 Dakotas, supplemented by a third in 1955, purchased for this work. The replacement of the DC-3s by Curtiss C-46s in 1957 put TSA's charter operations on a world-wide basis, Bangkok, Calcutta and Singapore being among the destinations served.

The airline received its first four-engined equipment in 1960, replacing the C-46s and forcing the airline to move its main base from Stockholm to Malmö's Bulltofta Airport where there was more room for expansion. Additional DC-6s and DC-6Bs were introduced during the next four years, a total of thirteen of these aircraft being in service prior to their replacement in 1965 by nine ex-Eastern Airlines Douglas DC-7Bs, and two ex-South African Airways aircraft of this type, which form the present fleet with three Boeing 727-134s, the airline's first aircraft to be purchased as new. At the present time, TSA's operations are mainly inclusive tour charter services for Scandinavian, Swiss and German travel agencies. A travel agent, Nyman and Schulz, owns the airline.

Livery F: white, orange, unpainted   **T:** white, orange
Fleet
Douglas DC-7B

SE-ERA	Stockholm	SE-ERI	Linköping
SE-ERB	Göteborg	SE-ERK	Borås
SE-ERC	Malmö	SE-ERL	Eskilstuna
SE-ERD	Norrköping	SE-ERM	Gävle
SE-ERE	Västerås	SE-ERN	Sundsvall
SE-ERG	Hälsingborg		

Boeing 727-134

SE-DDA	Midnight Sun	SE-DDC	Polar Circle
SE-DDB	Northern Light		

BALAIR
Balair AG

Switzerland

The present Balair was formed in 1948 as a flying school, and in 1950, on moving to Basle-Mulhouse airport, started to act as ground handling agents for a number of foreign airlines flying into Basle. Although airline activity did not start until a Vickers 'Viking' was purchased for charter flying in 1957, a predecessor company of the same name had operated from 1926 until its merger with Ad Astra Aero in 1931 to form Swissair.

Balair today operates inclusive tour charters to England, the Mediterranean and Northern Europe, together with long distance charters, also airline contract flying on Swissair's domestic and international passenger and freight scheduled services. The present fleet includes Douglas DC-3, DC-4, DC-6B and Fokker 'Friendship' and Convair 990 aircraft. Swissair holds 40% of Balair's share capital.

HB-AAI, a Swissair Fokker Friendship while on lease to Balair

Livery F: white, red, grey   **T:** red and white

Fleet

HB-ILD	Douglas DC-4 Freighter	HB-AAV	Fokker F-27 Friendship
HB-ILU	,, ,,	HB-AAW	,, ,,
HB-IBR	,, DC-6B	HB-AAX	,, ,,
HB-IBU	,, ,,	HB-ITD	Douglas DC-3 Dakota
HB-IBZ	,, ,,	HB-ICH	Convair 990 Coronado
HB-AAU	Fokker F-27 Friendship		

HB-IBU, a Douglas DC-6B of Balair, the Swiss charter operator

SWISSAIR
Schweizerische Luftverkehr AG

Switzerland

The Swiss Air Transport Company Ltd. was formed in 1931 on the merger of Balair of Basle and Ad Astra Aero of Zürich. Balair dated from 1925 but Ad Astra Aero was formed six years earlier as the Ad Astra Swiss Air Transport Company. It operated in competition with the Aero-Gesellschaft Comte Mittelholzer & Co. and Avion Tourisme, both also founded in 1919. Ad Astra Aero bought up its two rivals the following year and became the Swiss Air Transport Company—Ad Astra Aero-Avion Tourisme (Ad Astra Aero for short) with a fleet of sixteen aircraft.

On its formation in 1931, Swissair owned thirteen aircraft, mostly of Fokker manufacture, but the new airline soon purchased new aircraft. First to come, in 1932, was the single-engined four-seat Lockheed 'Orion' which at that time was the fastest aircraft type flying in Europe and which Swissair, its first European operator, used on a Zürich–Munich–Vienna service. This was followed in 1934 by the 15-seat Curtiss 'Condor' with which Swissair became the first European airline to employ stewardesses. The following year marked the start of all-year operations on the Zürich–Basle–London service, worked with Douglas DC-2's.

By the outbreak of war in 1939, when all operations had to be suspended, Swissair had a fleet of five DC-3's, three DC-2's, a de Havilland DH-89 'Dragon

HB-ICA, one of Swissair's Convair 990A Coronado's flying over the Alps

Rapide', a Fokker F-VIIa and a Comte AC-4. The fleet was enlarged when operations were resumed in 1945 after almost six years of suspension (despite Switzerland's neutrality during World War II) by the addition of several DC-3's. The following year Swissair's first four-engined aircraft—DC-4's—were introduced and with them the airline started its first trans-Atlantic service between Geneva and New York in 1949.

During the period between the DC-4 and the first jet arrivals, Douglas DC-8's in 1960, the airline continued to operate Douglas products, DC-6B's and DC-7C's, supplemented by Convair 440 'Metropolitans' for short-haul routes. The airline also operates Convair 990A 'Coronado', Sud Aviation 'Caravelle' and Douglas DC-9 jets. The recently-delivered twelve DC-9's replaced the 'Metropolitans'. The make-up of the Swissair fleet is, therefore, very similar to that of Scandinavian Airlines System with which an agreement was signed in 1958 covering the pooling of certain worldwide services and technical co-operation. Another technical co-operation agreement was made, this time between KLM Royal Dutch Airlines, Swissair and Scandinavian Airlines System in May 1968, to apply to DC-9 fleets, whereby Swissair maintains all the engines, and its own and KLM's airframes, and to the Boeing 747 'jumbo' jet, whereby KLM will maintain all three fleets' airframes, and SAS, the engines.

The winter and spring of 1968 marked a period of further expansion of Swissair's route network with the addition of Malaga and São Paulo as destinations, and two new services: to New York via Frankfurt, and to Johannesburg via Nairobi and Dar-es-Salaam. During 1968, the modernization of the fleet continued with the introduction of the larger Douglas DC-8-62 replacing the earlier DC-8 Series 30, and the replacement of the DC-9-15s by the larger DC-9-30. Fourteen DC-9s are operated, also four DC-8-62s, with three more on order. Also ordered are two Boeing 747 'Jumbo' jets.

Since 1947 Swissair has been the national airline of Switzerland, and it was in that same year that the present financial structure which reserves 30% of the share capital for public institutions and the remainder for private enterprise was created.

Member of the International Air Transport Association

Swissair's Douglas DC-9-32 registered HB-IFF *Fribourg*, used on the airlines shorter routes

International services (mainly from Geneva and/or Zürich with connections from Basle and Berne, also Geneva or Zürich when necessary) to:
Abidjan, Accra, Algiers, Amsterdam, Ankara, Athens, Baghdad, Bangkok, Barcelona, Beirut, Belgrade, Bombay, Brussels, Bucharest, Budapest, Buenos Aires, Cairo, Calcutta, Casablanca, Chicago, Cologne, Copenhagen, Dakar, Dar-es-Salaam, Düsseldorf, Faro, Frankfurt, Hamburg, Helsinki, Hong Kong, Innsbruck, Istanbul, Johannesburg, Karachi, Khartoum, Lagos, Lisbon, London,* Madrid, Malaga, Manchester, Manila, Milan, Monrovia, Montreal, Moscow, Munich, Nairobi, New York, Nice, Palma, Paris*, Prague, Rio de Janeiro, Rome, Rotterdam, Santiago, São Paulo, Stockholm, Stuttgart, Tehran. Tel-Aviv, Tokyo, Tripoli (Libya), Tunis, Vienna, Warsaw, Zagreb
*direct service to Basle as well as Zürich and Geneva

Domestic services from Geneva to:
Basle, Berne, Zürich
                        from Zürich to:
Basle, Berne, Geneva

There are also all-cargo services

Livery F: white, red, grey
       T: red and white

Fleet

Convair 440 Metropolitan

HB-IMB	Fribourg	HB-IML	Glarus
HB-IMF	Ticino	HB-IMM	Valais
HB-IMG	Appenzell I. Rh.	HB-IMN	Zug
HB-IMK	Neuchâtel	HB-IMP	Thurgau

Convair CV.990A Coronado

HB-ICA	Bern	HB-ICE	Vaud
HB-ICB	Luzern	HB-ICF	Schaffhausen
HB-ICC	St. Gallen	HB-ICG	Winterthür
HB-ICD	Basel-Land	HB-ICH	St. Gotthard

Sud Aviation S.E.210 Caravelle III

HB-ICS	Uri	HB-ICX	Chur
HB-ICT	Schwyz	HB-ICY	Lausanne
HB-ICU	Aargau	HB-ICZ	Bellinzona
HB-ICW	Solothurn		

Douglas DC-8–50

HB-IDB	Basel-Stadt	HB-IDD	Nidwalden

Douglas DC-8–62 (* -62F Jet Trader)

HB-IDE	Geneva	HB-IDG	Matterhorn
HB-IDF	Zürich	HB-IDH*	Neuchâtel

Douglas DC-9–32

HB-IFF	Fribourg	HB-IFN	Obwalden
HB-IFG	Valais	HB-IFO	Appenzell A. Rh.
HB-IFH	Opfikon	HB-IFP	Glarus
HB-IFI	Zug	HB-IFR	Ticino
HB-IFK	Kloten	HB-IFS	Grisons
HB-IFL	Appenzall I. Rh.	HB-IFX	Lausanne
HB-IFM	Thurgau	HB-IFY	Bellinzona

SAAL
Syria
Syrian Arab Airlines

Syrian Arab Airlines was formed in 1961 by the Government of Syria, through the Syrian Economic Organisation, on the withdrawal of Syria from the United Arab Republic. For less than a year prior to this, operations had been the responsibility of United Arab Airlines which had been formed in 1960 by the merging of the privately-owned Syrian Airways with Misrair, the State-owned Egyptian Airline.

Syrian Airways had commenced operations in 1947, but, due to heavy losses, services had to be suspended in 1948. The airline resumed operations in 1951 with some assistance from Pan American World Airways, but it was not until 1953 that international services to neighbouring capitals were re-introduced.

Since its formation SAAL has acquired jet aircraft in the form of Sud Aviation 'Caravelles'. The current fleet includes these aircraft and Douglas DC-6B's, DC-4's and DC-3's.

The airline opened a route to Rome and Munich in 1963, and extended it to London the following year. Other European capitals now included in the service list are Athens and Luxembourg.

International services from Damascus to:
Athens, Baghdad, Bahrain, Beirut, Delhi, Dhahran, Doha, Dubai, Istanbul, Jerusalem, Karachi, Kuwait, London, Luxembourg, Munich, Nicosia, Paris, Prague, Rome, Sharjah, Tehran

Domestic route points:
Aleppo, Damascus, Daraa, Deir-ezzor, Hama, Homs, Kamishly, Lattakia, Nabk, Palmyra

Livery F: white, green, grey   **T:** white, green
Fleet
YK-ACA	Douglas DC-3 Dakota	
YK-ACB	,,	,,
YK-ACC	,,	,,
YK-ADA	DC-4 Skymaster	
YK-ADB	,,	,,
YK-AEA	,, DC-6B	
YK-AEC	,,	,,
YK-AED	,,	,,
YK-AFA	Sud-Aviation S.E.210 Super Caravelle	
YK-AFB	,,	,,
YK-AFF	,,	,,

TUNIS-AIR
Tunisia
Société Tunisienne de L'Air

Tunis-Air was formed in 1948 with Air France backing, and the French airline was, until Tunisia's independence in 1957, the major shareholder. Today, the Tunisian Government holds 51per cent and Air France 49per cent of the total share capital. A fleet of four Sud Aviation Caravelle 3s, 2 Douglas DC-4 Skymasters and a DC-3 Dakota is operated on domestic, regional and international routes, the most recent additional destinations being London and Copenhagen, from Tunis' Carthage Airport.

TS-IKM, a Caravelle III of Tunis-Air at Tunis

International services from Tunis to:
Algiers, Amsterdam, Brussels, Casablanca, Copenhagen, Djerba, Frankfurt, Geneva, London, Lyon, Marseille, Nice, Paris, Rome, Tripoli, Zürich

Livery F: white, red, unpainted   **T:** white, red

Fleet
Douglas DC-3 Dakota
TS-AXZ
Douglas DC-4 Skymaster
TS-AMP   TS-BLH
Sud Aviation S.E.210 Caravelle III
TS-IKM   TS-ITU   TS-MAL   TS-TAR

THY   Turkey
Turk Hava Yollari-Turkish Airlines

Originally formed in 1933 as Devlet Hava Yollari (Turkish State Airlines), a branch of the Turkish Air Force, THY took over DHY's services, which were mainly DC-3 operated, in 1956. The new airline was owned by the Turkish Government, 94per cent, and by the British Overseas Airways Corporation, 6per cent, now reduced to 4per cent with the remaining 2per cent held by private interests. A fleet of five Vickers Viscount 700s was bought in 1957, followed in 1960 by ten Fokker Friendships, five built by Fokker, and five by Fairchild, the Dutch manufacturer's American licensee. Douglas DC-9-30s were introduced in 1968, prior to which a DC-9-10 was leased from Douglas. The Viscounts and Friendships are now used on domestic services. It is hoped that the DC-9s will help THY to play an increasing part in the growth of the Turkish tourist industry. Member of the International Air Transport Association

International services from Istanbul:
Athens, Beirut, Brussels, Frankfurt, Munich, Nicosia, Rome, Tel-Aviv, Vienna, Zürich

Fleet
Vickers Viscount 794
TC-SEC	TC-SEL	TC-SES	TC-SET

Douglas DC-9–30 (*leased)
TD-JAA*	TC-JAB	TC-JAC

Fokker F-27 Friendship Series 100 (*Fairchild-built version)
TC-KOC*	TC-KOR*	TC-KOZ*	TC-TEK	TC-TON
TC-KOD*	TC-KOP*	TC-TAY	TC-TEZ	TC-TOY

AEROFLOT   Union of Soviet Socialist Republics
Grazdenskij Wozdusznyj Flot

Aeroflot is the world's largest airline, although this is largely due to its being operated on a quasi-military basis and having, therefore, much more in common with an air force transport command than a purely commercial airline. Also, size can be partly accounted for by the airline undertaking the whole range of commercial aviation activities, as opposed to the specialisation of airlines elsewhere, and also due to the amount of maintenance required by Soviet-built equipment. The exact size of the airline, and a complete list of its services can only be guessed.

Aeroflot first came into existence in 1932 as the successor of Dobroflot, which had been formed in 1923 at the start of the first five-year plan, and the amalgamation of several small pioneer airlines. Dobroflot, then Aeroflot, grew rapidly until expansion was halted, along with most air services, by the invasion of 1941. In spite of this growth, and the fact that in 1923, Dobroflot had had the then high figure of 6,000 route miles, in 1940, the pre-war peak year, Aeroflot carried only 0.16% of all Soviet traffic in its fleet of mainly twin-engined types, including DC-2s.

During the war, the airline received Douglas DC-3 Dakotas from the United States as part of a lend-lease programme, and during, and after, the war, DC-3s were built in Russia as the Li-2. After the war, the Li-2 formed the backbone of the Aeroflot fleet, even after two Russian-designed aircraft, the Ilyushin Il-12 and Il-14, were introduced in the late 1940s and early 1950s respectively. Both the Russian designs were twin-engined, piston types as Aeroflot was, until the mid-1950s and the end of the Stalinist era, little more than a glorified air taxi service for government officials, and it was not considered worth wasting resources on the development of DC-4 and DC-6 equivalent aircraft, a concentration of effort on the production of a jet airliner being preferred.

During the period immediately after World War II, Aeroflot assisted East European nations, occupied by Russia, in the development of national airlines, in each case ownership being shared between Aeroflot and the respective government, and a standard package of Li-2 aircraft being used.

Aeroflot's first jet, the Tupolev Tu-104, was introduced in 1956, and other jets, including the Tupolev Tu-124, a short-range 104, followed, along with turboprop airliners including the Ilyushin Il-18, Antonev An-24 and Tupolev Tu-114. A new jet in current use is the Ilyushin Il-62, which is similar to the BAC VC-10 in appearance. Equivalent aircraft of 'Jumbo', airbus and SST specifications are under development. In 1967, routes to Montreal and Tokyo were inaugurated with Air Canada and Japan Air Lines' assistance respectively. In 1968, a joint Pan American/Aeroflot New York–Moscow service was started.

International route points (generally served from Moscow):
Accra, Algiers, Amsterdam, Baghdad, Belgrade, Berlin (East), Brussels, Bucharest, Budapest, Cairo, Colombo, Conakry, Copenhagen, Damascus, Djakarta, Havana, Helsinki, Kabul, Karachi, Khartoum, London, Montreal, New Delhi, New York, Paris, Peking, Prague, Rabat, Rangoon, Sofia, Stockholm, Tokyo, Ulaan Baator, Vienna, Warsaw

Domestic route points:
Adler, Aktyubinsk, Ashkhabad, Astrakhan, Baku, Batumi, Beltsy, Brest, Bruy, Bryansk, Bugulma, Cheboksory, Chelyabinsk, Chevovets, Dnepropetrovski, Donetzk, Elista, Gorky, Grodno, Groznyy, Guryer, Ivanova, Kalingrad, Kastruma, Kazan, Kharkov, Khersan, Kiaipeda, Kiev, Kirivoi, Kirovaback, Kirovogrock, Kishinev, Leningrad, Lugansk, Lvov, Magnitogorsk, Makhachkala, Minerainyevody, Minsk, Moscow, Nalehir, Nukus, Odessa, Oktyabrskoye, Orel Lipetsk, Orenburg, Orsk, Penza, Perm, Petrograd, Plast, Riga, Roa, Rustar, Sebastopol, Seratov, Simferopol, Stalingrad, Sukhumi, Sverdlovsk, Tallin, Tambov, Tblisi, Tyumen, Ufa, Uralsk, Urgench, Ulyanovsk, Varonezh, Velikye Luki, Vinnitsa, Viskoe, Vitebsk, Volgagrad, Yarnai, Yereran, Yerlakh, Zaporoshye, Zhdonov

Fleet
The following types are operated:
Antonov An-2, An-12, An-14 and An-24
Ilyushin Il14, Il-18 and Il-62
Kamov (helicopters) Ka-15, Ka-18 and Ka-26
Lisunov Li-2
L-200 Morava
Mil (helicopters) Mi-1, Mi-2, Mi-4, Mi-6, Mi-8 and Mi-10
Super Aero 145
Tupolev Tu-104, Tu-114, Tu-124 and Tu-134
Yakovlev Yak-12

UNITED ARAB AIRLINES   United Arab Republic

United Arab Airlines, Egypt's Government-owned airline, began life in 1932 as Misr Airwork with one DH 60 trainer. Assistance was given at that time by Airwork, a British company. The new airline's first scheduled service was opened in 1933 and linked Cairo, Alexandria and Mersa Matruh with a fleet of DH-89 'Dragons'. Three years later the fleet consisted of nine aircraft: two 'Dragons', five 'Rapides' and two DH-86 'Express' aircraft. By 1939, the route network had grown to include many important destinations in the Middle East.

After the war the airline introduced Vickers 'Vikings' and its name was changed to Misrair in 1949. This was changed again to the present title in 1961, but in the intervening period the airline operated 'Viscounts' and in 1960 became the first Middle East airline to operate jet airliners, de Havilland 'Comet' 4C's. The present fleet includes seven of these aircraft. Three Boeing 707-366C aircraft were delivered in October, 1968.

A small number of Antonov An-24s is also operated on loan from Misrair, the domestic airline, and the Egyptian Air Force.

Member of the International Air Transport Association

United Arab Airlines operates seven of these Hawker Siddeley (de Havilland) Comet 4C's on its international routes; shown here gaining height is SU-ALE

Services from Cairo to:
Accra, Addis Ababa, Aden, Alexandria, Asmara, Baghdad, Bahrain, Beirut, Bombay, Dar-es-Salaam, Entebbe, Frankfurt, Geneva, Jeddah, Jerusalem, Kano, Khartoum, Kuwait, Lagos, London, Mogadishu, Moscow, Nairobi, Paris, Port Said, Prague, Rome, Zürich

Livery F: white, green, grey
T: white with red and black

Fleet
Douglas DC-3 Dakota
SU-AJJ	SU-AKZ			

Douglas DC-6B
SU-ANJ	SU-ANL	SU-ANN	SU-ANO	SU-ANP
SU-ANK	SU-ANM			

Hawker Siddeley (de Havilland) Comet 4C
SU-ALC	SU-ALL	SU-AMV	SU-ANC	SU-ANI
SU-ALE	SU-ALM			

Boeing 707-366C
SU-AOU	SU-AOV	SU-AOW		

AIR GREGORY
Air Gregory Ltd

United Kingdom

Air Gregory was formed in 1966 as Gregory Air Services with aircraft of a basic operational weight of more than 12,500lb, those below this being operated by the parent company, Gregory Air Taxis Ltd., which was formed in 1963 to provide a 24-hour service free of the restrictions imposed on the user's time by airline schedules. Operating initially from Denham, the demand for the latter company's air-taxi services was such that within eight months new operating centres had to be established at Liverpool and Sunderland, and, a few months later, Luton. In this time, the fleet grew from one single-engined aircraft to the present four Piper Twin-'Comanche' twin-engined aircraft, one Piper 'Aztec' one H.S.125 executive jet and a de Havilland 'Dove' aircraft, and three Hughes and one Sud helicopters. Gregory Air Taxis was the first air-taxis operator to have an Air Operators' Certificate which means that Gregory's aircraft and maintenance facilities are subject to inspection by the Board of Trade in the same way as those of an airline. At one time Gregory operated an H.S. 125 executive jet on behalf of Air Hanson, prior to Gregory operating a similar aircraft on its own account, but this arrangement came to an end after the plane was impounded by the Algerian authorities following an incident in which the pilot was forced to fly the plane to Algeria at gunpoint.

Gregory Air Services sold its Newcastle based DC-3, which it operated since its formation, at the end of 1966, and intended to operate two ex-British Eagle 'Viscounts' on inclusive tours charters from Bristol and Cardiff, but this plan had to be abandoned because the company encountered difficulties due to the Government's fiscal policy. Also during this period, air-taxi operations had to be restricted to the Denham base, now the centre for all activities other than H.S.125 (operating from Luton).

The present title was adopted in early 1969 when the Bristol Street Group acquired a 60 percent interest in the company. Its founder, Ken Gregory, holds the remaining 40 per cent.

Air Gregory also has a Cessna dealership.

Member of the National Air Taxi Association

Livery: white with red

Fleet

G-ANMJ	Hawker Siddeley (de Havilland) Dove 1B
G-ASMR	Piper PA-30 Twin Comanche
G-ASON	,, ,,
G-ASRI	Piper PA-23 Aztec
G-ASYK	Piper PA-30 Twin Comanche
G-ASYO	,, ,,
G-AVOI	Hawker Siddeley HS.125
G-AVEE	Sud Aviation Alouette II
G-AVZC	Hughes 300
G-	Hughes 269A
G-	Hughes 500

AIR HANSON
Air Hanson Ltd

United Kingdom

Air Hanson is a division of the Hanson Transport Group (the activities of which include road haulage and vehicle leasing) and became operational with a Hawker Siddeley HS.125 executive jet which was operated by Gregory Air Services from March, 1966. A second HS.125 was leased from the manufacturers, starting in July, 1967, when the first aircraft was impounded by the Algerian Government at the end of June, 1967, after the crew had been forced to fly to that country. The aircraft was not released until mid-April, 1968, after considerable diplomatic activity.

At the present time, Air Hanson is reviewing the possibility of operating its own HS.125 (the leased aircraft having been returned) on executive charters depending on the successful outcome of negotiations for compensation due for the impounding of the aircraft. A Bell Jet Ranger is operated as a Hanson Group transport; this aircraft might be made available for charter if licensed maintenance facilities become available.

Livery: red and white

Fleet
G-ASNU   Hawker Siddeley HS.125
G-AVZH   Bell Jet Ranger

Air Hanson owns this Hawker Siddeley HS.125 executive jet which is operated by Gregory Air Services. Here it is alongside a "pier" in which passengers walk under cover, directly to their aircraft, at Gatwick

AIR ULSTER
Air Ulster Ltd

United Kingdom

Air Ulster began operations in May, 1968, with four ex-British United Douglas DC-3 Dakotas on the ex-Emerald Airways services from Belfast to Prestwick and Londonderry to Glasgow abandoned by that airline when it went into liquidation. Air Ulster was in fact first registered some two years before the start of operations, and Emerald Airways dated from 1965.

Air Ulster is owned by Rigby's Travel of Belfast, a firm of travel agents. It is planned to buy three or four Vickers Viscounts for the summer of 1969, when the DC-3s will operate cargo services. Charter services are a part of the airline's business which will increase once the Viscounts enter service making inclusive tour charters possible.

Domestic services
Belfast–Prestwick   Londonderry–Glasgow

Fleet
Douglas DC-3 Dakota
G-AKNB   G-AMWA   G-ANAE   G-A

AUTAIR
Autair Helicopters Ltd

United Kingdom

Autair's history of worldwide helicopter operations, including work in the Antarctic, began in 1952. At the present time helicopters are the only type of aircraft operated by the company, although in 1960 a commercial airline division had been formed with a Douglas DC-3 for air charter work, but this became an independent entity, Autair International Airways, in 1963. Currently Autair's fleet includes a Westland Whirlwind and seven Bell 47G and 47J types.

Fleet
Westland WS 55 Whirlwind 1
G-AOCF

Bell 47G (*J-2; †G-2)

G-ARXH	G-ATTO*	G-ATZX	G-AVKS†	G-AVZF†
G-ASDM	G-ATYV			

AUTAIR INTERNATIONAL
Autair International Airways Ltd

United Kingdom

The name Autair first appeared in 1952 when the company commenced helicopter operations specializing in foreign contract work, not only in Europe, the Middle East and Africa, but also in both the Arctic and the Antarctic. It was as a logical development of the company's aviation programme that it formed a Commercial Airline Division in 1960 which operated DC-3 aircraft supplemented shortly afterwards by 'Vikings'. Three years later this division of the company became a separate entity, Autair International Airways Ltd., leaving Autair to concentrate on its helicopter activities. Today the airline's activities include domestic scheduled services in the United Kingdom, first started to Blackpool in 1963, inclusive tour charters to Europe and the Middle East, and Berlin freight charters. The present fleet is comprised of Handley Page Heralds, BAC One-Elevens and the turbo-prop Hawker Siddeley 748's, although the company's first experience of turbo-prop equipment was with a Handley Page 'Herald' leased from the manufacturer in 1963 for three months pending delivery of the 'Ambassadors' and three of these were re-introduced in late 1966. The company was acquired by the Court Line Shipping Group of companies in 1965.

Autair International Airways is based at Luton, 30 miles from London via the M.1. Motorway, where it has been associated with Luton Corporation in the development of Luton as another airport for London. The airline has introduced a Luton–Hull service and for this has played an active part in preparing Hawker Siddeley's airfield at Brough, 11 miles from Hull, for commercial aviation. In addition, the airline has taken over many of the services into Tees-Side originally operated by BKS, before that airline dropped Tees-Side from its route network. Autair also operates services from Carlisle and Dundee. The company's maintenance base at Luton is also used by several other airlines, in addition to which, engineering assistance is provided for the Kingdom of Libya Airlines. The airline moved its scheduled services' terminus from Luton to Heathrow in April, 1969.

G-ATMI is one of two Hawker Siddeley 748 turbo-prop airliners operated by Autair International

Services
London-Blackpool-Glasgow   Hull-Jersey   Hull-Guernsey   London-Hull

Other route points:
Amsterdam, Belfast, Carlisle, Dundee, Isle of Man, Tees-side,

Livery F: white, blue, grey
　　　　T: blue and white

Fleet
BAC One-Eleven Series 400
| G-AVOE | G-AVOF | G-AWBL | G- | G- |

Hawker Siddeley HS 748 Series 2
| G-ATMI | G-ATMJ |

Handley Page H.P.R.7 Herald 101
| G-APWB | G-APWC | G-APWD |

BKS
BKS Air Transport Ltd

United Kingdom

　　Commencing operations in 1952 as an air charter operator with a DC-3 aircraft based on Southend, BKS (the title came from the initials of the three founder-directors), soon entered the scheduled service field and pioneered passenger and freight services from the North-East of England to London, Belfast, and the Channel Islands as well as introducing direct provincial-continental links from Newcastle, Tees-side (recently dropped) and Leeds/Bradford. An indication of the airline's success can be gained from the fact that between 1957 and 1962, there was a 200% increase in passengers, and a 1,000% increase in freight carried. A major activity throughout the history of BKS has been the carriage of racehorses—the airline having flown more race-horses than any other airline in the world, some 18,000).

BEA acquired a 30% interest in BKS in 1964, increased at the end of 1966 to 50%. At present BKS services from the North-East provide connections with a large number of BEA European services. One of the latest developments in the airline's route structure is a London–Bilbao service, although passenger and horse charter flights remain prominent in the company's operations.

Apart from the DC-3, the airline has also operated Vickers 'Vikings', Bristol 170's, 'Ambassadors', and Hawker Siddeley 748's. Two 'Ambassadors' were in store pending sale or conversion to horse freighters.

In November, 1967, a new holding company, British Air Services, was formed with BEA holding a 66% interest, and former non-BEA Cambrian and BKS shareholders having the remainder. BKS is now a wholly-owned subsidiary of British Air Services Ltd., and the two Hawker Siddeley 'Tridents' delivered early in 1969 carry BAS livery.

Member of the British Independent Air Transport Association

BKS introduced two Hawker Siddeley Trident 1E jets in early 1969 here is an impression of how they look

Services from Edinburgh to:
Belfast
        from Leeds/Bradford to:
Amsterdam, Belfast, Dublin, Düsseldorf, Guernsey, Jersey, London, Ostend, Paris
        from London to:
Bilbao
        from Newcastle to:
Basle, Belfast, Bergen, Dublin, Jersey, London, Ostend, Paris

Livery F: white, red, grey **T:** red and white

Fleet
de Havilland (Airspeed) AS.57 Ambassador (*horse freighter)
G-ALZR*   G-ALZT*   G-ALZW   G-AMAC
BAC (Bristol) Britannia 102
G-ANBD   G-ANBH   G-ANBK   G-APLL
Vickers (BAC) Viscount (*leased from BOAC) (type No. in parenthesis)
G-AOYH (806)   G-APEY (806)   G-ATTA (745)
G-AOYL (806)   G-APNF (776)*   G-AVED (798)
G-AOYO (806)   G-APTA (702)   G-AVIY (786)
Hawker Siddeley Trident 1E
G-AVYC   G-AVYD

BRITANNIA
Britannia Airways Ltd

United Kingdom

It was as Euravia that Britannia Airways first started operations in 1962 with a fleet of three ex-El Al 'Constellations' for use on the inclusive tour charter services which the airline was to fly for its parent, Universal Sky Tours. The fleet of 'Constellations' soon grew to eight and, in 1964, the airline adopted its present title to coincide with the introduction of turbo-prop Bristol 'Britannias', of which the airline now has seven. The following year the two companies were acquired by Thompson Industrial Holdings Ltd.

Although Britannia inclusive tour charters now depart from Glasgow, Manchester and Newcastle as well as Luton, the airline's main operating base is at this latter airport, selected originally for its siting close to the M1 motorway, convenient for passengers from London and the Midlands. The airline has co-operated with Luton Corporation in the development of the airport.

Inclusive tour charters still form 70% of the airline's business, mainly to Spain, Italy and Yugoslavia for Universal Sky Tours although charters are also flown for other tours organizers, and the remainder of the company's earnings include those from *ad hoc* and service charters and also the carriage of Mecca Pilgrims (20% of Britannia's receipts are in foreign currency). The airline had four Boeing 737's delivered in 1968, and more of these aircraft will be purchased as part of a 'Britannia' replacement programme.

Another Britannia 102 operator is Britannia Airways of Luton which has seven some of which may be sold soon

Livery F: white, blue, grey
T: blue and white (emblem: Britannia)

Fleet

BAC (Bristol) Britannia 102

G-ANBA	G-ANBF	G-ANBJ	G-ANBL	G-ANBO
G-ANBE	G-ANBI			

Boeing 727- 304

G-AVRL	G-AVRM	G-AVRN	G-AVRO

BRITISH AIR FERRIES
British Air Ferries Ltd

United Kingdom

British Air Ferries is one of the three air transport operating subsidiaries of the Air Holdings Group (P&O 20%, Furness Withy 20%, British & Commonwealth 46%, Whitehall Securities 8%, Eagle Star 6%), and has its origins in 1962 as British United Air Ferries, a company created at the time of formation of Air Holdings. The present title was adopted in 1967.

The predecessors of BAF, prior to 1962, were the Channel Air Bridge services of Airwork (a predecessor of British United Airways) which that airline had acquired when it bought Mr. Freddie Laker's Air Charter in 1958, Air Charter being Channel Air Bridge's parent, and the vehicle ferry services of Silver City Airways, a subsidiary of the Peninsular and Orient Steamship Company (P&O), which company's merging of its aviation interests with Airwork led to the formation of Air Holdings. Silver City had been formed in 1948, and was the first airline in the world to provide a car ferry service.

G-APNH *Menai Bridge*, one of five Carvairs operated by the Air Holdings subsidiary, British Air Ferries

114

During the few years of its life, British United Air Ferries operated Aviation Traders (another ex-Air Charter company) ATL-98 Carvairs (Douglas DC-4 conversions) and Bristol 170 Mk. 32 Freighters on a dense network of cross-Channel and Channel Islands services from Lydd, Southend and Southampton, with deep penetration services to Switzerland, a new type of service designed to combat the competition from the much improved sea ferries, and also services from Manchester, Coventry and Sheffield to the Continent. Falling traffic and rising losses led to the abandonment of all services except the cross-Channel routes from Lydd and Southend in 1967. Today the airline operates Bristol 170s from Lydd and Carvairs from Southend.

The other Air Holding Group company in air transport is SAFEAIR, operating 16 Bristol 170 Freighters on cargo and car carrying services across New Zealand's Cook Straits.

A Bristol Freighter, G-APAV *Viceroy*, of British Air Ferries

International services from Lydd to:
Deauville, Le Touquet, Ostend
from Southend to:
Calais, Ostend, Rotterdam

Livery F: white, yellow, blue, grey
T: white, yellow, blue

Fleet
Aviation Traders ATL-98 Carvair (from Southend)

G-APNH	*Menai Bridge*	G-ASKG	*Channel Bridge*
G-ASDC	*Pont de Rhin*	G-ASKN	*Pont d'Avignon*
G-ASHZ	*Maasbrug*		

Bristol 170 Mk. 32 Freighter (from Lydd)

G-ANVR	*Valiant*	G-APAU	*City of Edinburgh*
G-ANVS	*Versatile*	G-APAV	*Viceroy*
G-ANWK	*City of Leicester*		

BRITISH EAGLE
United Kingdom
British Eagle International Airlines Ltd

Eagle Aviation Ltd. was founded by Harold Bamberg in 1948 as an air charter operator with a fleet of two converted 'Halifax' bombers. During the Berlin Air Lift the number of aircraft increased to four, and afterwards the 'Halifaxes' were replaced by Avro 'Yorks'.

In 1952 the Government permitted a slight relaxation of the restrictions which had prevented the operation of scheduled services by independent airlines. Eagle did not hesitate to make the most of the still somewhat limited opportunities thus presented and, with the fleet of Vickers 'Vikings' which had replaced the 'Yorks', introduced services from London to Göteburg, Belgrade, Pisa, Rimini, La Baule and Dinard. Most of the more successful routes were seasonal and it was the quest for year-round operation that forced the airline to form an overseas subsidiary, Eagle Airways (Bermuda) Ltd., to operate a daily service from Bermuda to New York with 'Viscount' aircraft.

In order to secure its position Eagle proposed low fare services from London to several colonial destinations, but of these the only result was a London–Bermuda–Nassau service, modified later to include a twice weekly service to Miami, and a weekly service through Bermuda to Jamaica. In order to develop these services and build up a background from which the company could fly services across the North Atlantic, Eagle reached an agreement with the Cunard Steamship Company in which Cunard acquired the shareholding of the Eagle companies. Following this agreement, the company became Cunard Eagle Airways and, with two Boeing 707 aircraft, became the first British independent airline to operate jet aircraft. A licence was granted by the Air Transport Licensing Board to fly services from the United Kingdom to New York, but this was revoked on appeal by BOAC. The success of the airline's mid-Atlantic and Caribbean services lead BOAC to approach Cunard and, as a result of the subsequent negotiations, a new airline, BOAC-Cunard was formed in which Cunard held 30% of the £30million capital, and BOAC the remainder. The new company took over CE's Atlantic licences, the two Boeings and some aircrews.

The result of this was that the United Kingdom group of Companies, which had been geared for a year for trans-Atlantic operation, were left with a large engineering staff for the Boeing 707's which had been transferred to BOAC-Cunard, a handful of European routes, relatively little trooping, and a fleet of two 'Britannia' 300 series, three DC-6's and two 'Viscount' 700 series.

The fate of the airline hung in the balance from June, 1962, until March, 1963, when Harold Bamberg and his associates purchased 60% of the airline's share capital from Cunard, with an option on the remaining 40%, which was exercised at the end of 1966, and changed the name to British Eagle International Airlines. After initial reconstruction difficulties BEIA became the fourth largest British Airline, had a network of domestic and international routes and again operated jets with a fleet of BAC 'One-Elevens' and Boeing 707's.

The airline became part of the Eagle Group as a result of a re-organisation early in 1967 which divided the company's activities into a number of separate companies covering the Knightsbridge Air Terminal, catering, and engineering activities as well as airline operations. Also at this time, the Group moved into the general aviation business with the acquisition of the British dealership for Beech Aircraft from Short Brothers and Harland. Late in 1968, the airline went into liquidation. The firm may be restarted during 1969 if support can be obtained, as a smaller One-Eleven/Britannia operator; for this reason it is included here. The 707's and two One-Eleven's have been returned to their owners.

BEA   United Kingdom
British European Airways Corporation

British European Airways was formed under the Civil Aviation Act, 1946, to operate services in Europe and the British Isles, including those of 110 Wing, 46 Group, Royal Air Force. Early in 1947 these services were followed by those of Railway Air Services, Scottish Airways, Channel Islands Airways, Isle of Man Air Services and Great Western and Southern Air Lines, which together had formed the Associated Airways Joint Committee Companies.

The airline's fleet, immediately after its formation, contained a motley assortment of 'Dakotas', 'Rapides', Avro 19's, and even 'Jupiters' which were in fact ex-German three-engined Ju 52/3m's. This fleet was soon supplemented by new 'Vikings' and in 1952 the 'Ambassador' was introduced; it was to be the last piston-engined mainline aircraft to enter service with the airline.

BEA was the first airline to operate turbo-prop airliners by using the now famous 'Viscounts' which were designed to BEA's specifications. Today there are still 34 'Viscount' 800's in the airline's fleet which also includes the turbo-prop 'Vanguard' some of which are being converted into an all-cargo aircraft called the 'Merchantman', and 'Argosy', which will be phased out as the Merchantmen enter service in late 1969, and the jet 'Comet' 4B and 'Trident'. Also in the fleet are BAC 'Super One-Elevens' (One-Eleven 500's) which will replace many BEA 'Viscounts', especially on the German domestic services. The 'Argosy' is the only modern airliner designed primarily for cargo operations, a notable feature being its twin-boom design which enables loading and unloading to take place at the same time through opposite ends of the fuselage. BEA became the first airline to make an automatic landing in regular service on the 10th June, 1965, when a 'Trident' from Paris made an automatic landing at London (Heathrow). An improved version of the 'Trident', the 'Trident 2E', was introduced in 1968, and will replace BEA's 'Comets'. Twenty-six 130-seat 'Trident' 3B's are also on order.

Apart from its European services, BEA has an extensive domestic network which includes services to the North of Scotland, the Scottish Isles, and the Isles of Scilly. This latter service is operated by a wholly owned subsidiary, BEA Helicopters Ltd., which operates four 25/26-seat Sikorsky S-61N's on services which include the ferrying of supplies to drilling rigs in the North Sea.

Although BEA Helicopters Ltd. was only formed in 1964, it replaced the BEA Helicopter Experimental Unit which was formed in 1947. The unit operated experimental postal services at first, but later operated passenger services, mainly as feeder services to airports, until these were withdrawn as an economy measure in 1956.

During the winter of 1967-68, BEA, in association with the member companies of the Air Taxi Operators Association, instituted a scheme known as the BEA Air Taxi Plan under which the constituent companies provide, on request, air taxi connections with BEA scheduled flights. The founder members, with their aircraft, are:

Gregory Air Services Ltd., operating Aztec, Twin Comanche and HS.125 aircraft;

Loganair Ltd, operating Aztec and Islander aircraft;

London Aviation Ltd., with Twin Comanche and Cessna 310 aircraft;

Mid-Fly Ltd, operating Aztec aircraft;

Northern Executive Aviation Ltd, also operating Aztec aircraft, and

Truman Aviation Ltd, operating Apache and Twin Comanche aircraft.

Today the Corporation carries $7\frac{1}{4}$ million passengers annually in its 100 plus fleet of modern aircraft over a network of some 39,000 route miles ranging from Helsinki in the north to Cairo in the south, and from Lisbon in the west to Beirut in the east. BEA is the largest commercial operator outside the U.S.A.

Member of the International Air Transport Association

The Hawker Siddeley Trident IC was designed specifically for BEA

The turbo-prop Vickers Vanguard is a familiar sight on BEA's domestic routes

International services from London to:
Alghero, Amsterdam, Ankara, Athens, Barcelona, Basle, Bergen, Beirut, Berlin, Biarritz, Bordeaux, Bremen, Brussels, Cairo, Catania, Cologne/Bonn, Copenhagen, Corfu, Dinard, Dublin, Dubrovnik, Düsseldorf, Faro, Frankfurt, Geneva, Gibraltar, Göteburg, Hamburg, Hanover, Helsinki, Istanbul, Jerusalem*, Klagenfurt, Lisbon, Madrid, Malta, Milan, Moscow, Naples, Nice, Nicosia, Oporto, Oslo, Palermo, Palma, Paris, Prague, Rome, Salzburg, Sassari, Shannon, Stavanger, Stockholm, Stuttgart, Tangier, Tel-Aviv, Tripoli, Turin, Valencia, Venice, Vienna, Warsaw, Zürich
*Cyprus Airways

International services from Birmingham to:
Amsterdam, Barcelona, Düsseldorf, Paris
                    from Glasgow to:
Palma, Paris
                    from Manchester to:
Amsterdam, Barcelona, Brussels, Copenhagen, Düsseldorf, Palma, Paris, Zürich

Domestic services from London to:
Aberdeen, Belfast, Birmingham, Edinburgh, Glasgow, Guernsey*, Isle of Man
(C), Jersey*, Leeds/Bradford (B), Liverpool (C), Manchester, Newcastle (B),
Teeside (B)
*connections from Aberdeen, Belfast, Birmingham, Edinburgh, Glasgow,
Manchester
(C)–operated by Cambrian Airways   (B)–operated by BKS Air Transport Ltd.
                    from Belfast to:
Birmingham, Glasgow, Jersey, Manchester
                    from Birmingham to:
Edinburgh, Glasgow, Guernsey, Jersey
                    from Edinburgh to Jersey
                    from Glasgow to:
Guernsey, Jersey, Manchester
                    from Manchester to:
Birmingham, Guernsey, Jersey
Southampton–Jersey   Guernsey–Jersey
Penzance–Isles of Scilly (H)
(H)–BEA Helicopters Ltd.

The Hawker Siddeley Argosy is the only modern airliner designed for all-cargo
services only. G-ASXO, a series 220 version

BEA's fleet includes many Comet 4B's, short-range sisters of the 4C

BEA Helicopters Ltd. operate Sikorsky S61N's on Britain's only scheduled helicopter service, Penzance–Isles of Scilly

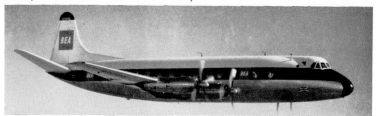

BEA operates 34 Vickers Viscount 800's; here is G-AOHL in flight before its sale to BKS

Scottish
Glasgow, Edinburgh, Aberdeen, Inverness, Benbecula, Stornoway, Wick, Orkney, Shetland*
Glasgow, Campeltown, Islay*†   Glasgow, Tiree, Barra*†
*connections from: Belfast, Birmingham, London, Manchester
†connections from: Aberdeen, Edinburgh

Germany—internal services from Berlin:
Bremen, Cologne, Düsseldorf, Hamburg, Hanover, Frankfurt, Munich, Stuttgart

Livery F: white, black, grey   **T:** white

Fleet
de Havilland Heron
G-ANXA   G-ANXB
Vickers Viscount 802

G-AOHG	G-AOHK	G-AOHO	G-AOHV	G-AOJD
G-AOHH	G-AOHL	G-AOHR	G-AOHW	G-AOJE
G-AOHI	G-AOHM	G-AOHS	G-AOJB	G-AOJF
G-AOHJ	G-AOHN	G-AOHT	G-AOJC	G-AORD

Vickers Viscount 806 (*806 luxury version for German domestic routes)

G-AOYG	G-AOYM*	G-AOYR*	G-APEX*	G-APKF*
G-AOYI	G-AOYN*	G-AOYS*	G-APIM*	G-APOX*
G-AOYK†	G-AOYP	G-AOYT*	G-APJU	

(† leased to Cyprus Airways—blue livery)

Vickers Vanguard Type 951

G-APEA	G-APEB	G-APEC	G-APED	G-APEF

Vickers Vanguard Merchantman Type 953

G-APEG	G-APEJ	G-APEM	G-APEP	G-APET
G-APEH	G-APEK	G-APEN	G-APER	G-APEU
G-APEI	G-APEL	G-APEO	G-APES	

Hawker Siddeley (de Havilland) Comet 4B

G-APMA	G-APMD	G-APMG	G-ARGM	G-ARJL
G-APMB	G-APME	G-ARCP	G-ARJK	G-ARJN
G-APMC	G-APMF			

Hawker Siddeley HS.121 Trident 1C

G-ARPA	G-ARPF	G-ARPK	G-ARPP	G-ARPU
G-ARPB	G-ARPG	G-ARPL	G-ARPR	G-ARPW
G-ARPC	G-ARPH	G-ARPM	G-ARPS	G-ARPX
G-ARPD	G-ARPI	G-ARPN	G-ARPT	G-ARPZ
G-ARPE	G-ARPJ	G-ARPO		

Hawker Siddeley Argosy A.W.650 Series 222

G-ASXM	G-ASXN	G-ASXO	G-ASXP	G-ATTC

Hawker Siddeley HS.121 Trident 2E

G-AVFA	G-AVFD	G-AVFG	G-AVFJ	G-AVFM
G-AVFB	G-AVFE	G-AVFH	G-AVFK	G-AVFN
G-AVFC	G-AVFF	G-AVFI	G-AVFL	G-AVFO

26 Hawker Siddeley Trident 3Bs are on order

BAC Super One-Eleven 501

G-AVMH	G-AVML	G-AVMP	G-AVMU	G-AVMX
G-AVMI	G-AVMM	G-AVMR	G-AVMV	G-AVMY
G-AVMJ	G-AVMN	G-AVMS	G-AVMW	G-AVMZ
G-AVMK	G-AVMO	G-AVMT		

Options are held on a further 12 aircraft

BEA Helicopters Ltd
Westland Sikorsky S-55

G-ANFH	G-AOCF

Sikorsky S-61N

G-ASNL	G-ASNM	G-ATJB	G-ATFM

BEAS
British Executive Air Services Ltd
United Kingdom

British Executive Air Services operates from its base at Oxford's Kidlington Airport with a fleet of eight Brantly B2B helicopters, and two Brantly 305s. The company's aircraft are employed on a variety of tasks, including air taxi work, aerial photography and filming.

Fleet
Brantly B2B

G-ASUN	G-ATFG	G-AVLA	G-AVJN	G-AWDU
G-ASXE	G-ATFH			

Brantly 305

G-ASXF	G-A

BRITISH MIDLAND
British Midland Airways Ltd

United Kingdom

British Midland's history goes back to 1938 when the airline's predecessor, Derby Aviation, established flying schools at Derby and Wolverhampton. This activity continued through the following war years during which time Derby trained 14,000 pilots. Indeed, pilot training on DH 'Chipmunks' still forms part of British Midland's activities today.

Scheduled services started during the 1946 holiday season when de Havilland 'Rapide' services between Derby and Jersey were operated. Other routes followed, to Glasgow and the Isle of Man, while DC-3's replaced the 'Rapides' and allowed the airline to undertake an increasing amount of charter work. Derby's first four-engined aircraft were three 20-seat Handley Page 'Marathons', and shortly after these were retired three Canadair C-4 'Argonauts' entered service, proving particularly useful on the inclusive tour and *ad hoc* charter work which continues as part of the company's business. Expansion of Derby Aviation included the acquisition of three other companies: Executive Air Transport of Birmingham, Mercury Airlines of Manchester (including Mercury's services to the Isle of Wight and the West Country), and Midland Airport Services of Birmingham.

At one time Derby operated services from Northampton, Swansea and Carlisle, but these proved to be uneconomic and were abandoned. Services are now operated from the main operating base at the East Midlands Airport, Castle Donington, where the airline moved in 1965—the same year as Derby adopted the British Midland title—also from Leeds/Bradford, Cambridge, Luton, and Gloucester/Cheltenham Spa.

British Midland Airways was appointed handling agent at Manchester in 1967 for several Middle East airlines which use the airport as an alternative to London when it is closed by fog. Also during 1967, the airline introduced 'Viscounts' and sold its Handley Page 'Herald'.

A merger is planned with Invicta Airways.

Services from Castle Donington to:

Barcelona, Belfast, Dublin, Edinburgh*, Glasgow, Guernsey and Jersey (some flights via Luton,) Isle of Man, Isle of Wight, Newquay, Ostend, Palma
Cambridge–Jersey and Guernsey, Gloucester/Cheltenham Spa–Jersey and Guernsey, Manchester–Ostend
(*some flights via Leeds/Bradford)

Livery F: white, light and dark blue, grey
T: white, light and dark blue

Fleet

G-AGJV	Douglas DC-3 Dakota	
G-ANTD	,, ,,	
G-AODG	Vickers Viscount 736	
G-APNE	,, ,,	831
G-ASED	,, ,,	
G-AVJA	,, ,,	815
G-AVJB	,, ,,	
G-AWCV	,, ,,	760
G-AWGV	,, ,,	745

BOAC   United Kingdom
British Overseas Airways Corporation

British Overseas Airways Corporation began operations in 1940 on the nationalization of Imperial Airways Ltd. and British Airways Ltd. which themselves owed their formation to the amalgamation of several operating companies. Handley Page Transport Ltd., Instone Air Line Ltd., Daimler Hire Ltd., and British Marine Air Navigation Ltd. went to form Imperial Airways Ltd. in 1924; and Hillman's Airways Ltd., Spartan Air Lines Ltd., and United Air Lines Ltd. joined to form British Airways Ltd. in 1935. Both airlines had operated services to the Continent and were nationalized as a result of the Cadman Report which recommended that the two airlines should not compete on the same routes and should maintain a close working liaison.

Imperial Airways had also developed routes to the Empire, between Cairo and Basra (on the Persian Gulf) in 1927, Karachi in 1929, Calcutta, Rangoon and Singapore in 1933, and Brisbane in 1935, the complete journey taking 12½ days on a route which was often altered to avoid political trouble-spots. The Singapore–Brisbane section was operated by the then newly formed QANTAS Empire Airways. Concurrently another route was developed which reached Mwanza (on Lake Victoria) in 1931, and Nairobi and Capetown in 1932, the journey taking 10½ days. There was also an east-west route across Africa from Khartoum to Kano.

In 1924 the £1-million Imperial Airways absorbed 1,760 miles of cross-Channel routes, an assortment of 18 aircraft and a staff of 250. Services from Cairo to Basra were inaugurated with the first new aircraft to be ordered for the Empire routes, the three-engined dH 66 'Hercules' which carried 7 passengers for 525 miles at 110 m.p.h. When absorbed by BOAC, Imperial had equipped itself with the Short 'Empire C' class flying boats, of which it had taken the then unprecedented step of ordering 28 straight off the drawing board; capable of carrying 24 passengers at 165 mph, these aircraft weighed 18½ tons. This was the first heavier-than-air aircraft to operate a commercial service across the Atlantic.

During the war BOAC used flying boats on its African routes which connected at Khartoum with a new horseshoe shaped route from Cape Town to Australia. After Japan invaded Malaya, BOAC and QANTAS flew non-stop on the 3,512 mile route from Ceylon to Perth, Western Australia. Other war services included, with unarmed military aircraft in civil markings, a Scotland–Sweden run which flew over hostile territory carrying personnel in both directions, and bringing ball bearings to Britain. BOAC also used 'Liberators' to return to North America the crews who had ferried new aircraft to the British Isles.

In 1946, British European Airways took over the European routes while British South American Airways Corporation took over services to South America including those of British South American Airways Limited. But in 1949 BOAC re-absorbed BSAA after the unexplained failure of that airline's 'Tudor' aircraft.

March 1950, saw the introduction of the first of a fleet of 25 Handley Page 'Hermes' aircraft; these replaced 'Solents' and 'Yorks' on the African routes while 'Stratocruisers' proved popular on the Atlantic. In 1952, BOAC became the first commercial airline to fly jet aircraft using de Havilland 'Comet' 1's, but after several disasters the Certificate of Airworthiness for this plane was withdrawn in 1954. This was a tragedy for BOAC which had already sold some of the 'Hermes', but the rest of the fleet was rapidly returned to service while the

South American services were cancelled, and for the next few years the airline had to buy aircraft where it could.

In 1957 BOAC introduced the first trans-Atlantic turbo-prop service using Bristol 'Britannias', and a year later, 'Comet' IV's introduced the first trans-Atlantic jet service.

The South American services were re-introduced in 1960, but withdrawn again as an economy measure in 1964. A service to Brazil, Uruguay, Argentina and Chile was then inaugurated by British United Airways.

In 1962 BOAC and the Cunard Steamship Company Ltd. formed a new company, BOAC-Cunard to operate services to the Caribbean and the East Coast of the U.S.A. This airline's services passed to BOAC in 1966 when Cunard sold its interest to the Corporation. BOAC, through a wholly-owned holding company, BOAC Associated Companies Ltd., also has an interest in several other airlines. These are (with interest in brackets): Bahamas Airways Ltd. (15%), British West Indian Airways Ltd. (10%), Cathay Pacific Airways Ltd. (15%), East African Airways Corporation (50% plus), Fiji Airways Ltd. (25%), Gulf Aviation Ltd. (55%), Malaysian Airways Ltd. (32%), and Turkish Airlines Corporation-THY (4%).

A new activity of BOAC is the development of hotels, often in conjunction with local interests, to provide accommodation for the increased number of air travellers in the future. At present, BOAC has an interest in hotels under development in Bahrain, Ceylon, Guyana, Jamaica, Kenya, Mauritius and Scotland, with several more planned. Also recently, the airline has been studying the possibilities of using hovercraft for feeder services in the Caribbean, the Persian Gulf and the Pacific, which would be operated by BOAC–Associated Companies. The expansion of the route network of BOAC has not been neglected amidst all this other activity, a new service to Jeddah, and a service to New York via Belfast, being developments of 1968, and following the introduction of a popular new London–Sydney, via New York, San Francisco, Honolulu and Fiji, service in 1967.

Today, with a modern jet fleet of Boeing 707's, Vickers VC10's and Super VC10's, BOAC has a future assured by an order for eleven Boeing 747 Jumbo jet airliners, and options on a twelfth 747, and eight BAC/Sud 'Concorde' and six Boeing 2707 SST's.

Member of the International Air Transport Association

Services

The following are served direct from Great Britain and Europe:
Abadan, Accra, Amman, Antigua, Auckland, Baghdad, Bahrain, Bangkok, Barbados, Beirut, Bermuda, Blantyre, Bogota, Bombay, Boston, Brisbane, Cairo, Calcutta, Caracas, Chicago, Colombo, Dar-es-Salaam, Darwin, Delhi, Detroit, Dhahran, Doha, Dubai, Entebbe, Fiji, Frankfurt, Freeport, Georgetown, Hong Kong, Honolulu, Jeddah, Johannesburg, Kano, Karachi, Khartoum, Kingston, Kuala Lumpur, Kuwait, Lagos, Lima, Lusaka, Mauritius, Mexico City, Miami, Montego Bay, Montreal, Nairobi, Nassau, Ndola, New York, Perth, Rangoon, San Francisco, Singapore, Sydney, Tehran, Tel-Aviv, Tokyo, Toronto, Trinidad, Tripoli, Zürich

Connections are made to numerous other destinations

Livery F: white, blue, grey
   T: blue (emblem: speedbird)

The popular BOAC Super VC10 takes-off from Heathrow Airport, London

Fleet

Boeing 707-436 (*series 336C; †series 379C)

G-APFB	G-APFH	G-APFM	G-ARRB	G-ASZG*
G-APFC	G-APFI	G-APFN	G-ARRC	G-ATWV*
G-APFD	G-ARFJ	G-APFO	G-ARWD	G-AWHU†
G-APFF	G-APFK	G-APFP	G-ASZF*	G-AVPB*
G-APFG	G-APFL	G-ARRA		

BAC (Vickers) VC10

G-ARVA	G-ARVE	G-ARVH	G-ARVJ	G-ARVL
G-ARVB	G-ARVF	G-ARVI	G-ARVK	G-ARVM
G-ARVC	G-ARVG			

BAC (Vickers) Super VC10

G-ASGA	G-ASGE	G-ASGI	G-ASGL	G-ASGO
G-ASGB	G-ASGF	G-ASGJ	G-ASGM	G-ASGP
G-ASGC	G-ASGG	G-ASGK	G-ASGN	G-ASGR
G-ASGD	G-ASGH			

A BOAC Pratt and Witney-powered Boeing 707-336 freighter, being hauled "dead" by a powerful tug

BRITISH UNITED (BUA)   United Kingdom
British United Airways (Holdings) Ltd

British United's history goes back to 1928 when Airwork was formed to provide a full range of technical services for private fliers. To this end the company bought land at Heston and built and operated an airfield there which was for many years one of Europe's leading aviation centres. As a result of the experience gained of airfield and aircraft operation, Airwork participated in the formation of Egypt's Misrair, and Indian National Airlines, and after the war, Sudan Airways.

During the Second World War, Airwork was engaged on military aircraft maintenance, airfield operation, flying training, and other work of a similar nature. A subsidiary company, Airwork General Trading, was formed and its activities as a major contractor included the manufacture of wings for the 'Blenheim' bomber.

Airwork started its own airline operations after the war, which, like most independent airlines, were virtually restricted to charter work, in Airwork's case mainly to Africa, and trooping after the Berlin Air Lift had demonstrated to the British Government the advantages of air transport. The company used 'Vikings' on its contract work and four 'Hermes' for trooping services. At this time another operator, Hunting-Clan, operated similar services and the two companies worked in close association from 1952 when a slight easement of the restrictions permitted independent airlines to have other services, such as colonial coach-class services, which the two airlines operated to East, West and Central Africa, and Hunting-Clan's all-freight, Europe-Africa, Africargo service.

It was not until 1960, however, that the two concerns merged to form British United Airways. Before this, Airwork had already taken over serveral other companies, including Transair and Air Charter in 1958, and Morton Air Services in 1959. Transair had specialized in newspaper and mail services to Western Europe while Air Charter was best known for its Channel Air Bridge vehicle and passenger service, but also included Aviation Traders Ltd. Morton Air Services was, and still is, a charter company which itself had absorbed Olley Air Service, a firm engaged on similar work which dated back to 1933. Two other acquisitions followed in 1962: Jersey Airlines, the highly successful Channel Islands independent, and Silver City Airways, the first airline to operate vehicle ferry services.

British United was re-organized in 1962 under a parent company, Air Holdings Ltd., which included amongst its major shareholders British and Commonwealth Shipping (the majority shareholder in Hunting-Clan), and P. & O. (the owners of Silver City Airways). Under the re-organization all the vehicle ferry services became the responsibility of British United Air Ferries Ltd., while the Channel Islands services were transferred to British United (CI) Airways Ltd. This latter company also became responsible for the Isle of Man services and in April 1967 a new title, British United Airways (CI) was adopted. Airwork International was formed from a merger between Airwork Helicopters Ltd. (which as Fisons-Airwork had pioneered helicopter crop-spraying in Britain) and Bristow Helicopters Ltd., to become the largest helicopter operator in the World. Its fleet operates in many parts of the world on oil exploration, aerial surveys, and any form of commercial aviation suitable for helicopter operation.

In 1968, one of the Air Holdings Group's principal shareholders, British and Commonwealth Shipping, acquired British United Airways, British United Airways (CI), Morton Air Services and Bristow Helicopters, from the Air Holdings Group, leaving that Group with Air Ferry, British Air Ferries (the

The highly popular BAC One-Eleven was designed largely to BUA specifications

renamed British United Air Ferries), the New Zealand-based SAFEAIR Ltd., and all the allied companies within the group dealing with travel and aviation fringe activities (Airwork, etc). The Eagle Star Assurance Company (also an Air Holdings shareholder), and Alan Bristow, founder of Bristow Helicopters and Managing Director of BUA, are minor shareholders in the new British United Group, organized under a new parent, British United Airways (Holdings) Ltd. Other changes which followed the acquisition of BUA by British and Commonwealth included the re-organization of the Channel Islands and Isle of Man services under a new company, British United Island Airways Ltd—BUIA—which operates the former BUA(CI), BUA (Manx) and Morton Air Services fleets.

British United Airways Ltd. is Britain's largest independent airline carrying over 2 million passengers annually. It operates extensive scheduled services including its Interjet services from Gatwick to Belfast, Glasgow and Edinburgh; it was on this service that BUA became the first operator of regular jet services from both Gatwick and from the new airport for Glasgow at Abbotsinch, and also the first airline to operate domestic jet services. The airline can, with its fleet of second generation jet VC10's for its African and ex-BOAC South American services, and BAC 'One-Elevens' for domestic and European services, claim to have one of Britain's most modern jet fleets. British United has five BAC Super 'One-Eleven' 500s in service, with three more on order.

Member of the International Air Transport Association

Livery F: white, yellow, blue, grey
     T: white, yellow, blue

British United operates four VC10s on charter and on South American and African scheduled services. This one is in the livery adopted during the winter of 1966-7

International rail/air services
Belgian Arrow: London–Brussels, Bruges, Ghent
Silver Arrow: London–Paris

International services from London to:
Accra, Algiers, Amsterdam, Barcelona, Bathurst, Buenos Aires, Dinard, Düsseldorf, Entebbe, Freetown, Genoa, Ibiza, Lagos, Las Palmas, Le Touquet, Lisbon, Lusaka, Malaga, Montevideo, Nairobi, Ndola, Palma, Quimper, Rio de Janeiro, Rotterdam, Salisbury, Santiago, São Paulo, St. Brieuc, Tenerife
Connections are made between the European services and services within the British Isles, also between European and African and South American services
from Jersey to:
Dinard/St. Brieuc, Paris*, Quimper
*connection from Guernsey
also:
Glasgow/Newcastle–Amsterdam–Düsseldorf, Ostend–Guernsey–Dinard/St. Brieuc, Belfast/Exeter–Paris, Southampton/Exeter–Dublin/Cork, Blackpool–Dublin

Domestic services from London to:
Alderney, Guernsey, Jersey, Swansea
Interjet–Belfast, Edinburgh, Glasgow
from Channel Islands to:
Belfast, Blackpool, Coventry, Exeter, Glasgow, Leeds/Bradford, Manchester, Southampton, Swansea
Jersey–Guernsey   Guernsey–Alderney
from Isle of Man to:
Belfast, Birmingham, Blackpool, Coventry, Edinburgh, Glasgow, Leeds/Bradford, Newcastle
from Belfast to:
Blackpool, Exeter, Southampton
from Blackpool to:
Coventry, Leeds/Bradford, Manchester
from Edinburgh/Glasgow to:
Southampton, Exeter; Glasgow–Newcastle
from Exeter to:
Manchester, Plymouth, Southampton, Swansea
also:
Manchester–Southampton

Fleet   British United Airways
BAC (Vickers) VC10

G-ARTA	G-ASIW	G-ASIX	G-ATDJ

BAC One-Eleven 502 Series

G-	G-	G-	G-	G-
G-	G-	G-		

BAC One-Eleven 201 Series

G-ASJA	G-ASJD	G-ASJF	G-ASJH	G-ASJJ
G-ASJC	G-ASJE	G-ASJG	G-ASJI	G-ASTJ

Bristol Britannia 307

G-ANCD	G-ANCE

Bristol Britannia 317

G-APNA	G-APNB

Vickers Viscount 833

G-APTB	G-APTC	G-APTD

Bristow Helicopters' Westland WS55 No. G-ANUK

Fleet British United Island Airways
Vickers Viscount 831
G-APND

British United Island Airways operates eight Handley Page Heralds; here is
G-APWF while in BUA (C.I.) livery

Handley Page H.P.R.7 Herald 201

G-APWE	G-APWG	G-APWI	G-ASKK	G-AVEZ
G-APWF	G-APWH	G-APWJ		

Douglas DC-3 Dakota

G-AKNB	G-AMJU	G-AMYV	G-AMYX	G-ANAE
G-ALPN				

Douglas DC-3 Dakota

G-AMHJ	G-AMSV	G-AMYJ	G-AOBN	G-AOUD
G-AMRA				

de Havilland Heron

G-ANSZ	G-AOGO	G-AOXL	G-ASUZ	G-ASVA
G-ANWZ				

de Havilland Dove

G-AJBI	G-AMYO	G-ANAN	G-ANVC	G-AOYC
G-AKJR				

Fleet   Airwork International (incorporating Bristow Helicopters)

Westland Wessex W.S.58 60

G-ATBY	G-ATCA	G-ATCB	G-ATSC	G-AVEW
G-ATBZ				

Westland-Sikorsky W.S.55 Series 3

G-ANJV	G-AOHG	G-APWN	D-HOBI	EP-HAC
G-ANUK	G-AOZK	G-APWO	D-HODE	EP-HAE
G-AODB	G-APDY	G-ATKV	EP-HAA	EP-HAF
G-AODP	G-APRW	G-ATLZ	EP-HAB	

Sud-Aviation SE 3160 Alouette III

EP-HAD

Westland-Sikorsky W.S.51 Series 2

5N-ABV	5N-ABW	5N-AGA	5N-AGL

Hiller 360-UH12A

G-AMDN	G-ANOA

Hiller 360-UH12B

G-APJN	G-ASTM	G-ASVI	G-ATKG	S/N497
G-APSH	G-ASTR	G-ASVJ	G-ATLG	S/505N
G-APTM	G-ASVH	G-ASVK	G-AVAJ	S/N598
				S/N726

Hiller 360-UH12C

G-APMP	G-APMS	G-APNR	G-ASTP	9Y-TCE
G-APMR				

Hiller 360-UH-12E4

| G-ATDW | 5N-ABY | 5N-ABZ | 5N-AGE | |

Hiller 12E

| G-ATUG | G-ATVN | GP-HAM | 5N-AGB | 5N-AGG |
| G-ATUM | | | | |

Bell 47G-2A (*47G)   VR=Romania

| G-ASYW | VR-BAT* | VR-BAV* | VR-BAW* | VR-BBB |

Auster JIN

G-APOA

Scottish Aviation Twin Pioneer

5N-ABQ

Riley Dove

5N-AGF

Agusta-Bell 206A Jet Ranger   EP=Iran

| G-AVII | G-AVSW | G-AVSY | G-AVSZ | EP-HAM |
| G-AVSV | G-AVSX | | | |

CALEDONIAN
Caledonian Airways Ltd

United Kingdom

In the eight years which have elapsed since Caledonian's formation in 1961 with one DC-7C the airline's fleet has grown until it now has four Bristol 'Britannias' and two Boeing 707-320 convertible passenger/cargo jet airliners, delivered in 1967 and 1968, with three BAC 'One-Eleven' 500s now in course of delivery. One of the airline's main activities has been the flying of North Atlantic charter flights and Caledonian was the first non-American airline to be granted permission to fly an almost unlimited number of charter flights into the United States.

European inclusive tours and trooping flights have also featured in Caledonian's activities, and, in addition, the airline has flown scheduled services on behalf of several major airlines. It was only natural, therefore, that the airline should seek scheduled services of its own, but although a licence has been obtained for a Glasgow–Barcelona service the airline will not operate scheduled services until a worthwhile number of destinations can be served. The airline applied unsuccessfully for North Atlantic scheduled service licences in 1968.

Caledonian Airways has two Boeing 707-399Cs in its fleet; they were delivered in 1967

Ownership of Caledonian is divided among several companies, including Great Universal Stores, Lyle Shipping Company, Industrial & Commercial Finance Corporation (a consortium of Britain's "big four" banks), National Commercial and Schroders', Scottish Aviation International (a new York-based group), Hogarth Shipping and Airways Interests (Thompson) which includes a group of employees and the airline's founders.

Livery F: white, blue, grey
T: blue (emblem: lion rampant)

Scheduled service:
Glasgow–Barcelona

Fleet

G-AOVJ	*County of Aberdeen*	BAC (Bristol) Britannia 312	
G-ASTF	*County of Perth*	,,	Britannia 314
G-ATMA	*County of Midlothian*	,,	,,
G-ATNZ	*County of Inverness*	,,	,,
G-AVKA	*Flagship Bonnie Scotland*	Boeing 707-399C	
G-AVTW	*County of Ayr*	,, ,,	
G-A	*Isle of Skye*	BAC One-Eleven 500	
G-A	*Isle of Eriskay*	,, ,,	
G-A	*Isle of Iona*	,, ,,	
G-A	*Isle of Arran*	,, ,, (on option)	

CAMBRIAN
Cambrian Airways Ltd

United Kingdom

This Welsh airline's name is derived from the old Latin name for the West—Cambria—and it has borne the name since 1935 when S. Kenneth Davies, a Welsh Businessman and aviation enthusiast, founded the airline with a de Havilland 'Moth' for use on training and pleasure flights and military charter work which included target towing. The attitude of the general public to aviation at that time resulted in a profit of only £2–19–6d by the third year of operation.

Civil flying ceased on the outbreak of war in 1939, but after the cessation of hostilities a Cambrian aircraft had the distinction of making the first post war civil flight in the United Kingdom when, on 1st January, 1946, a three-seat Auster flew from Cardiff to Bristol with a reel of wire rope and a prototype aircraft seat as cargo. Shortly afterwards Cambrian became the first British independent airline to be granted a licence for a scheduled service, between Cardiff and Weston-super-Mare, for which a six-seat de Havilland 'Rapide' was acquired.

Although after the war BEA operated services from Cardiff to Weston, Bristol and Southampton, they were uneconomic and it soon abandoned them, leaving Cambrian as the only airline flying to and from Wales except for a short period when BEA operated, with Cambrian as handling agents at Cardiff, an experimental helicopter service to Liverpool and Wrexham. The experiment ended in 1951 but Cambrian continued the Liverpool service with the 'Rapides'. In 1953 Cambrian took over the Bristol activities of Morton Air Services, and

A Viscount of Cambrian Airways sporting the airline's new livery

began operating from Bristol to Southampton, Paris and the Channel Islands. Channel Islands—Cardiff had been introduced by Cambrian in 1949.

In 1953 de Havilland 'Doves' were introduced, to be followed during the next few years by 'Herons' and DC-3 'Pionairs' as the airline kept pace with the expansion in air travel. In 1956 an operating agreement was entered into with BEA, to be followed in 1958 by BEA acquiring a one-third interest in the airline. At the same time, John Morgan, another Welsh businessman, also acquired an interest in the company. Unfortunately that year also saw a recession in the airline business and Cambrian was forced to take drastic measures, including the sale of the entire fleet of aircraft. Operations were resumed on a limited scale in 1959 with a fleet of aircraft hired from BEA and the airline's expansion has continued since including the introduction of services to the new airport at Cork in 1961 and in 1963 Cambrian took over BEA's services to the Isle of Man and Liverpool. It was at this time that turbo-prop Vickers 'Viscounts' were acquired allowing the airline to expand into the inclusive tours' field.

In November, 1967, Cambrian became a wholly-owned subsidiary of British Air Services Ltd., a holding company in which BEA has a 66% interest, and the former non-BEA Cambrian and BKS shareholders hold the remaining stock.

Today, the Cambrian red dragon motif which is carried on the tail of all the airline's aircraft is a familiar sight at 30 airports in the ten countries served.

Member of the British Independent Air Transport Association

Livery F: white, red, grey

T: white (emblem: dragon)

Services from Bristol/Cardiff to:
Belfast, Cork, Dinard, Dublin (CS), Glasgow, Guernsey, Jersey, Paris

C—Cardiff only   S—includes flights via Swansea

from Liverpool to:
Belfast, Cork, Guernsey/Jersey, Isle of Man, London

from Isle of Man to:
Belfast, London, Manchester

Swansea–Guernsey/Jersey   Manchester–Glasgow

London–Cork   Southampton–Paris   Bournemouth–Paris

Fleet

Douglas DC-3 Dakota-Pionair C-47

G-AGHM	G-AGHS	G-AHCZ	G-ALCC	G-ALXL

Vickers Viscount 701

G-ALWF	G-AMOA	G-AMOG	G-AMON	G-AMOP
G-AMNZ	G-AMOE	G-AMOH		

CHANNEL AIRWAYS
Channel Airways Ltd

United Kingdom

Channel Airways was founded in 1946 as East Anglian Flying Services Ltd. by the present chairman and managing director, Squadron Leader R. J. Jones, who used his RAF demobilization gratuity to purchase an elderly de Havilland 'Puss Moth' three-seat aircraft with which he flew pleasure trips from a field adjoining a holiday camp at Herne Bay.

The following year the new airline moved to Southend Airport, which had re-opened for civilian flying only a few days previously, and now some 75 per cent of Channel's flying is from its base at Southend—one of today's busiest provincial airports. By the end of the 1948 holiday season the fleet had grown to eight aircraft, including five 'Rapides', a Miles 'Aerovan' and an 'Airspeed Courier' as well as the 'Puss Moth', while the experience gained on flying inclusive tour charters to Ostend, Squadron Leader Jones decided to commence scheduled operations to Ostend and Jersey the following year.

A slump that occurred in 1951 forced Jones to reduce his full-time staff to one and confine the airline's activities to pleasure trips. However, business improved sufficiently by 1953 for scheduled services to be re-introduced with additional services to Shoreham, Guernsey and Paris from Southend, and services from Portsmouth to Jersey and Paris. Further progress was made in 1956 when de Havilland 'Doves' were introduced and a Southend–Rotterdam service was inaugurated. During the next few years, aircraft operated by the company included Bristol 170 Freighters, 'Vikings', DC-3's, a DC-4 and, in 1962, a few months after changing to its present title, Channel purchased from Tradair, two 'Viscount' 700's which were to be the first of many of this type. The 'Viscounts' allowed the airline to expand further into the inclusive tour charter field.

At present Channel operates a fleet of 'Viscount' 812's, 'One-Elevens' and 'Tridents' from Southend, Stansted, Bournemouth, Southampton and Ipswich. The airline also has plans for improved domestic services from Southend, including a "bus-stop" service to Edinburgh and Aberdeen (begun in January, 1969) and also intends to operate domestic and international scheduled services from the proposed new airport for London at Stansted which is recognized as being in Channel's catchment area. Portsmouth was dropped from Channel's network after that city's airport was closed to aircraft of HS748 size and larger. Channel Airways currently carries over $\frac{1}{2}$ million passengers a year and often operates more than 700 flights in a week. Early in 1967, Channel Airways was appointed British dealer for SIAI-Marchetti, the Italian light aircraft manufacturer.

Services from Southend to:

Düsseldorf, Guernsey, Hanover, Jersey, Ostend, Paris, Rotterdam

Services to Southend connecting with the above services from East Midlands (Castle Donington), Ipswich, Rochester

from Southampton and Bournemouth to:

Guernsey, Jersey

Livery F: white and grey with black
　　　T: black and gold

Vickers Viscount 812

G-APPU	G-AVHE	G-AVIW	G-A	G-A
G-ATUE	G-AVHK	G-AVJL	G-A	
G-ATVR				

BAC One-Eleven series 408

G-AVGP	G-AWEJ	G-AWGG	G-A	G-A
GA-				

Hawker Siddeley Trident 1E-140

G-AVYB	G-AVYE

DAN-AIR
Dan-Air Services Ltd

United Kingdom

Formed as a wholly-owned subsidiary of Davies and Newman Ltd., an old established firm of brokers, Dan-Air commenced charter operations in 1953 with a DC-3 based at Southend. A second DC-3 was acquired the following year and both aircraft are still in service. Three ex-Royal Air Force 'Yorks', were also purchased in 1954 but not delivered until some time later. In fact the first of them arrived from Scottish Aviation, the company which converted the aircraft to Dan-Air's requirements, just before the airline moved its operating base to Blackbushe Airport, Hampshire, early in 1955.

The first main expansion of the airline's activities away from charter work occurred in 1956 when it was awarded an Air Ministry freight contract for a service between England and Singapore. Dan-Air ordered two more 'Yorks' to operate the service. It introduced its first scheduled service between Blackbushe and Jersey the same year. During the next few years several different types of aircraft were operated by the company, 'Doves', 'Herons', and Bristol Freighters as well as the DC-3's already mentioned, while from 1959 onwards the airline's network of scheduled services expanded to include Bristol, Cardiff, Liverpool, Newcastle upon Tyne, Plymouth, Carlisle and the Isle of Man as well as several European destinations. Other activities included a new freight service for the Air Ministry to the Woomera Rocket Range in Australia after the Singapore contract expired, and from 1959 to 1961 Dan-Air's 'Yorks' operated BEA's London–Manchester–Glasgow freight service.

At present Dan-Air operates a fleet of DC-3's, Comet 4's, a DC-7B freighter and 'Ambassadors', one of which, G-ALFR, came to the airline from BEA via Napier who used it as a flying test bed for their Eland turbo-prop engine. The fleet is employed on a much enlarged network of scheduled service and contract flights.

Dan-Air's fleet includes four de Havilland Ambassadors; this one is G-AMAE

International services
Newcastle–Liverpool–Amsterdam   Bristol–Cardiff–Ostend
Bristol–Cardiff–Liverpool–Newcastle–Kristiansand–Stavanger
London–Ostend

Domestic services
Cardiff–Isle of Man   Bristol–Swansea–Isle of Man
Glasgow–Isle of Man   Newcastle–Carlisle–Isle of Man
London–Jersey

Livery F: white, red, grey   **T:** white

Fleet
Hawker Siddeley (de Havilland) Comet 4
G-APDJ   G-APDK   G-APDN   G-APDO

Douglas DC-7B/F
G-ATAB

de Havilland (Airspeed) Ambassador A.S.57–2
G-ALZO   G-ALZY   G-AMAE   G-AMAH

Douglas DC-3 Dakota
G-ALXK   G-AMPP   G-AMSS   G-AMSU

One of the four ex-BOAC Comet 4's operated by Dan-Air, G-APDO

INVICTA AIRWAYS
Invicta Airways Ltd

United Kingdom

Formed in 1964, Invicta Airways commenced operations the following Spring and now operate a fleet of 'Viscounts' and DC-4's and five 'Vikings', mainly on inclusive tour and freight charter work, but also on a scheduled service to Ostend from Manston in Kent where the airline has its new passenger terminal, administrative offices and a fully equipped hangar. In 1967, an interest in the airline was acquired by Travel Trust and two ex-British Eagle 'Viscounts' were purchased.

A merger with British Midland Airways is planned.

The Invicta fleet includes four Douglas DC-4's like this one, at Manston

Scheduled service: Manston–Ostend

Fleet
Douglas DC-4 Skymaster
G-ASEN	G-ASPM	G-ASPN	G-ASZT*
*on hire			

Vickers Viscount 755
G-AOCB	G-AOCC

KING AVIATION
King Aviation Ltd

United Kingdom

King Aviation was formed by the present managing director, John S. King, in 1963 to provide a business aircraft management service for those companies which wished to have the advantages of their own aircraft without the disadvantage of being responsible for maintenance and having to employ a full time pilot. The company entered the air-taxi business in 1965 when it moved to its present base at the East Midlands Airport at Castle Donington.

Member of the National Air Taxi Association

Livery: white with red

Fleet

G-APXM	Piper PA22-160 Tripacer
G-ASKW	Piper PA23 Apache 235
G-ATDC	,, PA-23 Aztec C
G-ATNY	Cessna 337 Super Skymaster
G-AVKN	Cessna 401

G-ATNY, a Cessna Super Skymaster twin-engined aircraft operated by King Aviation on air-taxi duties

LAKER AIRWAYS
Laker Airways Ltd

United Kingdom

Mr. Freddie Laker, a former managing director of Air Holdings Ltd., founded Laker Airways early in 1966 as Britain's first air-package contract carrier, with an initial fleet of two Bristol 'Britannia' 102's which were leased to scheduled service airlines. Inclusive tours' operators taking advantage of this service include Lord Brothers (a Laker subsidiary), and Wings Ltd. At present a fleet of four BAC 'One-Elevens' is operated; a VC10, which had been leased to MEA having been sold to British United Airways.

One of Britains' newest airlines, Laker, operates BAC One-Elevens on inclusive tour charters

Livery F: white, red, black, grey   **T:** black

Fleet

G-AVBW	BAC One-Eleven series 320L	
G-AVBX	,,	,,
G-AVBY	,,	,,
G-AVYZ	,,	,,

LLOYD INTERNATIONAL
Lloyd International Airways Ltd

United Kingdom

Lloyd International Airways takes its name from that of Mr. C. B. M. Lloyd who was a major shareholder and joint managing director of the company from its formation in 1961 until 1964 when he sold his interest. Wheelock Marden, a well-established firm of Far-East traders, then acquired a one-third interest in the company. The other joint managing director at this time was Mr. A. L. MacLeod, present managing director and Lloyd's partner in a shipbroking business.

The airline was formed to provide air transport for crews of ships owned by the Mavroleon companies in the Far-East. This activity failed to provide an economic level of utilization for the company's aircraft, and expansion was made into other fields, embracing inclusive tour and Ministry of Defence charters. As a result, the airline's fleet expanded from the original, ill-fated DC-4, destroyed in a refuelling accident, to the present fleet of three Bristol 'Britannias', a second DC-4 having been sold in late 1968. Two of the Bristol 'Britannias' were ex-BOAC 312's while a third is an ex-BUA 317. An interesting feature of the Company's operations is the ground maintenance engineer, nicknamed the "flying spanners" carried on some long distance flights to deal with any difficulties which may arise as well as providing assistance with cargo stowing.

During 1965 an application was made for a Europe–Far-East all-cargo service, but although permission was granted by the Hong Kong authority, the Air Transport Licensing Board refused permission. In spite of this setback, Lloyd International does not rule out the possibility of scheduled services in the not-too-far-distant future. The airline had had a Douglas DC-8-63F on order for its planned Far East all-cargo services, but as two further attempts to obtain the required licences failed, this aircraft had to be cancelled. A new venture for the company is the operation of a Dassault 'Fan Jet Falcon' eight-seat executive aircraft for charters.

The brunt of Lloyd International's work load is borne by the airline's three Bristol Britannia 300's which are used on both passenger and freight duties

Livery F: white, blue, grey   **T:** white and blue

Fleet
BAC (Bristol) Britannia 312 (*series 317)
G-AOVP   G-AOVS   G-APNA*
Dassault Fan Jet Falcon
HB-VAW

LOGANAIR
Loganair Ltd

United Kingdom

Originally formed as the Aviation Division of Duncan Logan (Contractors) Ltd., a civil engineering group, Loganair started operations in 1962 carrying the directors and staff of the group between construction sites and to business meetings using a Piper 'Aztec' twin-engined aircraft. Because of the demand for this kind of service the company has expanded by the addition of another 'Aztec' for air-taxi duties to the present fleet of two 'Aztecs', two Britten-Norman BN-2 'Islanders' and a Beech 18.

Loganair operates from the Glasgow Airport at Abbottsinch, and included among its flying activities are a newspaper service to Stornoway, some military contract work, a weekday Glasgow–Blackpool service for the Post Office Savings Department carrying computer cards and an ambulance service for the Inner Hebrides. Two Britten-Norman BN-2 'Islander' aircraft are used on the Glasgow–Oban–Mull service.

Member of the Air Taxi Operators Association and of the BEA Air Taxi Plan

The Scottish air taxi operator, Loganair, operates this Piper Aztec aircraft

Services
Glasgow–Oban–Mull

Fleet
G-ASER	Piper PA-23 Aztec B
G-ASUG	Beech 18
G-ASYB	Piper PA-23 Aztec B
G-ATJV	Piper PA-28 Cherokee Six
G-AVRA	Britten-Norman BN-2 Islander
G-AVRC	,, ,,

LONDON AVIATION
London Aviation Ltd

United Kingdom

It was as Polyfoto Air Taxi Services Ltd that London Aviation was formed, the present title being adopted in 1968. The firm currently operates air-taxi and executive charter services from Elstree, near Watford, Hertfordshire. The company started operations in October, 1962 and three years later it acquired the London School of Flying. The present fleet comprises four Piper and one Cessna aircraft.

Member of the Air Taxi Operators Association and BEA Air Taxi Plan

Fleet

G-ASWW	Piper PA-30 Twin Comanche
G-ATMT	,, ,,
G-ATSV	Cessna 310C
G-ATYF	Piper Twin Comanche 160
G-AVJJ	,, ,,

MANAGEMENT AVIATION
Management Aviation Ltd

United Kingdom

Management Aviation operates a fleet of four Hiller UH-12C and UH-12E helicopters from its base at Bourn, near Cambridge, on executive charter work.

Fleet

Hiller UH-12C (*type UH-12E)

G-ARTG	G-ASIH*	G-ATED*	G-ATDM*

McALPINE AVIATION
Sir Robert McAlpine & Sons Ltd

United Kingdom

Originally starting operations as the aviation division of Sir Robert McAlpine and Sons Ltd, the civil engineering contractors, McAlpine Aviation entered the executive charter and air-taxi business in 1963. Today the company operates six aircraft, two Piaggio 166B's, two Piper 'Aztecs', and two Helio 'Super Couriers', on services which include the operation of the Piper 'Twinair' service for Trans World Airlines in the United Kingdom.

McAlpine Aviation also provides a complete range of services for business aircraft owners at the company's maintenance base at Luton Airport. The company holds the British dealership for both Helio and Riley 'Dove' aircraft; it also has a Piper dealership.

Another Piper Aztec operator is McAlpine Aviation, the air taxi division of the famous civil engineering group

Fleet

Helio Super Courier
G-ARLD   G-ATGM

Piaggio P.166B Portofino
G-ASPC   G-AVSM

Piper PA-23 Aztec C
G-ATXG   G-AVKZ

MID-FLY
Mid-Fly Ltd

United Kingdom

Mid-Fly Ltd. currently provides an air-taxi service from its base at Elmnon, Birmingham, with a Piper 'Aztec', a de Havilland 'Dove' and a Piper 'Cherokee' 180. The air-taxi service started in 1964 with two DH 'Rapides' which were supplemented the following year by the 'Aztec'. The 'Rapides' were also intended to be used for aerial photography and pleasure flights, but as these plans failed to materialize, the aircraft were sold. The 'Dove' and the 'Cherokee' have since been added.

Mid-Fly owns the Birmingham Air Centre at Elmdon where the company provides flying training on a fleet of three Cessna 150's, and a maintenance service for light aircraft owners. Both activities date from 1964.

The company became a wholly owned subsidiary of Air Gregory in February 1969.

Member of the Air Taxi Operators Association and BEA Air Taxi Plan

Fleet

G-APZU   Hawker Siddeley (de Havilland) Dove Mk. IV
G-ARYF   Piper PA-23 Aztec B
G-ASWR   Piper Cherokee 180

MONARCH
Monarch Airlines Ltd

United Kingdom

Monarch Airlines is the newest British air charter operator, having been formed in June, 1967, and operations commenced on April 5, 1968, with two ex-Caledonian Airways Bristol 'Britannia "Whispering Giant" turbo-prop airliners. The airline is owned 80% by Cosmos Tours Ltd, and 18% by the Chairman, Mr. G. P. Jackman, and it is intended to operate general freight and passengrr charters as well as inclusive tour charters for Cosmos Tours. The airline has an associate company, Airline Engineering, which undertakes aircraft overhaul and maintenance work at Luton.

Livery F: white, black, yellow
     T: black

Fleet
Bristol Britannia 312
G-AOVH   G-AOVI

NORFOLK AIRWAYS
Norfolk Airways Ltd

United Kingdom

Norfolk Airways currently operates a Piper 'Aztec' and a Cessna 172 on air-taxi work from its base at Norwich, and a subsidiary company, Rig Air, operates a Twin 'Comanche' and another Cessna 172. The company also uses an Auster for aerial survey work and during the summer months operates the airfield at Clacton for pleasure flights. During some twelve years of operations Norfolk Airways has also undertaken contract flying in Africa.

Fleet (*Rig Air Fleet)

G-ATBV	Piper PA-23 Aztec	G-ATUN*	Cessna 172
G-ATEN*	Piper PA-30 Twin Comanche	G-AVVZ	,,

NORTHERN AIR TAXIS
Northern Air Taxis Ltd

United Kingdom

Based at the Leeds/Bradford Airport at Yeadon, Northern Air Taxis Ltd. is the largest air-taxi operator in the north of England, handling in the region of 200–250 passengers a week during the summer months. The company was founded in 1964 by Ernest Crabtree with a fleet of two aircraft. It has since grown to six, three Piper 'Aztecs', a Cessna 310, and two single-engined Cessna's.

Northern Air Taxis Ltd. operates its own maintenance service at Yeadon, where it also provides special facilities for the company's passengers.

A gathering of the Northern Air Taxi Services fleet outside the company's base, together with some of the aircraft maintained by the firm

Fleet

G-ARWF	Cessna 310G	G-AVLV	Piper Aztec C
G-ASTD	Piper Aztec C	G-AWBP	Cessna 182
G-ASTE	,, ,,	G-AWGW	,, 172

NORTHERN EXECUTIVE
Northern Executive Aviation Ltd
United Kingdom

Northern Executive Aviation Ltd. currently operates a Piper 'Cherokee Six' and three 'Aztecs' from the company's base at Manchester Airport, where it is also the Northern Area dealer for Piper aircraft.

Operations began in 1962 with a Piper 'Cherokee 160' which was supplemented by an 'Aztec' in 1965, and replaced by a 'Cherokee Six' in 1966. Initially only air-taxi work was undertaken, but today Northern Executive Aviation Ltd. includes aerial photography and light freighting in its programme.

Member of the National Air Taxi Association

Fleet

Piper PA-23 Aztec C (*Turbo Aztec C)
G-ATJR   G-ATPR*   G-AWIY
G-ATRW Piper Cherokee Six

RENT-A-COPTER
Rent-a-Copter Ltd
United Kingdom

Rent-a-Copter was formed in 1962 to provide a helicopter charter service which, apart from air-taxi work, also covers crop spraying, aerial photography and constructional lifting. Initially the fleet consisted of two Hiller 12C helicopters, and today it is formed of a Hiller F.H. 1100 and a Hughes 300, having employed a Hiller 12E, an E4 and another 12C in the meantime.

The company's main operating base is at Bourn, near Cambridge, and there is a co-operative combined fleet agreement with Management Aviation Ltd.

Fleet

G-ASTZ	Hughes 300	G-AVTG	Hiller FH.1100

SCILLONIA
Scillonia Airways Ltd

United Kingdom

Scillonia Airways was formed in 1965 with a fleet of four de Havilland 'Dragon Rapides'. The company commenced operations linking Newquay, Penzance, and the Isles of Scilly for the summer of 1966. Three Britten-Norman BN-2 'Islander' aircraft will be introduced as soon as their performance meets the airline's requirements.

Other activities of Scillonia include passenger and freight charters and a service within Eire, and the transport of shell-fish to France from Cornwall.

Services
Newquay–Isles of Scilly   Penzance–Isles of Scilly

Livery F: white, blue
T: white

Fleet

G-AHAG	de Havilland D.H.89A Dragon Rapide	
G-AHGC	,,	,,
G-AJCL	,,	Dragon Rapide 6
G-ALGC	,,	Dragon Rapide
Britten-Norman BN-2 Islander		
G-A	G-A	G-A

SKYWAYS
Skyways Coach Air Ltd

United Kingdom

Founded by the present managing director, Eric Rylands, who had had experience of coach/air travel while with the Lancashire Aircraft Corporation and Skyways Limited, Skyways Coach Air commenced operations during September 1955, with a DC-3 service between the main operating base at Lympne in Kent and Beauvais in Northern France. There were coach connections between London and Lympne, and between Paris and Beauvais. Although services to Lyons, Vichy, Montpellier, Tours and Clermont Ferrand are operated, this route remains the most important. Services were also commenced from the East Midlands Airport at Castle Donington, but they were withdrawn at the end of the 1966 summer season because of IATA pressure to increase fares to a level the airline considered would be unattractive to its passengers.

Skyways Coach Air is currently operating Douglas DC-3s with twin Rolls-Royce Dart turbo-prop powered HS 748's. The Transport Holding Company acquired a 50% interest in the airline during January 1968.

Services from Lympne to:
Beauvais, Clermont Ferrand, Lyons, Montpellier, Tours, Vichy

Livery F: white, blue, grey
T: blue

A Hawker Siddeley 748 of Skyways Coach Air, the first company to operate the 748 Series I, unloads its passengers at Lympne in Kent

Fleet

G-AGYZ*	Douglas DC-3 Dakota
G-AMSM	,, ,,
G-AMWW	,, ,,
G-ARMW	Hawker Siddeley H.S.748 Series 1
G-ARMX	,, ,,
G-ARRW	,, ,,
G-ASPL	,, ,,

*freight

SKYWORK
Skywork Ltd

United Kingdom

Skywork was formed in 1964 as Lennard Aviation Ltd., the present title being adopted in October, 1966. The main activity is pilot training with some air-taxi work. The operating base is London (Stansted) Airport.

Fleet

G-ASSB	Piper PA-30 Twin Comanche

SLINGSBY AIR CHARTER
Slingsby Air Charter Ltd

United Kingdom

Formed as Williams Air Charter, Slingsby Air Charter currently provides an air-taxi service from the company's base at the Leeds/Bradford Airport at Yeadon using a Riley 65 and a Cessna 310G. The company also undertakes aerial photography work. training, and light freight charters with these aircraft. Operations began in 1964 with one Riley-modified Cessna 310.

Slingsby Air Charter operates this Cessna 310 on air-taxi services from Yeadon (Leeds/Bradford) Airport

Fleet

G-ASSZ	Riley 65	G-ASYV	Cessna 310G

SOUTHWEST AVIATION
South-West Aviation Co Ltd

United Kingdom

South-West Aviation dates from August, 1966, when it was formed at Exeter to operate executive and freight charters, and to operate local air services. Applications have been made for scheduled service licences. Currently the airline operates two Short Skyvans, one of which is an ex-Ansett-ANA series 2 converted to series 3 (Garrett-power), an ex-British Midland Douglas DC-3, a Beech Travel Air and a Piper Aztec.

Fleet

G-ATPF	Short Skyvan 2
G-AWCS	,,　　,,　3
G-APBC	Douglas DC-3 Dakota
G-	Beechcraft Travel Air
G-	Piper PA-23 Aztec

STRATHAIR
Strathallan Air Services Ltd
United Kingdom

Strathair was formed in December, 1964, with a single-engined Helio 'Courier' which was used on air-taxi work. This aircraft had the advantage of a very short take-off and landing, but it suffered from payload limitations and the restrictions placed on single-engined aircraft for public transport flying, and as a result it was soon replaced by a Piper 'Aztec'.

The present fleet operated by Strathair includes a Piper 'Aztec' and a 'Twin Comanche', both of which are owned by Scottish business houses, and Strathair's own de Havilland 'Dove' which is used both for executive charters and as a light freighter. During 1966 Strathair acquired licences for both a Dundee–Edinburgh–Prestwick and an Inverness–Dundee–Edinburgh service, the former being operated for six weeks, but then withdrawn due to lack of support, while the Inverness–Dundee–Edinburgh service is not yet operated.

Services

Inverness–Dundee–Edinburgh

Fleet

G-ASDD   de Havilland Dove Mk. 5

G-ATLC   Piper PA-23 Aztec (owned by Scottish Malt Distillers Ltd.)

G-ATWG   „ PA-30 Twin Comanche (owned by West Highland Woodlands
                                                              Ltd.)

TAMAR AIRWAYS
Tamar Airways Ltd
United Kingdom

Tamar Airways was formed by Bainbridge-Scott Limited in August, 1966, to fill the gap left in scheduled services to the West of England by the bankruptcy of British Westpoint Airlines. The company holds a licence for a service between Gatwick Airport (London) and Plymouth with Britten-Norman 'Islander' aircraft, but these plans have been postponed for the time being.

Service (not operated)
London–Plymouth

Fleet

G-   Britten-Norman BN-2 Islander
G-   „   „

TRANSGLOBE
Transglobe Airways Ltd
United Kingdom

Transglobe Airways Ltd. was formed in 1959 under the name of Air Links with a single DC-3 for charter work. A second DC-3 was acquired in 1961, and these aircraft were replaced the following year by the last Handley Page 'Hermes' to fly on commercial operations. This in turn was superseded in 1964 by several 'Argonaut' aircraft.

The company's new title was assumed in 1965 to coincide with the introduction of Bristol 'Britannia' aircraft which, apart from taking over charter and trooping operations from the 'Argonauts', allowed Transglobe to expand its activities into the inclusive tours field. Canadair CL 44's with swing tails to assist in the speedy loading of cargo when operated in the all-cargo role were delivered in 1968.

A 42% interest in the company was bought by the Bolton Steamship Co. early in 1967. Transglobe went into liquidation in late 1968, but may be revived if Seaboard World Airlines, from whom the CL-44's were being lease-purchased, can find British financial support.

TRANS MERIDIAN
Trans Meridian (London) Ltd

United Kingdom

Trans Meridian Flying Services Ltd. was formed in January, 1962, and operated two Douglas DC-4 'Skymasters' on charter services. These aircraft were replaced three years later by a Douglas DC-7B convertible passenger/freight aircraft, and this in turn was replaced by two Douglas DC-7C/F freighters in January, 1966. A third DC-7C/F was added in spring, 1968, after the airline had been reorganized and renamed from Trans Meridian Flying Services Ltd in March of that year. It is now intended that Trans Meridian will concentrate more on the cargo aspect of its operations, becoming Britain's first all-cargo airline. Canadair CL-44s are for DC-7C/F replacement and expansion of the airline.

The operating base of Trans Meridian is at Luton Airport, Bedfordshire.

Fleet

G-ATMF	Douglas DC-7C/F	G-AWWB Canadair CL-44D
G-AVXH	,, ,,	
G-AWBI	,, ,,	Five more CL-44Ds are on option

TRUMAN AVIATION
Truman Aviation Ltd

United Kingdom

Truman Aviation was formed in 1963 as an agent for Piper aircraft and as an air-taxi operator with a Piper 'Cherokee 180B'. This aircraft was replaced in 1964 by a 'Twin Comanche', which in turn was replaced by a similar aircraft in 1966. In addition Truman's have taken over the operation of an 'Apache 235' for a customer, and this aircraft is also used as a reserve for air-taxi work.

The company holds a 75-year lease on Tollerton Airport at Nottingham, which it is developing for private fliers, and to this end has built a new control tower, installed runway lights, and made other improvements.

Member of the Air Taxi Operators Association and BEA Air Taxi Plan

Fleet

| G-ASKW | Piper PA-23 Apache 235 |
| G-ATSZ | „ PA-30 Twin Comanche |

AMERICAN AIRLINES
American Airlines Inc

United States of America

American Airlines is one of the largest airlines in the western hemisphere, and as such it has been largely responsible for the specification of several famous aircraft types, including the Douglas DC-3 Dakota, the Convair 340, the Douglas DC-7, the Lockheed Electra and the Convair 990 development of the Convair 880.

American's history dates from the formation of the Aviation Corporation in 1929 by the acquisition of several small, often one-route, airlines, the oldest of which, the Robertson Aircraft Corporation, acquired through its parent company, the Universal Aviation Corporation, dated from 1921 and operated a Chicago–St. Louis–Omaha service, but most of the small airlines were formed during the 1926–1929 period. The others were Colonial Air Transport, operating New York–Boston and Albany–Buffalo–Cleveland, and Canadian Colonial Airways (New York–Montreal); Embry-Riddle Aviation Corporation (Chicago–Cincinnati); Interstate Airlines (Chicago–Atlanta and St. Louis–Evansville); Gulf Air Lines (Atlanta–Houston–New Orleans); Texas Air Transport (Dallas–Galveston); and the Universal Aviation Corporation (Tulsa–Dallas); Central Air Lines (Kansas City–Wichita–Tulsa); Continental Airlines (Cleveland–Louisville), and finally Northern Air Lines (Cleveland–Chicago–Kansas City). Some of these airlines were themselves subsidiaries of larger concerns. Colonial Air Transport and Canadian Colonial Airways were both subsidiaries of the Colonial Airways Corporation, and Gulf Air Lines and Texas Air Transport were subsidiaries of Southern Air Transport. The Universal Aviation Corporation, apart from Robertson Aircraft, included under its wing Braniff Air Lines, which had been formed in 1928 by Paul and Tom Braniff to operate the Tulsa–Dallas service. The service was acquired by Universal in 1929.

The following year, 1930, American Airways Inc. was formed as a subsidiary of the Aviation Corporation and set about the task of rationalizing the wide assortment of equipment and integrating the widely scattered network of services. Further acquisitions followed, including Standard Airlines, with a Los Angeles–El Paso service, from Western Air Express, this in October, 1930, and from E. L. Cord in 1932, both Century Air Lines, with a network of mid-west routes, and Century Pacific Lines. An Act of Congress in 1934 forced the Aviation Corporation to isolate its manufacturing and operating interests, and as a result, American Airlines was formed as a separate and independent entity that same year. The new airline started life with a network of services stretching from the Atlantic to the Pacific coasts of the United States.

America started towards expansion on to international routes in 1942, when a licence was awarded for services from El Paso and Dallas to Mexico City, although not until after the war could these services be started due to the wartime shortage of equipment. A further step towards expansion on to international routes was the purchase from American Export Lines of a 51% interest in American Export Airlines, which dated from 1937 when it was formed to operate services to Europe and the Mediterranean area, but had only received a temporary permit for services to Lisbon by 1940. In October, 1945 however, AEA introduced the first commercial New York–London landplane service with Douglas DC-4s. In 1948, American's interest in AOA was increased to 62%, and the title American Overseas Airlines adopted. In 1950, AOA was sold to its old rival, Pan American World Airways.

The 1950s saw a policy of rationalization of services for American, which meant the dropping of many small towns from American's route network as they were handed over to the feeder, or local service, airlines; the reason being that a large trans-continental airline cannot serve these places as economically as a small, locally-based carrier. Further steps were also taken during this period to strengthen the airline's trans-continental network by the introduction of a Chicago–San Francisco service in 1955, and a little later, a non-stop New York–San Francisco route. During the early 1960s, the possibility of a merger with another of the very large American domestic trunk operators, Eastern Air Lines, was investigated, but although in 1962 the shareholders of both companies agreed to the idea, the Civil Aeronautics Board rejected the proposal in 1963.

At present, a network of services is operated by American stretching from coast to coast, and Toronto to Mexico City, with worldwide charter flights. A fleet of Boeing 707s, 720s and 727s, Convair 990s, Lockheed Electras and BAC One-Elevens (American has the largest fleet of these aircraft) is operated, with ten Boeing 747 Jumbo Jets, and 25 McDonnell-Douglas DC-10 airbuses on order, and options held for a further 25 DC-10s, six BAC/Sud Concorde and six Boeing 2707 SSTs.

Member of the International Air Transport Association

Route points:
Albany, Baltimore, Boston, Buffalo, Charleston, Chicago, Cincinnati, Cleveland, Columbus, Dallas, Deyton, Detroit, El Paso, Fort Worth, Houston, Indianapolis, Joplin, Knoxville, Little Rock, Los Angeles, Louisville, Memphis, Mexico City, Milwaukee, Nashville, New York, Oklahoma City, Philadelphia, Phoenix, Pittsburgh, Providence, Rochester, San Antonio, San Diego, San Francisco, Springfield, St. Louis, Syracuse, Toronto

Livery: unpainted

Fleet:
Boeing 707-323C

N7555A	N7563A	N7596A	N	A	N	A
N7556A	N7564A	N7597A	N	A	N	A
N7557A	N7565A	N7598A	N	A	N	A
N7558A	N7566A	N7599A	N	A	N	A
N7559A	N7567A	N	A	N	A	N	A
N7560A	N7568A	N	A	N	A	N	A
N7561A	N7569A	N	A	N	A	N	A
N7562A	N7595A					

Boeing 707-123B (*series 123)

N7501A	N7513A	N7524A	N7573A	N7584A
N7502A*	N7514A*	N7525A	N7574A	N7585A
N7503A	N7515A	N7526A	N7575A	N7586A
N7504A	N7516A	N7550A	N7576A	N7587A
N7505A	N7517A	N7551A	N7577A	N7588A

N7506A	N7518A	N7552A	N7578A	N7589A
N7507A	N7519A	N7553A	N7579A	N7590A
N7508A	N7520A	N7554A	N7580A	N7591A
N7509A	N7521A	N7570A	N7581A	N7592A
N7510A	N7522A	N7571A	N7582A	N7593A
N7511A	N7523A	N7572A	N7583A	N7594A
N7512A				

Boeing 720-023B

N7527A	N7532A	N7537A	N7541A	N7545A
N7528A	N7533A	N7538A	N7542A	N7546A
N7529A	N7534A	N7539A	N7543A	N7548A
N7530A	N7535A	N7540A	N7544A	N7549A
N7531A	N7536A			

Convair 990 Coronado

N5601	N5605	N5613	N5615	N5618
N5603	N5606	N5614	N5616	N5620
N5604	N5608			

Boeing 727-23

N1901	N1929	N1972	N1981	N1990
N1902	N1930	N1973	N1982	N1991
N1903	N1931	N1974	N1983	N1992
N1905	N1932	N1975	N1984	N1993
N1906	N1933	N1976	N1985	N1994
N1907	N1934	N1977	N1986	N1995
N1908	N1935	N1978	N1987	N1997
N1909	N1936	N1979	N1988	N1998
N1910	N1970	N1980	N1989	
N1928	N1971			

22 Boeing 727-223s are on order

BAC One-Eleven Series 400

N5015	N5021	N5027	N5033	N5039
N5016	N5022	N5028	N5034	N5040
N5017	N5023	N5029	N5035	N5041
N5018	N5024	N5030	N5036	N5042
N5019	N5025	N5031	N5037	N5043
N5020	N5026	N5032	N5038	N5044

Lockheed Electra L-188A

N6101A	N6115A	N6121A	N6128A	N6133A
N6102A	N6116A	N6122A	N6129A	N6134A
N6106A	N6117A	N6123A	N6130A	N6135A
N6111A	N6118A	N6125A	N6131A	N7142C
N6112A	N6119A	N6126A	N6132A	N7143C
N6114A	N6120A	N6127A		

AMERICAN FLYERS United States of America
American Flyers Airline Inc

One of the oldest established American supplemental (charter) carriers, American Flyers dates from 1939 when Reed Pigman, the airline's late president, started operations with a five-seat Spartan 'Executive'. After the Second World War ended, the airline acquired Douglas DC-3's for operation on low-fare charter flights.

In 1951, American Flyers became the first charter airline to operate CAM (domestic trooping) flights, and today, in common with many other American charter operators, military contracts form a considerable part of the airline's business. The first four-engined aircraft, a Lockheed 'Constellation', was acquired in 1960, and the turbo-prop Lockheed 'Electras', which the airline currently uses on North Atlantic charters, were first placed in service in 1963. The present fleet also includes two Boeing 707-320's, delivered early in 1966 and 1967.

American Flyers currently operates from Fort Worth, Texas, on military and civil charters, including inclusive tours over both the Atlantic and the Pacific. A proposal for a merger with another American charter operator, Universal Airlines (formerly Zantop Air Transport) has been presented to the Civil Aeronautics Board for approval.

N182H Lockheed Electra of American Flyers at Fort Worth, Texas

Livery F: white, red, grey **T:** red

Fleet

N182H	Lockheed L-188C Electra	N126US	Lockheed L-188C Electra
N122US	,,	,,	N8400A	Boeing 707-385C
N124US	,,	,,	N8401A	,, ,,
N125US	,,	,,		

BRANIFF INTERNATIONAL
United States of America
Braniff Airways Inc

The original airline, Braniff Air Lines, was formed in 1928 by Tom Braniff, an Oklahoma financier, and his brother Paul, with the fleetname, Tulsa–Oklahoma City Airlines, and a Stinson Detroiter as equipment. The following year, the airline became part of the Universal Aviation Corporation, which was a predecessor of American Airlines.

The present airline was formed in 1930, completely independent of Universal Aviation, and operated a Tulsa–Wichita service, followed by a service to Chicago in 1931. Further expansion of the airline came in 1934 when the United States' Government opened postal contracts to competitive bidding, and Braniff gained the Dallas–Chicago contract, and in 1935 purchased the Dallas–Amarillo contract from Harman Airlines; passenger services were extended to Lexington that same year.

The title Braniff International was first adopted in 1948 to mark the airline's expansion on to the route from Houston to Havana and Lima, although a service to Mexico City and Buenos Aires had been operated for a short period in 1946, until suspended by the Mexican authorities. In 1951, Miami was added to the Havana route, and, in 1955, Panama and Bogota were added to the fast expanding route network, along with a Dallas–New York service.

A merger with Mid-Continent Airlines in 1952 helped Braniff's expansion. Mid-Continent had been formed in 1936, and at the time of the merger, operated to 35 cities in 12 states. A more recent acquisition has been Pan American Grace Airways (PANAGRA) from Pan American World Airways and the W. R. Grace Company, each of which held 50per cent of the capital. PANAGRA had been formed in 1929, and operated services from the United States to South and Central America.

Today Braniff operates a fleet of Boeing 707s, 720s and 727s, Douglas DC-8s, Lockheed Electras and BAC One-Elevens throughout the United States and Central and South America. Two Boeing 747 Jumbo Jets are on order, and options are held for three BAC/Sud Concorde and two Boeing 2707 SSTs. The Greatamerica Corporation, an investment trust, holds 80.9per cent of the airline's capital. The airline undertakes a large volume of military contract work, including flights to Europe, and its most remarkable feature is its livery, which comprises 11 different colours, and each aircraft has its fuselage painted completely in one of these.

The American airline, Braniff, paints the fuselages of its aircraft in one of several colours; here in flight is N7272, a blue Boeing 727

Member of the International Air Transport Association

Domestic route points:
Amarillo, Atlanta, Austin, Birmingham, Brownsville, Chicago, Colorado Springs,
Corpus Christi, Dallas, Denver, Des Moines, Fort Smith, Fort Worth, Houston,
Kansas City, Little Rock, Lubbock, Memphis, Miami, Minneapolis, St. Paul,
Nashville, New Orleans, New York, Newark, Oklahoma City, Omaha,
Portland, St. Louis, San Antonio, Seattle, Shreveport, Tulsa, Washington,
Wichita

International services from Houston, Los Angeles, Miami, New York and
San Francisco to:

Acapulco, Antofagusta, Asuncion, Bogota, Buenos Aires, Cali, Guayaquil,
La Paz, Lima, Mexico City, Montevideo, Panama City, Quito, Rio de Janeiro,
Santiago, São Paulo

Chicago–London and Frankfurt (with Pan Am)

Livery T: white
      F: a range of eleven colours, denoted in the **fleet** list by the following
      key letters by the registration number:

r–red   y–yellow   l–light blue   m–medium blue   d–dark blue   g–green
        p–light green   o–orange   b–beige   t–turquoise   c–ochre

Fleet
Douglas DC-8–62

N1803y	N1804m	N1805p	N1806r	N1807g

Boeing 707-320C

N7095c	N7097t	N7099d	N7102o	N7104g
N7096y	N7098o	N7100g	N7103d	

Boeing 707-227

N7072l	N7073y	N7074p	N7075l

Boeing 720-027

N7076d	N7077c	N7078d	N7079o	N7080b

Boeing 727-27C (*series 27, **162 †62C)

N7270t	N7275d	N7280m	N7287r	N7293r*
N7271y	N7276t	N7281p	N7288b	N7294g*
N7272l	N7277y	N7282o**	N7289y	N7295b
N7273o	N7278g	N7284d†	N7290g	N7296r
N7274c	N7279o	N7286l†	N7292o	

BAC One-Eleven 203

N1541m	N1544o	N1547d	N1550c	N1552o
N1542d	N1545l	N1548y	N1551r	N1554c
N1543c	N1546 b	N1549t		

Lockheed L-188 Electra (*may be unpainted)

N9701C*	N9703Cy	N9706Co	N9708C*	N9710Cc
N9702C*	N9704Cd	N9707C*	N9709C*	

Aircraft marked* will be painted in order: light green, beige, red, new blue
and green—order has no bearing on registration

CAPITOL INTERNATIONAL AIRWAYS

United States of America

Capitol International Airways Inc

Capital International Airways started its existence in 1946 providing aircraft sales, service and maintenance, as well as flight training, at Nashville, Tennessee. The business was at that time owned by Jesse Stallings—currently president, but then an American Airlines' pilot—and a partner, but when his partner left the business Stallings resigned from American Airlines and Capitol commenced air charter services with a single war-surplus aircraft as Capitol Airways.

The airline grew steadily over the years operating non-scheduled services, which, as for most American charter (or 'supplemental') operators included a large volume of military contract work on which the airline used C-46's and Hawker Siddeley Argosy freighters. This situation still exists, although, again in common with many other charter operators, inclusive tour and other civil charter work is taking an increasing proportion of the airline's business. At present Capitol has six Curtiss C-46's on LOGAIR work (scheduled freight services between military bases within the United States). In addition to LOGAIR and MAC work, several of the Capitol fleet are committed to the Civil Reserve Air Fleet.

The current Capitol International Airways fleet includes five Douglas DC-8's, 11 Lockheed 'Super Constellations', and C-46's. The airline was owned by Jesse Stallings (87.5%) and R. S. Farrar (12.5%) until it went public recently. The main operating base is at Wilmington, Delaware with headquarters at Nashville.

The Capitol Airways fleet includes this Douglas DC-8F ''fan'' (i.e. Turbo-jet)

Fleet

Douglas DC-8 series 31

N1800	N1801	N1802

Douglas DC-8 series 54F (*series 55F)

N4904C	N4905C*	N4906C*	N4907C	N4908C

Lockheed L-1049A Super Constellation

N1006C	N4715G	N5401V	N5403V	N9718C
N1007C	N4903C	N5402V	N5404V	N9720C
N1008C				

Curtiss C-46

N9890Z	N9892Z	N9893Z	N66326	N68964
N9891Z				

FLYING TIGER LINE
The Flying Tiger Line Inc

United States of America

The Flying Tiger Line was formed in 1945 by a group of war veterans, including Robert Prescott, the airline's president. The group had fought in Burma, China, and India as the "Flying Tigers". The airline's first aircraft were Budd Conestogas, and these were replaced in 1946 by Douglas C-47 Dakotas and C-54 Skymasters, which the airline used on a military airlift to Japan, which, at that time, was the largest contract for air freight ever awarded to an airline. Flying Tigers received some Curtiss C-46 Commandos in 1949, the year in which the airline received authority to operate scheduled cargo services from coast to coast in the USA.

Today, Flying Tiger is the world's largest airline on all-cargo scheduled operations, which are flown throughout the United States, having been the first all-cargo airline at the time of its formation. The current fleet of Boeing 707s and Douglas DC-8s replaced Canadair CL-44s, a notable feature of which were their swing tails for easy cargo loading, and Lockheed Super Constellations, themselves the successors of Douglas DC-6As. Apart from scheduled operations, freight charters are operated on a worldwide basis, and some inclusive tour charters are also operated, including some to Europe.

Associate Member of the International Air Transport Association

Flying Tiger Line's Boeing 707 registered N322F (of series 349C) flies over wooded landscape

Domestic services from Los Angeles to:

Birmingham, Boston, Buffalo, Chicago, Cleveland, Detroit, Hartford, Milwaukee, New York, Philadelphia, Portland, San Francisco, Seattle

Livery: blue and red on unpainted

Fleet

Boeing 707-349C

N322F	N323F	N324F	N325F

Douglas DC-8–63F

N7080FT	N7084FT	N7088FT	N7091FT	N7094FT
N7081FT	N7085FT	N7089FT	N7092FT	N7095FT
N7082FT	N7086FT	N7090FT	N7093FT	N7096FT
N7083FT	N7087FT			

OVERSEAS NATIONAL AIRWAYS
Overseas National Airways Inc

United States of America

Overseas National Airways was formed in 1950 with a fleet of five DC-4's, used on military contracts in connection with the Korean War. Several years later, the airline was awarded a contract to carry supplies and personnel from Los Angeles, San Diego and Denver to Cape Kennedy (then known as Cape Canaveral). During 1957 ONA acquired four DC-6AC's and commenced civil charter operations. Military contracts continued to provide most of the airline's work load however, and two years later, as a result of the award of a very large contract, one DC-6B and twelve Douglas DC-7's were added to the fleet.

In October 1963, the airline voluntarily suspended operations, not resuming them until the same month two years later, when a group of employees obtained new financial backing for the airline. This enabled jet equipment—two Douglas DC-8's—to be ordered; they were delivered in June and July, 1966. In September of that year, the airline was awarded authority to operate domestic and trans-Atlantic inclusive tours charter. Currently, ONA's operations are divided between military contracts, inclusive tours, ad hoc passenger charters and civilian freight charters.

The current Overseas National fleet includes two Douglas DC-8-55s, four DC-9-33s and nine ex-National Lockheed L-188 Electras; three DC-8-63Fs are in course of delivery.

The main base is at New York.

Fleet

Douglas DC-8–55 (*series DC-8–63F)

N851F	N852F	N863F*	N F*	N F*

Douglas DC-9–32

N931F	N932F	N933F	N934F

Lockheed L-188 Electra

N280F	N282F	N284F	N286F	N289F
N281F	N283F	N285F	N287F	

N852F *Contender*, one of the two Douglas DC-8-55F's in the Overseas National fleet

PAN AM
Pan American World Airways Inc

United States of America

The history of Pan American World Airways goes back to 1927 when the chairman of the airline until May 1968, Juan Trippe, founded Pan American Airways with a fleet of two three-engined Fokker F-VII's operating between Key West, Florida, and Havana, Cuba, a distance of 90 miles. By 1928 the new airline was flying to South America, with the twin-engined Sikorsky S-38 amphibian, an aircraft developed with Pan Am's requirements in mind, as were the Sikorsky S-40s and S-42s that followed during the next few years.

In February 1929, Pan American and the W. R. Grace company formed Pan American–Grace Airways (PANAGRA) to operate services to South America, mainly on the west coast. The first PANAGRA service was inaugurated in May 1929, to Peru, using Fairchild FC-2s. Santiago and Buenos Aires were added to the network in that first year. In 1966, Pan Am's 50per cent interest in PANAGRA was sold to Braniff, which also acquired the Grace shareholding and absorbed PANAGRA into its route network.

Also during 1928 the airline took a step towards its twin ambitions of providing trans-Atlantic and trans-Pacific services by engaging the famous aviation pioneer, Charles Lindbergh, to chart routes for these services. They followed over the Pacific in 1935 with the Martin M-130 flying boat *China Clipper* and on the North Atlantic route with the first scheduled service in 1939 with *Dixie Clipper*, a Boeing B 314 flying boat.

In 1950, Pan Am bought out an old rival on the North Atlantic, American Overseas Airlines, from the then owners, American Air Lines and American

Export Lines, a shipping company which had formed AOA as American Export Lines in 1937.

Other firsts by the airline include the first 'Round-the-World' service in 1947 with a Lockheed 'Constellation', and the first order for American jet airliners, Boeing 707's, in 1955. A New York–Moscow service was introduced in July 1968.

Pan American World Airways (the title adopted in January 1950) has a financial interest in several other airlines; Avianca (38%), Ariana (49%) and Phillippine Air Lines (20%). Pan Am also markets the French Dassault 'Falcon' business jet in the U.S.A., owns Intercontinental Hotels, a worldwide chain of 40 hotels, and manages a missile range. In 1967, 20% of Pan Am's fleet was operating military charters.

In common with many of the world's leading airlines Pan Am, which is the world's largest purely international airline, has ordered the Boeing 747 'Jumbo' jet airliner, and has options on eight BAC/Sud Concordes and 15 Boeing 2707 SST's. The present fleet includes Boeing 707s, 720s, and 727s (for Caribbean and German domestic services) and the Sikorsky S-61 helicopters introduced in spring 1968.

Member of the International Air Transport Association

N707PA, *Clipper America*, a Pan American Boeing 707.

Atlantic services from New York to:
Abidjan, Accra, Amsterdam, Ankara, Barcelona, Baghdad, Beirut, Belgrade, Berlin, Brussels, Conakry*, Copenhagen, Cotonou, Dakar*, Dar-es-Salaam, Douala, Düsseldorf, Entebbe, Frankfurt, Glasgow, Hamburg, Helsinki, Istanbul, Johannesburg, Keflavik, Kinshasa, Lagos, Lisbon, London, Monrovia*, Moscow, Munich, Nairobi, Nice, Oslo, Paris, Prague, Rabat*, Santa Maria, Shannon, Stockholm, Stuttgart, Tehran, Vienna

*all flights via Boston

Connections from Houston, Dallas, New Orleans, Chicago, Detroit, Atlanta, Washington, Baltimore, Philadelphia

Latin American services:
Asuncion, Brasilia, Buenos Aires, Caracas, Guatemala, Managua, Maracaibo,

Merida, Mexico City, Panama, Port of Spain, Rio de Janeiro, San José, San Juan, San Salvador, São Paulo, Tampa, Tegucigalpa

Certain of these flights are direct from Miami, New Orleans, and Houston

There are also flights from San Francisco via Los Angeles

Atlantic services from Baltimore, Chicago, Cleveland, Denver, Detroit, Hartford, Los Angles, Philadelphia, San Francisco, St. Louis, Washington to:

Frankfurt, Lisbon, London, Paris, Rome
Many of these flights are direct, others are via New York, Paris, London, Boston and Chicago

Pacific services from Los Angeles, Portland, San Francisco, Seattle to:

Honolulu, with connections from Boston, New York, Washington, Detroit, Chicago, Dallas via American Airlines

from Los Angeles, Portland, San Francisco, Seattle to:

Wake Island, American Samoa, Bangkok, Djakarta, Fiji, Guam, Hong Kong, Manila, Saigon, Singapore, Sydney, Tahiti, Tokyo, Wake Island

Caribbean services from New York or Miami to:

Antigua, Aruba, Barbados, Barranquilla, Belem, Curaçao, Fort de France, Georgetown, Kingston, Maracaibo, Montego Bay, Panama City, Paramaribo, Pointe à Pitre, Port au Prince, Port of Spain, St. Croix, St. Lucia, St. Maarten, St. Thomas, San Juan, Santo Domingo

German internal services from Berlin (West) to:

Cologne, Düsseldorf, Frankfurt, Hamburg, Hanover, Munich, Nuremberg, Stuttgart

Alaska service
Portland-Seattle–Fairbanks

Air cargo services are operated in addition

Livery F: white, blue, grey
     T: white and blue

A Pan American Boeing 727 of the type operated on German domestic routes and in the Caribbean

Fleet

Boeing 727 -21 (*-21C)

N314PA	*Clipper Sam Houston*
N315PA	*Clipper White Falcon*
N316PA	*Clipper Buena Vista*
N317PA	*Clipper De Soto*
N318PA	*Clipper Inca*
N319PA	*Clipper Ponce de Leon*
N320PA	*Clipper Berlin*
N321PA	*Clipper Köln/Bonn*
N323PA	*Clipper Frankfurt*
N324PA	*Clipper München*
N325PA	*Clipper Düsseldorf*
N326PA	*Clipper Nuremburg*
N327PA	*Clipper Hanover*
N328PA	*Clipper Hamburg*
N329PA	*Clipper Lightfoot*
N339PA*	*Clipper Stuttgart*
N340PA*	*Clipper Talisman*
N341PA*	*Clipper Plymouth Rock*
N342PA*	*Clipper Golden Age*

Boeing 707-321

N401PA*	*Clipper Dauntless*
N402PA*	*Clipper Black Hawk*
N403PA*	*Clipper Goodwill*
N404PA*	*Clipper Seven Seas*
N405PA*	*Clipper Stargazer*
N406PA*	*Clipper Kingfisher*
N407PA*	*Clipper Celestial*
N408PA*	*Clipper Morning Star*
N409PA*	*Clipper Eclipse*
N410PA*	*Clipper Argonaut*
N412PA*	*Clipper Empress of the Skies*
N414PA*	*Clipper Ann McKim*
N415PA*	*Clipper Monsoon*
N416PA*	*Clipper Paul Jones*
N417PA*	*Clipper Winged Racer*
N418PA*	*Clipper Yankee Ranger*
N419PA*	*Clipper Gem of the Skies*
N420PA*	*Clipper Monarch of the Skies*
N421PA*	*Clipper Charmer*
N422PA*	*Clipper Mount Vernon*
N423PA*	*Clipper Glory of the Skies*
N424PA*	*Clipper Golden West*
N425PA*	*Clipper Virginia*
N426PA*	*Clipper National Eagle*
N427PA*	*Clipper Crystal Palace*
N428PA*	*Clipper Star of Hope*
N433PA*	*Clipper Glad Tidings*
N434PA*	*Clipper Queen of the Sky*
N435PA*	*Clipper Celestial Empire*
N446PA‡	*Clipper Climax*
N447PA‡	*Clipper Onward*
N448PA‡	*Clipper Pacific Raider*
N449PA‡	*Clipper Red Rover*
N450PA‡	*Clipper Borinquen*
N451PA‡	*Clipper Union*
N452PA‡	*Clipper Golden Fleece*
N453PA*	*Clipper Universe*
N454PA*	*Clipper Radiant*
N455PA*	*Clipper Waverly*
N457PA‡	*Clipper Phoenix*
N458PA‡	*Clipper Titian*
N459PA‡	*Clipper Western Continent*
N460PA‡	*Clipper Sovereign of the Skies*
N461PA‡	*Clipper Rising Sun*
N462PA‡	*Clipper Eagle*
N463PA‡	*Clipper Queen of the East*
N473PA‡	*Clipper Pride of America*
N474PA‡	*Clipper Morning Glory*
N475PA‡	*Clipper Sea Serpent*
N491PA*	*Clipper Chariot of Fame*
N492PA*	*Clipper Eagle Wing*
N493PA*	*Clipper Fortune*
N495PA*	*Clipper Morning Light*
N496PA*	*Clipper Northern Eagle*
N497PA*	*Clipper Victor*
N701PA	*Clipper Donald McKay*
N702PA	*Clipper Hotspur*
N703PA	*Clipper Dashaway*
N704PA	*Clipper Defiance*
N705PA	*Clipper Wings of the Morning*
N706PA	*Clipper Courier*
N707PA†	*Clipper Maria*
N710PA†	*Clipper America*
N711PA†	*Clipper Mayflower*
N712PA†	*Clipper Washington*
N714PA	*Clipper Golden Eagle*
N715PA	*Clipper Liberty Bell*
N716PA	*Clipper Flying Eagle*
N717PA	*Clipper Fleetwing*
N718PA	*Clipper Invincible*
N719PA	*Clipper Windward*
N720PA	*Clipper Fairwind*
N721PA	*Clipper Splendid*
N722PA	*Clipper Lark*
N723PA	*Clipper Viking*

N724PA	Clipper Mercury	N765PA	Clipper Gladiator
N725PA	Clipper Aurora	N766PA‡	Clipper Jupiter
N726PA	Clipper Westward Ho	N767PA	Clipper Challenger
N727PA	Clipper Mohawk	N778PA†	Clipper Skylark
N728PA	Clipper Peerless	N790PA‡	Clipper Courser
N729PA	Clipper Isabella	N791PA‡	Clipper Fidelity
N730PA	Clipper Bald Eagle	N792PA‡	Clipper Good Hope
N757PA	Clipper Pathfinder	N793PA‡	Clipper Messenger
N758PA	Clipper Resolute	N794PA‡	Clipper Undaunted
N759PA	Clipper Freedom	N795PA‡	Clipper Jupiter Rex
N760PA*	Clipper Evening Star	N796PA‡	Clipper Mermaid
N761PA*	Clipper Friendship	N797PA‡	Clipper North Wind
N762PA*	Clipper Endeavour	N798PA‡	Clipper Caribbean
N763PA*	Clipper Yankee	N799PA‡	Clipper Racer
N764PA*	Clipper Nautilus	*707-321B	†707-121B ‡707-321C

Boeing 720-023B

N780PA	Clipper Carib	N785PA	Clipper Balbao
N781PA	Clipper Flying Arrow	N786PA	Clipper Winged Arrow
N782PA	Clipper Flying Cloud	N787PA	Clipper Guiding Star
N783PA	Clipper Bonita	N788PA	Clipper Nonpareil
N784PA	Clipper Panama		

Douglas DC-8 series 30

N801PA	Clipper Queen of the Pacific	N811PA	Clipper Pacific Trader
N802PA	Clipper Cathay	N812PA	Clipper Blue Jacket
N803PA	Clipper Mandarin	N813PA	Clipper Bostonian
N804PA	Clipper Midnight Sun	N814PA	Clipper Caroline
N805PA	Clipper Nightingale	N815PA	Clipper Charger
N806PA	Clipper Northern Light	N816PA	Clipper East Indian
N807PA	Clipper Polynesia	N817PA	Clipper Derby
N808PA	Clipper Gauntlet	N818PA	Clipper Rambler
N809PA	Clipper Great Republic		
N810PA	Clipper Intrepid		

SATURN AIRWAYS
Saturn Airways Inc

United States of America

Saturn Airways was formed in 1948 as All American Airways to operate air charter flights with a fleet of Douglas DC-3's and Curtiss C-46's. The present title was adopted in 1960, the same year in which the airline became one of only two U.S. 'supplemental' carriers to became permanently licensed to operate trans-Atlantic charter flights. The airline acquired a fleet of Douglas DC-6's for these flights; they were later replaced by DC-7C's.

Since its inception, Saturn has operated civil and military charters, and in 1965, Saturn merged with Aaxico Airlines, an operator engaged entirely on military contract work. A major reason for this union was a decision by the U.S. Government to award military contracts only to airlines whose work load consisted of at least one-third civil operations. At the present time CAMS (domestic troop flights) and MACS (international troop flights) charter work forms a large percentage of Saturn's business.

A Douglas DC-7C of Saturn Airways, the American charter operator

Apart from military contracts, the activities of Saturn Airways at present include *ad hoc* and inclusive tour charters, and some domestic freight charters. In addition the airline operates inclusive tour charters from West Berlin, where three Douglas DC-7's are based for this work. The present Saturn fleet consists of Douglas DC-8-61's, Boeing 707's, introduced during 1967, and DC-7's. The president, H. J. Korth, formerly of Aaxico, holds a controlling interest in the airline.

Saturn's main base is at Miami.

Livery F: white, red, grey
     T: white

Fleet
Douglas DC-7C

N90773	N90778	N90802	N90803	N90804
N90774	N90801			

Douglas DC-8–61

N8955SU	N8956SU

Boeing 707-379C

N761U	N762U	N763U

SEABOARD
Seaboard World Airlines Inc

United States of America

Formed in September 1946, as Seaboard and Western Airlines, operations commenced the following May with a Douglas DC-4, which operated the first trans-atlantic flight of an all-cargo civil aircraft. The airline operated as a freight charter carrier until 1955 when it was awarded a five-year permit to operate scheduled services from New York, Philadelphia and Baltimore to Europe; the first flight took place in 1957. A year later, the airline was awarded a contract to carry United States and foreign airmail.

Although the scheduled freight services began to show a profit almost immediately, the airline made heavy losses on its other operations in 1959, and during 1960, had to be extensively re-organized to avoid bankruptcy. A return to profit-making operation was made by 1962, assisted by the introduction of a 'blocked-space' agreement with Deutsche Lufthansa, and the following year similar agreements were made with Swissair and BOAC. Under these agreements cargo space on Seaboard services is divided equally between the airline and one of the European carriers, who pays one-third of the operating cost whether its share of the cargo space is used or not.

Also during 1962, the airline introduced the first of its turbo-prop Canadair CL-44's, and these were replaced during 1966 by Douglas DC-8 freighters. Seaboard operates scheduled and charter services, also Military Airlift Command (MAC) charter work.

Livery F: white, red, grey
   T: white

Fleet

Boeing 707-345CF
N7321S   N7322S

Douglas DC-8 Series 55CF
N801SW   N803SW   N804SW   N805SW   N806SW
N802SW

Douglas DC-8–63CF
N8631W   N8632W

TRANS INTERNATIONAL
United States of America

Trans International Airlines Inc

Trans International Airlines was formed in 1948 as Los Angeles Air Service, the present title being adopted in 1960. TIA was the first American non-scheduled airline to become a public company, and at present is the operating subsidiary of Trans International Airlines Corporation. Previous owners include the Studebaker Corporation between 1962 and 1964, and, prior to the present parent, Glenkirk Inc.

The airline's present fleet includes three Douglas DC-8 jet airliners, the first of which was taken on strength in 1963, and three more are on order. TIA has played a prominent part in the development of inclusive tour charters in the United States, and authority has been obtained for domestic, South American, Caribbean, Pacific and North Atlantic ITC's. Although at present military contract work totals 60% of TIA's business, the rate of growth for the period between 1962 and 1965 was only 21% as against 217% for civil charters.

Livery F: white, green, grey
   T: green

A Trans International Douglas DC-8 shortly after take-off

Fleet

N6924C	Lockheed L1049 Super Constellation	
N7776C	,,	,,
N9751C	,,	,,
N9752C	,,	,,
N33258T	Douglas DC-8–55F	
N8008D	,,	51
N8008F	,,	54F
N8960T	Douglas DC-8–61F	
N8961T	,,	,,
N8962T	,,	,,

TWA   United States of America
Trans World Airlines Inc

In 1925, Congress passed the Kelly Act enabling air mail contracts to be let to privately-owned companies. The first of Trans World Airlines' ancestor companies, Western Air Express, was then formed. The airline's bid was successful and it became one of the five companies to be chosen out of more than 5,000 applicants to carry the air mail contract. The initial route was between Los Angeles and Salt Lake City, a distance of 575 miles, on which the airline operated a variety of aircraft during its early years, including the Douglas 'Cruiser' biplane and three-engined Fokkers.

Amongst the other American airlines in existence at this time were Maddux Airlines, which flew Fokkers on routes from Los Angeles to San Diego and San Francisco, and Transcontinental Air Transport (TAT), an airline formed in 1929 which retained Charles Lindbergh as consultant and operated a trans-United States rail/air service. During 1929 control of Maddux passed to Transcontinental while Western Air Express took over Standard Airlines, a Los Angeles operator. The following year TAT-Maddux and Western Air Express merged to form Transcontinental and Western Air Express. This airline became known as 'TWA' although the present title was not adopted for another twenty years.

During the next few years the airline expanded, but still on domestic routes. Aircraft operated in this period included the Douglas DC-2 and DC-3, and the airline became the first to fly the Boeing 'Stratoliner', the first pressurized airliner, with which TWA gained experience on trans-ocean routes when these aircraft, with TWA crews, were pressed into war service by the United States Government.

Before the outbreak of war, TWA, with Lockheed, had participated in the design of the Lockheed 'Constellation', and with the airline it commenced its trans-Atlantic scheduled services in 1946, initially between New York and Paris via Shannon.

Trans World Airlines today operates the largest single Boeing fleet in the world with a fleet of 707's and 727's and has ordered twelve 747 'Jumbo' jet airliners. Other aircraft in the fleet include Douglas DC-9's and Convair 880's. The airline ordered 44 Lockheed L-1011 airbuses, the first airline to do so, in the spring of 1968, with an option on another 44, with six BAC/Sud Concorde and ten Boeing 2707 SST's also on option. Management assistance is given to Ethiopian Airlines and Saudi Arabian Airlines, while Trans-Mediterranean Airways receives technical assistance. The airline owns the Hilton International Hotel chain which has some 50 hotels, and which was purchased in May, 1967.

Member of the International Air Transport Association

International Services from New York to:

Algiers, Athens, Azores, Bangkok, Bombay, Cairo, Dhahran, Frankfurt, Geneva, Hong Kong, Lisbon, London, Madrid, Milan, Paris, Rome, Shannon, Tel-Aviv, Tripoli, Tunis, Zürich

Connections from Boston, Chicago, Cleveland, Denver, Detroit, Kansas City, Los Angeles, Oklahoma City, Philadelphia, Pittsburgh, St. Louis, San Francisco, Tulsa, Washington

Some flights from these cities are via New York, and some from Washington and Chicago by-pass New York

Domestic route points:

Albuquerque, Amarillo, Atlanta, Baltimore, Boston, Chicago, Cincinnati, Cleveland, Columbus, Dayton, Detroit, Hartford, Indianapolis, Kansas City, Las Vegas, Los Angeles, Louisville, Miami, Nashville, New York, Oakland, Oklahoma City, Phoenix, Pittsburgh, St. Louis, San Francisco, Springfield, Tulsa, Tucson, Washington, Wichita

Air cargo services are operated in addition

A Boeing 707 *Starstream* jet airliner of Trans World Airways way above the clouds

Livery F: white red, grey
T: white,

Fleet

Boeing 707-131 (*series 131B, †331, ‡331B, §331C)

N731TW	N750TW*	N770TW†	N790TW§	N16738‡
N732TW	N751TW*	N771TW†	N791TW§	N16739‡
N733TW	N752TW*	N772TW†	N792TW§	N18701‡
N734TW	N754TW*	N773TW‡	N793TW‡	N18702‡
N735TW	N755TW*	N774TW‡	N795TW†	N18703‡
N736TW	N756TW*	N775TW‡	N796TW†	N18704‡
N737TW	N757TW*	N776TW‡	N797TW†	N18706‡
N738TW	N758TW*	N778TW‡	N798TW†	N18707‡
N739TW	N759TW*	N779TW‡	N799TW†	N18708‡
N740TW	N760TW‡	N780TW‡	N5771T§	N18709‡
N741TW	N761TW†	N781TW*	N5772T§	N18710‡
N742TW	N762TW†	N782TW*	N5773T§	N18711‡
N743TW	N763TW†	N783TW*	N5774T§	N18712‡
N744TW	N764TW†	N784TW*	N8705T‡	N18713‡
N745TW	N765TW†	N785TW*	N8715T‡	N28724‡
N746TW*	N766TW†	N786TW§	N8725T‡	N28726‡
N747TW*	N767TW†	N787TW§	N15710§	N28727‡
N748TW*	N768TW†	N788TW§	N15711§	N28728‡
N749TW*	N769TW†	N789TW§		

Boeing 727-31 (*series 31C)

N831TW	N844TW	N850TW	N856TW	N891TW*
N833TW	N845TW	N851TW	N857TW	N892TW*
N839TW	N846TW	N852TW	N858TW	N893TW*
N840TW	N847TW	N853TW	N859TW	N984TW*
N841TW	N848TW	N854TW	N889TW	N895TW*
N842TW	N849TW	N855TW	N890TW*	

Boeing 727-231

N12301	N12303	N12305	N12307	N12308
N12302	N12304	N12306		

Douglas DC-9-14

N1051T	N1055T	N1059T	N1063T	N1067T
N1052T	N1056T	N1060T	N1064T	N1068T
N1053T	N1057T	N1061T	N1065T	N1069T
N1054T	N1058T	N1062T	N1066T	N1070T

Convair 880 Coronado

N801TW	N808TW	N815TW	N820TW	N825TW
N802TW	N809TW	N816TW	N821TW	N826TW
N803TW	N810TW	N817TW	N822TW	N828TW
N804TW	N811TW	N818TW	N823TW	N830TW
N805TW	N812TW	N819TW	N824TW	N871TW
N806TW	N814TW			

UNITED
United Air Lines Inc

United States of America

United Air Lines is the largest, and, if the date of formation of its oldest ancestor airline is taken into account, the oldest, American airline. Indeed, probably only Aeroflot is larger than United.

The first of United's ancestor airlines, Varney Air Lines, was formed in 1926 to operate a feeder service to the trans-continental air mail service, at that time operated by the United States Post Office. Varney Air Lines used Swallow biplanes on this service, and only mail could be carried. The remaining three ancestor airlines were all formed in 1927, when the air mail services were handed over to private contractors. Boeing Air Transport gained San Francisco–Chicago, and National Air Transport received Chicago–New York, while Pacific Air Transport operated the Seattle–Los Angeles feeder. Boeing hastened its 40-A design into service for the air mail contract, and this aircraft was able to carry passengers as well as mail. Boeing and Ford Tri-motor 14 passenger aircraft followed in 1929, and in 1930, Boeing took the great step forward of introducing stewardesses and meal service on its flights.

In 1928, Boeing had acquired Pacific Air Transport as a step towards single-carrier operation of the trans-continental service, and, in March 1930, Varney and National were also acquired, United Aircraft and Transport being formed to manage the airlines from July 1931. Stout Airlines, the operator of services from Detroit to Chicago and Cleveland, soon became a part of United. Progress in the air was not forgotten during this very busy period, and the Boeing 247 was introduced in 1933, being the first twin-engined, all-metal, low-wing airliner. Back on the ground, an Act of Congress forbade the grouping of manufacturing and operating interests, and United Air Lines, divorced from Boeing, was the result.

After its formation as a separate entity in 1934, United immediately suffered the loss of several air mail contracts after the Post Office opened air mail contracts to competitive bidding that same year. Expansion of the airline continued, however, throughout the 1930s and 1940s. One of the more notable awards in the creation of the present vast route network was the first overseas route in 1946, to Hawaii. Also in 1946, United obtained the Los Angeles–Denver route of Western Airlines, six years after the Civil Aeronautics Board had forbidden any merger between the two airlines.

In 1947, United became the first airline to introduce the Douglas DC-6 pressurized airliner. Other similar 'firsts' since include the Douglas DC-8 in 1959, and Super DC-8 (Series 61) in 1967, the Boeing 720 in 1960 and 727 in 1962, and the airline was the first, and only, American airline to operate the Sud Aviation Caravelle jet airliner, which it introduced in 1961.

In 1961, United merged with another large American carrier, Capital Airlines, which was in some financial difficulties, after several years of failing to agree on the terms of the merger. The merger added an immediate 25% to United's revenues. Currently, the United fleet consists of Douglas DC-8, DC-8F and DC-8-61, Boeing 720, 727, 727QC and 737, and Caravelle jets, and Viscount turbo-prop airliners. Additional DC-8-61s, 727s and 737s are on order, and for the future, 18 Boeing 747 Jumbo jets are on order, with options held on six BAC/Sud Concorde and six Boeing 2707 SSTs.

Member of the International Air Transport Association

Route points:

Akron Canton, Allentown, Asheville, Atlanta, Bakersfield, Baltimore, Birmingham, Borse, Boston, Buffalo, Cedar Rapids, Charleston, Charlotteville, Chicago, Cleveland, Columbus, Dayton, Denver, Des Moines, Detroit, Elko, Ely, Eugene, Fort Lauderdale, Fort Wayne, Fresco, Grand Junction, Grand Rapids, Greenborough, Hartford, Honolulu, Huntsville, Jacksonville, Johnson City, Kansas City, Knoxville, Lincoln, Long Beach, Los Angeles, Medford, Memphis, Miami, Milwaukee, Minneapolis & St Paul, Mobile, Modesto, Monterrey, New Orleans, New York, Newark, Newport, Norfolk, Omaha, Pendleton, Pittsburgh, Philadelphia, Portland, Providence, Raleigh, Richmond, Rochester, Sacramento, Salt Lake City, San Diego, San Francisco, Santa Barbara, Seattle, South Bend, Spokane, Stockton, Tampa, Toledo, Vancouver, Visalia, Washington, West Palm Beach, Williamsburg, Williamsport, Youngston

Fleet

Vickers Viscount 745 (These aircraft are being sold upon replacement by Boeing 727 and 737 aircraft)

N7406	N7423	N7434	N7444	N7454
N7407	N7424	N7435	N7445	N7455
N7408	N7425	N7436	N7446	N7456
N7409	N7426	N7437	N7447	N7457
N7411	N7427	N7438	N7448	N7458
N7412	N7428	N7439	N7449	N7459
N7413	N7429	N7440	N7450	N7460
N7417	N7430	N7441	N7451	N7461
N7419	N7431	N7443	N7452	N7465
N7422				

Douglas DC-8–61

N	U	N	U	N	U	N	U	N	U
N	U	N	U	N	U	N	U	N	U
N	U								

Douglas DC-8–21 (*series 12)

N8001U	N8013U*	N8020U*	N8026U	N8032U
N8002U	N8014U	N8021U	N8027U	N8033U
N8003U	N8015U*	N8022U	N8028U	N8037U*
N8004U	N8016U	N8023U	N8029U	N8038U*
N8005U	N8017U	N8024U	N8030U	N8039U*
N8006U	N8018U	N8025U	N8031U	N8040U*
N8012U*	N8019U*			

Douglas DC-8–51 (*series 52, †series 54, ‡series 55)

N8007U	N8036U*	N8046U‡	N8062U*	N8067U‡
N8008U	N8041U†	N8047U†	N8063U*	N8068U‡
N8009U	N8042U†	N8048U†	N8064U*	N8069U‡
N8010U	N8043U†	N8060U*	N8065U*	N8070U‡
N8011U	N8044U‡	N8061U*	N8066U‡	N8071U‡
N8035U*	N8045U‡			

Boeing 720-022

N7201U	N7207U	N7213U	N7219U	N7225U
N7202U	N7208U	N7214U	N7220U	N7226U
N7203U	N7209U	N7215U	N7221U	N7227U
N7204U	N7210U	N7216U	N7222U	N7228U
N7205U	N7211U	N7217U	N7223U	N7229U
N7206U	N7212U	N7218U	N7224U	

Boeing 727-22

N7001U	N7019U	N7038U	N7057U	N7074U
N7002U	N7020U	N7039U	N7058U	N7075U
N7003U	N7021U	N7040U	N7059U	N7076U
N7004U	N7022U	N7041U	N7060U	N7077U
N7005U	N7023U	N7042U	N7061U	N7078U
N7006U	N7024U	N7044U	N7062U	N7079U
N7007U	N7025U	N7045U	N7063U	N7080U
N7008U	N7026U	N7046U	N7064U	N7081U
N7009U	N7027U	N7047U	N7065U	N7082U
N7010U	N7028U	N7048U	N7066U	N7083U
N7011U	N7029U	N7049U	N7067U	N7084U
N7012U	N7031U	N7050U	N7068U	N7085U
N7013U	N7032U	N7052U	N7069U	N7086U
N7014U	N7033U	N7053U	N7070U	N7087U
N7015U	N7034U	N7054U	N7071U	N7088U
N7016U	N7035U	N7055U	N7072U	N7089U
N7017U	N7037U	N7056U	N7073U	N7090U
N7018U				

Boeing 727-22QC (*series 22C)

N7401U	N7407U	N7413U	N7420U*	N7426U*
N7402U	N7408U	N7414U	N7421U*	N7427U*
N7403U	N7409U	N7415U	N7422U*	N7428U*
N7404U	N7410U	N7416U*	N7423U*	N7429U*
N7405U	N7411U	N7417U*	N7424U*	N7430U*
N7406U	N7412U	N7419U*	N7425U*	

Boeing 727-222

N7621U	N7622U	N7623U	N7624U	N7625U

Boeing 737-222

N9001U	N9011U	N9021U	N9031U	N9041U
N9002U	N9012U	N9022U	N9032U	N9042U
N9003U	N9013U	N9023U	N9033U	N9043U
N9004U	N9014U	N9024U	N9034U	N9044U
N9005U	N9015U	N9025U	N9035U	N9045U
N9006U	N9016U	N9026U	N9036U	N9046U
N9007U	N9017U	N9027U	N9037U	N9047U
N9008U	N9018U	N9028U	N9038U	N9048U
N9009U	N9019U	N9029U	N9039U	N9049U
N9010U	N9020U	N9030U	N9040U	N9050U

WORLD AIRWAYS   United States of America
World Airways Inc

World Airways was formed in 1948 as a supplemental carrier (air charter operator), but the new airline was unsuccessful and by 1950 it had accumulated liabilities of $250,000. It was at this stage in the airline's history that the present president, Edward J. Daly, acquired the airline for $50,000.

The airline embarked on a programme of continuous expansion, mainly on military charter work, until by 1962, the year when the first jet equipment was ordered, the 1950 fleet of two Curtiss C-46's had expanded to eight Douglas DC-6's and eleven Lockheed 'Constellations'. Today military contracts still form a considerable part of the airline's business, but increasing emphasis is being put on domestic, trans-Atlantic and Pacific inclusive tour charters. This is a relatively new type of business for American airlines dating mainly from 1962 when Congress passed Public Law 528 which enabled the Civil Aeronautics Board to certify carriers to operate charter flights to regions with a proven need for such services. For the future, World has ambitions to operate Pacific scheduled services.

The present fleet includes eight Boeing 707's and six Boeing 727's. The airline is the first non-scheduled airline to order the Boeing 747 'Jumbo' jet and secure options on the Boeing 2707 supersonic transport; in each case three aircraft are involved.

World became the second 'non-sched' in the United States to become a public company when Daly sold 19½% of his shareholding in spring, 1966. Two years later, in spring 1968, World became the first airline to own a bank when, through its wholly-owned subsidiary, Worldamerica Investors Corporation, it bought the First Western Bank and Trust Co. of California, which has 86 branches throughout the U.S.A., and assets of $900million.

World Airways operates a fleet of Boeing 707-373C on charter services. One of these aircraft is shown here at London (Gatwick) Airport

Livery F: white, red, grey (emblem: globe)
T: white

Fleet

Boeing 707-373C

| N368WA | N371WA | N373WA | N375WA | N376WA |
| N369WA | N372WA | N374WA | | |

Boeing 727QC

| N690WA | N692WA | N693WA | N694WA | N695WA |
| N691WA | | | | |

JAT
Jugoslovenski Aerotransport

Yugoslavia

JAT was formed in 1946 by the Government of Yugoslavia. The predecessor of JAT, Aeropout, ceased operations on the outbreak of World War II. In 1947, JAT started operations on domestic routes with Douglas DC-3's and before the year was out, was also operating international services to Romania, Hungary, and Czechoslovakia.

In 1949 all international services had to be restarted after suspension for much of 1948. The East European routes were suspended again the following year when Yugoslavia declared itself independent of the Soviet Bloc. The airline's route network mirrored this new policy and JAT concentrated on introducing services to important centres in Western Europe, although this policy was soon modified to re-include Prague and East Berlin. This policy also influenced the airline's equipment, in 1954 JAT introduced Convair 440 'Metropolitans' and ordered Douglas DC-6B's, although some Ilyushin Il-14's arrived in 1957.

Jugoslovenski Aerotransport's first jet aircraft, Sud Aviation 'Caravelles', were introduced in 1962 to replace Convair 440's on major European routes and to start new services to Moscow and Amsterdam. The present fleet consists of 'Caravelles', 'Metropolitans', Douglas DC-6B's and Il-14's. The route network covers the Middle East, both East and West Europe, as well as domestic services.

Member of the International Air Transport Association

International services from Belgrade to:
Amsterdam, Athens, Beirut, Berlin (East), Cairo, Copenhagen, Frankfurt, London, Moscow, Munich, Paris, Prague, Rome, Vienna, Warsaw, Zürich

Domestic route points:
Belgrade, Dubrovnik, Ohrid, Skopje, Tirana, Titograd, Zagreb

Fleet

Douglas DC-3 Dakota

YU-ABA	YU-ABF	YU-ABJ	YU-ACA	YU-ACC
YU-ABB	YU-ABG	YU-ABK	YU-ACB	YU-ACD
YU-ABD	YU-ABI	YU-ABM		

Douglas DC-6B
YU-AFB

Convair 340/440 Metropolitan

YU-ADB	YU-ADE	YU-ADL	YU-ADM	YU-ADN
YU-ADD	YU-ADK			

Sud Aviation S.E.210 Caravelle 6N

YU-AHA	*Dubrovnik*	YU-AHE	*Budva*
YU-AHB	*Bled*	YU-AHF	*Split*
YU-AHD	*Opatija*	YU-AHG	*Ohrid*

ZAMBIA AIRWAYS
Zambia Airways Corporation

Formed in 1963 as a subsidiary of Central African Airways Corporation after the break-up of the Federation of Rhodesia and Nyasaland, Zambia Airways Ltd. began operations on 1st July, 1964, with two Douglas DC-3's and three de Havilland Canada Beavers. The aircraft, crews and technical assistance were provided by CAA. Zambia Airways took over a CAA contract in 1966 for two BAC 'One-Elevens'; these aircraft were leased to British Eagle, and returned in December, 1967.

Zambia Airways Corporation, a statutory body formed by the Government, took over all scheduled services within the country from 1st September, 1967, when the former concern, Zambia Airways Ltd., left the Central African Airways group. Management for the corporation is undertaken by Alitalia, the Italian airline.

International services are operated from the corporation's headquarters at Lusaka to the United Kingdom, Italy and several East African countries with the BAC 'One-Eleven's, a Douglas DC-8 and a Vickers 'Viscount'. Domestic routes are worked by de Havilland Canada 'Beavers', Douglas DC-3's and 'One-Elevens'.

International services from Lusaka to:

Blantyre, Dar-es-Salaam, Gaberones*, London, Nairobi, Rome
† operated by Botswana National Airways

Domestic route points

Balovale, Chipata, Kalabo, Kasaba Bay, Kasama, Kitwe, Livingstone, Lukulu, Lusaka, Mankoya, Mansa, Mbala, Mongu Lealui, Ndola, Ngoma, Senanga, Sesheke

Fleet

9J-RFX	Douglas DC-3
9J-RFY	,, ,,
VP-YHH	de Havilland Canada DHC2 Beaver
VP-	,, ,,
9J-	Vickers Viscount
9J-RCH	BAC One-Eleven 207
9J-RCI	,, ,,

A Douglas DC-8 is leased from Alitalia (Italy)